The Destruction *of* Atlantis

Compelling Evidence of the Sudden Fall of the Legendary Civilization

FRANK JOSEPH

Bear & Company
Rochester, Vermont

Bear & Company
One Park Street
Rochester, Vermont 05767
www.InnerTraditions.com

The Library of Congress has cataloged the hardcover edition as follows:
Joseph, Frank.
  The destruction of Atlantis : compelling evidence of the sudden fall of the legendary civilization / Frank Joseph.
    p.   cm.
Includes bibliographic references and index (p.)
  ISBN 1-879181-85-1 (hardcover)
  1.   Atlantis. I. Title.

GN751 .J68 2002
001.94—dc21   2001056096

ISBN of paperback edition: ISBN 1-59143-019-4

Printed and bound in the United States by Lake Book Manufacturing, Inc.

10 9 8 7 6 5 4 3 2 1

Text design and layout by Priscilla Baker
This book was typeset in Stone serif with Gill sans as a display typeface

The
Destruction
of Atlantis

To Kenneth Caroli, Atlantologist extraordinaire

Contents

INTRODUCTION

Atlantis Madness

*Reading made Don Quixote a gentleman. Believing
what he read made him mad.*
George Bernard Shaw

The grizzled Arab in his full-length black *galabiya* grunted and mo-
tioned impatiently for my canteen. I hesitated. In North Africa fresh
water and life are one and the same, and I was alone, a heathen
American in a forsaken corner of Islamic Morocco, come to search the
gaunt ruins of a long-dead city for traces of an even older civilization.
My friend, who seemed hardly less ancient, did not speak English. I
knew no Arabic. He had, notwithstanding, appointed himself my
unsolicited guide to Lixus.

His mostly toothless expression twisted into the grimace of a
devious smile, and I reluctantly relinquished the army-surplus con-
tainer. He emptied it at our feet, the priceless liquid splashing to the
parched ground, then squatted to the Roman pavement. Mumbling
low, as if chanting a mantra, he pressed the palm of his right hand
onto the dust-laden stones and rubbed in a circular motion. Gradually, the dim outlines of a mosaic began to materialize from the drab
surface.

While the old man continued to rub, muttering all the while,

1

colors began to emerge from the porous stone: carnelian reds, corn-golden yellows, aqua blues, sea greens—the suggestion of a face took form. First, large, blue, commanding eyes, then bushy eyebrows. Then a powerful forehead, followed by long locks of golden hair, a bold nose, a mouth open, as though calling. The portrait expanded to become a vibrant scene with dolphin-filled seas behind the manifesting head. The figure began to fill out in shade and brilliance, revealing a bull neck, massive shoulders, and a strong trident. Here was the living face of the ocean god, Rome's Neptune, the Greek Poseidon, in a mosaic masterpiece preserved in all its original pieces and vivid colors for two millennia. The old man who conjured this apparition stopped rubbing the stones, and almost at once the vision began to fade. The bright hues lost their shine. The face grew indistinct, as though veiled by mist, then cloud. A moment more, and it was unrecognizable. As my spilled water quickly evaporated in the North African sun, the mosaic disappeared entirely, fading back into the indistinguishable brown-ish gray pavement. The precious contents of my canteen had been a libation, a small sacrifice to the god of waters, who revealed his timeless face only so long as the offering lasted.

My encounter with Neptune seemed to personify the quest that brought me from my home in Colfax, Wisconsin. Like the mosaic, the object of that search lies hidden, but the proper method may yet bring it back to life. I arrived in coastal Morocco specifically to study, photograph, and most of all experience a place called Lixus, the "City of Light," as the Romans left it. The ruins are not far from the broken-down town of Larache, fronting a dark blue Atlantic Ocean. Only the upper and most recent ruins of the archaeological zone were Roman.

The Romans' identifiable pillars and arches rest upon the stone-work of earlier, unknown architects. I traced one of these massive, perfectly square-cut monoliths with the palm of my hand and thrilled with a feeling akin to deja vu: the workmanship was uncannily reminiscent of other massive, ancient stones I had touched high in the Andes of South America and at the ocean bottom near the island of Bimini, fifty-five miles east of Florida. Before the Romans made a colony out of northwest Africa, it was the independent kingdom of Mauretania. Phoenicians from Carthage preceded the white-skinned Mauretanians. But who was building cities before *they* arrived?

A MATTER OF LIFE AND DEATH

Morocco was the midpoint in my single-minded search for the roots of an obsession. Weeks before, I was sitting on the red leather saddle astride a black horse riding through the desert sands in the shadow of the Great Pyramid. In the Upper Nile Valley, I heard my footsteps echo through the enormous Victory Temple of Ramses III. In Turkey, I stood on the battlements of Ilios and looked down on the great plain where Greeks and Trojans fought to the death. Everywhere, I collected pieces of a lost, prehistoric puzzle far greater than all the places I visited.

From the world's oldest known tomb, in Ireland, and Etruscan Italy's subterranean temple, beyond to Athens, where the Greek philosopher, Plato, first narrated the story that set me wandering, twenty-four centuries later, I was a driven man. Wherever I journeyed, I felt protected from men and events that on occasion threatened my life, and guided toward the answers I sought. But there were never enough answers. They were spread out like breadcrumbs before a hungry bird, always enticing me on to the next sacred site and the one beyond that.

I climbed Mount Ida, on Crete, to visit the cave were Zeus, king of the Olympian gods, had been born. There were other islands that needed visiting: In the Aegean, Santorini, its sickle shape all that remained of the volcanic explosion that vaporized a mountain, and Delos, birthplace of Apollo, god of light and enlightenment. In the broad Atlantic, Tenerife, its ominous mountain still trembling with seismic rage; Lanzarote, its tall, conical pyramids continuing to chart the progress of the sun after unknown millennia; and Gran Canaria, where I found the very signature of Atlas himself. My investigations went beyond the Old World, back across the sea to the colossal geoglyphs of fantastic animals and giant men drawn in the Peruvian desert, and to Bolivia's most enigmatic city, high in the mountains. There were Mexican pyramids to climb and, not far from home, I sought out the effigy mounds of birds and serpents from Wisconsin to Louisiana.

The price paid for these and many more life-changing travels sometimes went beyond money. On Lanzarote I almost drowned when the rising tide trapped me in a seaside cave. Later, that same day, I was saved from falling into the mouth of a volcano by my walking stick. In Tangiers, I escaped a gang of cutthroats. I was less lucky in Peru, when three men strangled me into unconsciousness and left me for dead in the streets of Cuzco.

Even though this book has gone to press, it is not finished, nor ever shall be, because my ongoing travels continually unfold new dimensions in an endless search for the story which can never be known in its entirety. All these adventures were and are bent to a primary purpose: *to re-connect with that which was lost.* Why I want to do so may be explained through sensible rationalizations—discovering the roots of civilization, the alchemical thrill of transforming dramatic legend into historical reality—or some such reasoned justification for incurring prodigious amounts of time, energy, money, and risk to my physical existence. But they would be only partial explanations. There is a visceral cause beyond the power of words to describe what has become the joyful obsession of my life; it exceeds mere intellectual curiosity.

This *idee fixe* is by no means mine alone. Other investigators have been and are still similarly enchanted. My fondest hope is that the readers of this book, at least to some degree, become so infected—for their own good, of course! The fever came upon me most gently. While browsing in a Chicago bookstore in the spring of 1980, I picked up a copy of L. Sprague de Camp's *Lost Continents*, the first book I read about Atlantis.[1] I knew next to nothing about the subject and regarded it as little more than a legendary sidelight of peripheral interest. De Camp wrote convincingly and entertainingly against the leading arguments for Atlantis-as-fact, debunking the claims with sound geology and accessible history. I liked his no-nonsense approach. Still, he provoked more questions than he answered, and left me with the feeling that there was more to the story than his cavalier dismissal of this myth that has endured for at least twenty-four centuries. I re-read *Lost Continents* and searched out every book in its bibliography. Some were ridiculous, others credible, but all offered something thought-provoking. Although I still regarded Atlantis as fantasy, I could not shake the possibility that some kind of reality lay behind the myth.

TO FIND THE PAST IS TO FIND OURSELVES

Perhaps an answer might be discovered in the writings of Plato, the fourth century B.C.E. philosopher. His *Dialogues* comprise the earliest known account of Atlantis. Examining the *Timaeus* and *Kritias*, I found it difficult to resist, as have so many readers, the impression that his was a straightforward retelling of actual events in a real place with flesh-and-blood characters. He wrote of an oceanic empire on a beautiful island inhabited by a brilliant people reveling in their glittering temples and palaces, suddenly obliterated by a geologic event on the scale of a nuclear catastrophe. Most modern scholars dismissed his narrative as allegory.

But like so many readers of the great thinker's words I sensed there was something more to it than that. I dissected Plato's *Dialogues* point by point, all the while building an expanding library of source material that almost kept pace with my voluminous note-taking. I investigated the wonders of plate tectonics, volcanology, underwater archaeology, comparative mythology, archaeo-biology, archaeo-astronomy, and history, especially history. I plunged into the study of the past, from the rise of *Homo erectus* and the Paleolithic Age to Predynastic Egypt and early Mesopotamia, beyond to the American cultures in the Valley of Mexico and the Andes. The more I learned, the more I wanted to know. Pursuit of Atlantis was frustrating and elusive, but enriching, because the answer to one question almost invariably posed several more.

After years of research, far from narrowing my investigation, it had broadened. I felt challenged and more determined than ever to solve the riddle to my own satisfaction. Before the end of the decade, the information I had accumulated was making a strong case for Plato's sunken city. It is impossible to determine, however, precisely at what point the certainty dawned on me that, yes, Atlantis was historical reality. No single piece of decisive evidence convinced me. Only as I reviewed the mass of collected and organized material, detecting common themes and recurring patterns, did an overall, objective view of the whole civilization begin to appear.

Like the various pieces in the mosaic of Neptune's head brought back to life by the old Moroccan, Atlantis gradually emerged in a total picture that could only be appreciated from the correct perspective. That perspective was formed by properly interrelating the various fragments of information. I did not force the facts to fit any preconceived notions. On the contrary, my conclusions grew entirely from the available data. I had not set out to prove or disprove the existence of Atlantis, but to find the reason for its hold on the human imagination. It was awesome to finally come to the realization that the place had existed after all. True, physical proof for its demise is scant and equivocal. But had I been arguing a habeas corpus case in any court of law, I knew I possessed more than sufficient evidence to bring in a guilty verdict. I could not imagine that my curiosity would eventually lead to so enormous a project. At first, I felt inhibited about writing a book about Atlantis. I am not a professional archaeologist, and the subject seemed far too broad for a specialist in any one field. The only person who could write *the* book on Atlantis had to be a genius proficient in a dozen different sciences.

My dilemma was the same as that faced by the astronomers Clube and Napier in their related research *The Cosmic Serpent:* "No one individual has the breadth of knowledge to analyze, in full scholarly depth, more than a fraction of the evidence which can be brought to bear on the theme. On the other hand, ever-increasing specialization of knowledge is a recipe for sterility and error: sterility because the comprehensive picture may go unrecognized, and even if it does not, error, because the specialist will tend to overemphasize the significance of this or that data in his own field. The specialist is right to attach importance to details; but one does not judge the theory of evolution simply by its application to the flying squirrels of Eastern Asia." No salaried archaeologist alive today would be allowed to touch the subject of Atlantis, save to debunk or diminish it. An explanation of the causes for their extreme reluctance concerning all things Atlantean to readers unfamiliar with the present, somewhat deplorable condition of modern American archaeology would require a sad book all its own. Actually, that book has already been written—*The Hidden History of the Human Race.*[2] Suffice it to say that a powerful dogma demanding that no one seriously consider certain taboo subjects rules today's hallowed halls of academia.

ANY PLACE BUT ATLANTIS

There are legitimate reasons for serious investigators, professional or not, to avoid mentioning the A-word. They have been told that Atlantis was founded by spacemen, that its magic ray is still sinking ships and downing aircraft in the Bermuda Triangle, that its alien inhabitants are alive today and reside under the North Pole, and many other fantasies, enough to make any sane researcher dismiss sober consideration of the sunken city as so much hallucination.

Atlantis has been linked with ancient Troy, the Bahamas, the Hebrides, northern Germany, even another planet. Establishment scientists that have investigated the tale suggest it was on Crete, while the latest interpretation by "diffusionists" postulates Antarctica. This confusion concerning the whereabouts of Atlantis is not new. As long ago as 1841, an exasperated T. H. Martin wrote in *Etudes sur le Timee de Platon*, "Many scholars embarking upon the search with a more or less heavy cargo of erudition, but with no compass other than their imagination and caprice, have voyaged at random. And where have they arrived? In Africa, in America, in Spitzbergen, in Sweden, in Sardinia, in Palestine, in Athens, in Persia, and in Ceylon, they say."[3] My investigation suggests the Atlanteans impacted all these places and more, so it should not be surprising that investigators find revealing clues to the lost civilization in widely separated locations. While some of these sites may have been Atlantean colonies or places of refuge for its survivors, the city itself cannot be identified with any of them. One of this century's saner Atlantologists, James Bramwell, stated succinctly, "Atlantis must be understood as located in the Atlantic Ocean or it is not Atlantis at all."[4]

In view of the wild claims made for "the lost continent," it is no wonder most professionals dismiss the very notion of Atlantis with contempt. The piles of speculative droppings that surround discussion of Plato's story comprise an obstacle course that every honest inquirer must hurdle to reach the truth. Someone other than an archaeologist or an occultist might, therefore, be more willing to sort out that truth buried under decades of official hostility and lunatic-fringe advocacy.

Perhaps my background as a student at Southern Illinois University's School of Journalism and, later as an investigative reporter with the *Winnetka Paper* prepared me for sifting fact from fantasy in order to make sense out of the ancient mystery. I felt that if I dealt with Atlantis as an archaeological detective story, perhaps the truth might be determined. It is, after all, a reporter's task to assemble as many pieces of evidence as possible, then arrange them into a coherent picture for the general public. Archaeologists, on the other hand, object to popularizations of their work, which, by its very nature, subjectively concentrates on individual pieces of the whole. They have abandoned the subject of Atlantis altogether, save for their efforts to explain it away, either as a complete fiction or a misinterpretation of ancient events in the Aegean Sea. In so doing, they leave the field of investigation open to researchers who lack their academic credentials.

ATLANTIS LIVES!

It was as a reporter, then, that I published *The Destruction of Atlantis* in 1987. The income it generated funded the next eight years of my overseas' research. During those extensive travels, the evidence I accumulated from around the world not only confirmed most of my original conclusions, but expanded them far beyond the chapters of the first edition. When the opportunity to republish it presented itself, I was determined to use the primary text as a foundation upon which to add these latest materials. The result is a substantially augmented presentation, five times larger than the original. Too many books on Atlantis contain nothing more than rehashed information that has been used numerous times before. *The Destruction of Atlantis* is unique, because it offers fresh evidence, most of it never-before available to general readers and new even to long-time students of the sunken civilization. It is presented here within the credible context of the Near-East Bronze Age, not removed, as it usually is, from recognizable history by sixty-five hundred years. Those pieces of evidence appearing in previous publications are held up in a new light. Some are discarded because they have been proved invalid by modern research; some refit into a new way of seeing Atlantis.

Dry recitations of documented theories will not resurrect the

Queen of Legends from her watery grave. A definite shift in consciousness is necessary and is presently underway. The dogmas of the past no longer rest on the firm footing they depended on for so long, as more and more researchers, some with outstanding scientific credentials, publicly voice their serious doubts concerning obsolete theories preached as holy writs of Academia. Establishment positions regarding humankind's supposedly first civilizations in Mesopotamia and the Nile Valley; the impossibility of ancient mariners to cross the oceans from Europe, the Near East, Africa, or Asia to the Americas; the lack of any contact between the ancient peoples of Mexico and Peru—these and similarly entrenched positions are eroding at an accelerating rate under the hard questions posed by a new generation of investigators. Awareness of Atlantis is next on the list of issues still too radical for consideration. But it is the single most explosive issue of them all, because its discovery could blow the Ivory Tower's official doctrine sky high. Perhaps that is why the defenders of Atlantis-as-myth are so unyielding. After so many decades of denial they have too much to lose.

My chief purpose in writing this book has been to make the lost civilization come alive in the reader's imagination. It is not enough to simply argue facts, no matter how convincingly. To make Atlantis live in the mind requires a persuasive factual basis on which to present an explanatory theory dramatized by a credible re-creation. The facts themselves need to be developed in such a manner that they seem more like clues to a fascinating mystery than the bloodless components of mere conjecture. The mystery, in turn, is examined by a theory that unifies all the evidence into a comprehensive solution. Using the factual elements of this unifying theory, I included a re-creation of what it might have been like to actually walk the streets of Atlantis, visit its temples and palaces, and witness its last day through the eyes of the Atlanteans themselves. It is hoped that such a re-creation will revivify a subject too long savaged by professional debunkers, half-baked historians, and self-styled psychics.

The factual Atlantis is fantastic enough. As such, this investigation makes no claims, ventures upon no speculation not supported by today's understanding of the past. It avoids the occult and extraterrestrial theories that discredit historic Atlantis among professionals and public alike. It relies exclusively on the better-established information and reasonably inferred conclusions of modern science, recognizable history, and comparative myth. If the Atlantis legend cannot be credibly transposed into an accessible, rational theory, resting largely on documented criteria, then it is, after all, only a legend not worthy of our curiosity. But once the paranormal speculations have been set aside, let us at least allow ourselves enough honesty to follow the facts wherever they may lead.

This is not to suggest that Atlantis lacks a genuinely mystical dimension. In truth, it was steeped in mysticism. The whole orientation of the Atlanteans' culture was aimed at obtaining spiritual empowerment through the mystical arts. It was not for nothing that their foremost mythic figure, Atlas, was revered as the founder of astrology. To be sure, even a reasoned examination cannot elude the Otherworldly aspects of the Atlantis story. To divest this investigation of them would be to miss Atlantis's reason for being—and the reason for its annihilation. But the mysticism found in these pages was not "channeled," nor conjured via some favorite crystal. I allowed whatever magic there might be here to arise of its own accord. The real sensation of wonderment derives not through paranormal uncertainties, but from realizing the historical certainty that Atlantis did indeed exist.

Why should the historical certainty of Atlantis be interesting or important? Aside from its place as the real cradle of civilization, Atlantis represents a warning we need to grasp to the bottom of our souls. Not since the Atlanteans elevated their society to its zenith has the world attained a similarly international civilization. But they so abused the fundamental principles of their greatness through arrogance and greed that their entire society crashed into horrific oblivion. The demise of a civilization (and hundreds have fallen before our own) is never painless.

Americans have no right to assume that their civilization will continue indefinitely, especially when they allow forces inimical to the basic survival of their society to proliferate. We need to consider our own behavior, not only as a nation, but as a species, to appreciate how vital an Atlantean comparison might be for today's so-called movers and shakers, before they and the rest of us are moved and shaken by the consequences of our own misdeeds. Atlantis is the supreme object lesson. We ignore it at our own peril.

IN THE SHADOW OF ATLANTIS

Atlantis can be restored to life through the collection and comparison of trace evidence. Since the capital's destruction was of so cataclysmic a nature, it is to a large extent through the literary, historical, and mythological evidence of those peoples touched by the Atlanteans that we are able to follow the story. If, by comparison, Rome had suddenly vanished at the zenith of her imperial greatness, leaving no material evidence of the city's existence, we would still know much about her from the surviving testimony of the societies she directly influenced. The surviving testimony of peoples touched by Atlantis during the height of her empire is no less revealing. Until Atlantis herself is discovered, her physical absence does not invalidate the possibility of her story.

The discovery of the planet Pluto is an analogous example: It was not actually seen until 1930, when the invention of more powerful telescopes made its observation possible. Pluto's existence had nevertheless been strongly suspected since the turn of the twentieth century, because astronomers already knew the motions of its neighbors, Uranus and Neptune, revealed gravitational perturbations that could not be attributed to the other planets. In other words, Pluto, though unseen for years, was believed to exist because of its observable effect on Uranus and Neptune. The physical laws of cause and effect are no less applicable to those of human history. Even though the material evidence of Atlantis has yet to be found, we may nonetheless learn the truth about her existence by observing her effect on other societies she influenced. In so doing, we point our investigation in that direction, until the eventual discovery and verification of Atlantean artifacts.

But Atlantis is far more than some archaeological problem. It is, in fact, more than we can entirely express in words, because it is the collective trauma of our species: the birthplace of earthly civilization detonated in a magnitude of terror and guilt that seared the memory of mankind from that time to this. Its supreme moment of horrific mass extinction echoes through all the generations since in the persistent nightmares of our collective unconscious as universally expressed through the myths of every human society. It is time we awoke from the nightmare. Let us heal that missing memory of our origins by recalling the great glory we achieved, but carelessly lost, before we repeat the process of self-destruction by making the same dreadful errors.

ONE

"In a Single Day and Night"

A Re-creation

And when, amid no earthly moans, down, down that
town shall settle hence, Hell, rising from a
thousand thrones, shall do it reverence.
From Edgar Allen Poe's "The City in the Sea"

A lone white sail emblazoned with the image of a black, predatory owl unfurled in a loud flap to inhale the first breath of dawn at sea. Behind the ship's high, curling stem, Elasippos—an ancient harbor-city on the continental coast—fell away in the rosy morning. A female eye painted indigo just above the waterline on either side of the prow stared serenely across the calm expanse of the water heaving gently like the dark breast of a titan. The ship was a freighter, single masted and square rigged, a cargo of bronzes packed amid branches and lashed with hemp to the in-boards.

There were chalices for sacred libations, tripods crawling with serpentine motifs, cauldrons fashioned like crowns, statuettes of gods and monsters. The crew of thirty-two men were as bronzed as the cargo they carried. They had crossed this eighty-league stretch

of Kronos Sea many times before. They knew the clear-sky weather
would hold, because their captain had sacrificed a young bull to
Poseidon at the quay. Most of the meat was taken by the officiating
priests. The ship's company was allowed a few morsels. The rest,
tossed into the water, went to the god. As the sun climbed to its
noontide, a lookout on the high bow called out, "Ships ahead!" All
eyes not occupied with immediate duties searched the western
horizon. Before long, the captain spotted a small armada of warships tacking in a wide zigzag against the same wind that mildly
blew his freighter on its course.

Soon the frightening designs of their sails were discernable—
grinning skulls, grasping ravens, the sea god's own crimson trident,
a golden lightning bolt—fearsome portents for the enemies of the
Distant West. The warships approached in lengthy, swaggering strides.
Like the freighter, painted eyes were carved above the waterline,
but, like the narwhal, pointed, serrated battering-rams jutted just
beneath the spreading bow waves. Both bow and stern posts curved
upward to end in the stylized heads of serpents or birds of prey.
Before the captain could order a change of heading to avoid the on-
rushing flotilla, the warships themselves simultaneously dispersed
to north and south in an orderly maneuver coordinated by flag
signals and trumpet calls that sounded more musical than military
over the shifting soundboard of the sea. Moments later, the vessels
passed hissing through the water to port and starboard, so close the
freighter's crew could appreciate the prodigious length and lolling
bulk of the swift warships.

Troops of warriors crowded the high gunwales, cheering a greet-
ing across the short space of water and waving their red horsehair
helmets. Figure-8 shields glinted in the afternoon sun, as the overshadowed freighter slithered in between the half-dozen battle cruis-
ers. The small fleet dropped quickly astern and eventually vanished
behind the eastern horizon. Fresh water flasks were passed around
for all hands, and rations of oranges, dates, and pomegranates were

equally distributed to officers and common seamen alike. A noisy raven was released from its little wooden cage and everyone watched Apollo's bird rise rapidly on its shiny black wings as it circled ever higher overhead. After a moment of apparent indecision, it dashed off straight toward the west. "To your oars!" the captain bellowed, his gaze still on the freed raven, now only a dark spot dwindling against the sky gathering with cloud. Not long after it was lost to even his eagle-eye, the bow-watch sang out, "Atlas!"

ARRIVING IN ATLANTIS

The captain ordered a slight change of course, and the steersman leaned on his tiller at the stern. The ship's ever-languid eyes stared directly ahead at the dark silhouette on the horizon. In less than an hour, the silhouette assumed the form of a shield laid upon the mirror surface of the sea, its middle boss rising steeply from the center. Moments later, the image changed again, this time to that of a colossal pillar, almost anthropomorphic in shape, vaguely suggesting the configuration of a giant down on one knee supporting the roof of the sky, for a partial overcast hung above the island. The great mountain's summit was lost in cloud, its bouldered shoulders hunched against heaven. Atlas, "He who upholds," was well named. The men were temporarily relieved of oar duty as a freshening breeze, like the unseen hand of the goddess Alkyone herself, sped the vessel to port. The freighter slid past several outcroppings of half-sunken rocks, one strangely fashioned by the incessant fingers of wind and wave to closely resemble a demasted ship not unlike their own—a circumstantial creation in stone washed over with Gorgon legends of Medusa. For sailors, it was a warning to beware these perilous waters.

Approaching the island-capital from the east, the freighter fell into the enormous shadow of Mount Atlas cast far out over the sea by a lowering sun that scattered the oppressive cloud cover. This view of the island from the sea never failed to impress observers. At once majestic and fearsome, newcomers, even from civilizations of great splendor, were invariably awed by the power, political, architectural, and geologic, that radiated from this rather eerie place. Especially to the governed, their Atlantean conquerors seemed to be larger-than-life human extensions of their homeland: culturally sophisticated, but not without an innate capacity for overpowering violence.

The Elasippos ship came within hailing distance of the beach, skirting the shoreline around to the south. The busy crewmen sometimes looked up from their duties to see a farmer and his family laboring in the wheat fields. There were airy villas of whitewashed walls and grand private homes with red- and orange-tiled roofs, some perched halfway up hillside acreages overlooking eastern ocean vistas. Coastal roads grew visible, and horse and cart traffic were joined by the occasional chariot of a wealthy landowner or palace official.

Soon, the great harbor was on right, and the sun, poised huge and carnelian, like a titan's burnished shield raised just over the edge of the world, sketched the broken overcast in bold streaks of scarlet, tinting wine-dark the waters through which the freighter coasted. The captain ordered the sail furled and the rowers back to their stations. Oars rose and fell rhythmically to the measured beat of the *hortator* upon his drum as the ship executed its lumbering turn toward shore. The captain, standing at his place in the high bow, marveled at the towering wall on the other side of the harbor. As often as he had seen it, the sight of such a colossal fortification never failed to awe. From the perspective of an incoming vessel, only Mount Atlas was more prominent. The battlements' vast extent were sufficient to make the capital unique, but the Atlanteans always did things on a grand scale that no one else could afford or duplicate.

Completing an unbroken circuit around the entire inner city, these castellated ramparts sloped gently upward from their contiguous base, making the whole work appear even higher than its forty feet. The effect was heightened by the placement of various stones arranged into colored bands that narrowed as they reached to the top of the wall. Black lava rock rose from the wall's base to little more than halfway up the front. The next course, about ten feet high, was made of white pumice below a top band, the narrowest, of red tufa. When viewed close-up, the rampart seemed to reach for the sky. The broad, black course had been made to dramatically contrast with gleaming sheets of highly polished bronze set into the walls. Massive, crenelated towers manned by special regiments of archers and spearmen abutted the wall and were spaced within a bow shot of each other, surrounding the entire capital, if need be, with impenetrable crossfire. The tower roofs were spacious enough to accommodate catapults that could throw a quarter-ton stone, a weighted sponge of flaming oil, or a large basket filled with lethal vipers onto the deck of an approaching enemy long before the ship could make land. If any did make their way to shore, their crews would be pounded into oblivion by a concentrated barrage.

The unchanging eyes of the freighter stared at the sprawling harbor, its gigantic docks crammed with lean triremes from the northerly kingdom of Mestor, famous even then for its circle of huge stones that counted the progress of the sun; pot-shaped trading ships from lands of the Inner Sea almost closed off in the west by the Pillars of Heracles; a luxurious yacht of gleaming white cedar and bronze appointments on emissary from newly conquered Etruria; scarred freighters creaking in their quays, weary with long, overocean voyages to and from copper mines of the Outer Continent; beautiful but dangerous-looking Confederation warships, like the rigs encountered en route, in the process of refitting; a whole shipful of musicians and their strange instruments from allied Libya; an Azaes merchantman with a heavily guarded cargo of costly dyed linens, rare perfumes, and huge feathers that glinted in the sunlight like azure metal.

THE CITY OF WORLDLY DELIGHTS

Oars up on command, the little freighter from Elasippos coasted expertly into dock. Ready hands caught thrown lines and beam ends squeaked into the wood pilings; bow and stern were secured. The discharged crew bounded ashore for the promise of high times, but their captain and first officer remained behind to supervise the unloading of the precious bronzes with the just-arrived palace recorder, wax ledger and silver-tipped stylus in his hand. Immediately behind the harbor works was a broad, extensive avenue that fronted and partially surrounded the lofty walls that guarded the city with their bold watchtowers at regular intervals. It was here, along this elaborate avenue, that the goods of the whole island-capital and much of the wealth of the world, civilized or not, were displayed, bartered, bought, and sold. It was Atlas' own marketplace, the economic heart of his empire that beat night and day; where virtually everything and practically anyone were for sale; where the riches of three dozen cultures flowed in an exciting disharmony of international voices, sights, and smells, at once garish and intoxicating.

Into this mercantile vortex the crewmen of the Elasippos freighter threw themselves, followed eventually by the captain and first officer. The variety of faces and often wildly dissimilar bodies that crowded this eternal bazaar were no less varied than the confused riot of glittering goods and myriad services that infested the market avenue itself. There were godlike giants with metallic-golden hair tied tightly behind their bold, strong heads. They had ice-blue eyes and voices like Atlas' when he bellows from the depths of his mountain. There were awed, dark brown little fellows bedecked with so many feathers one might imagine they flew across the ocean from their forest-kingdom of Maia. There were brusque, big-boned men from northerly Euaemon with hair like fire and tempers to match. Taller were the Eastern Continent's blue-black men, whose incomprehensible babbling was punctuated by the constant clatter of huge ivory collars hanging around their long necks.

These and more were the outsiders, some of them part of the Confederation, but most foreigners come to Atlantis for the profusion of material goods she spread out for the world. Native Atlanteans less frequently seen among the jostling crowds were the apparently wise, long-robed, long-bearded astrologers. They passed unheeding and unheeded through the joyful mobs. Graceful courtesans with purple-painted eyes flowed like filmy apparitions between the rows of bawling street merchants. Warriors in the Atlantean armed forces—infantrymen, bowmen, and marines—were common sights, their high, crimson, horse-hair helmets bobbing above the crowds. There were merchants, some native but most foreign, selling everything from stubby vats of aromatic spices to flasks of wine and hogsheads of beer, from fruits and fans to votive statuettes and perfumes. Through the crowds pushed farmers and shorehands, pickpockets and prostitutes, street musicians and beggars.

Beyond the flurry of the marketplace and the gargantuan wall that squeezed it next to the harbor, the capital lay in resplendent, monumental organization, like an empress' crown jewels on permanent display. The sacred city was strangely designed, unlike any other in the known world. It was laid out in concentric circles, alternating rings of land and water, each equidistant from the other. The water rings were joined by a system of canals that bisected the capital in all directions, with gates and outlets to the three capacious harbors on the south coast. Two land rings encircled a central island. Each ring was entirely surrounded by a high wall, the inner ring plated in a glinting excess of *orichalcum*. Displaying this costly metal was a deliberate extravagance meant to impess foreign visitors with the Atlanteans' almost barbaric opulence.

Orichalcum was the Atlanten name for the finest grade of copper on Earth, and they alone were its miners, shippers, and dealers. Thanks to their skill as sailors, they had discovered rich deposits of the ore in the freezing north of the Opposite Continent long ago. Since that discovery, the men of Atlantis never relinquished their hold on its source, which simultaneously made possible the Near Eastern Bronze Age and Atlantis's unparalleled prosperity. They ostentatiously displayed the metallurgical components that generated their great wealth, decorating the inner wall with orichalcum, the middle wall with tin, and the outer wall with bronze. Every kingdom in the Ancient World had to purchase the copper needed to make bronze from the Atlanteans, who jealously guarded its overseas sources as the highest state secret. And bronze was the most important component in contemporary weapons' manufacture. Without it, conquerors of new lands or defenders of their own could not hope to succeed.

AT THE CITADEL

The land ring directly behind the tricolored wall that encircled the city comprised the military headquarters of the Atlantean Empire. Here, its navy and marines set up extensive offices, training facilities, and barracks for every grade of officer, seaman, and foot soldier. Admirals and generals planned strategy; captains rehearsed their junior commanders and sailors in maritime proficiency; lieutenants drilled ranks of archers, spearmen, and slingers, and the more heavily armed warriors with sword and shield; horse soldiers and charioteers competed in tactical mobility with organized brigades of elephants; the huge animals, ferocious in spiked armor, grasped seven-foot long scimitars with their trunks.

Natural hot and cold springs were converted into luxuriously ornate baths for men and animals alike. From this circular headquarters the imperial power of Atlantean conquest spread over the world. But the land ring was not without temples (mostly to the gods of war) and enormous gardens that provided both supplies of food and numerous places of entertainment. Foremost of these was the largest racetrack ever built. It made a complete circuit around the middle of the land ring. All facilities were grouped on either side of the track. While the general public was ordinarily forbidden from entering this most important military zone, it was regularly open when races and other sporting events were staged to celebrate a special occasion, such as the Day of Poseidon, creator of the horse; an important victory; or to entertain a guest of particular merit. This military land ring was connected by stone bridges to the next, and each bridge was wide enough to accommodate two war chariots side by side.

Towers and gates guarded both sides of the bridges, which were splendidly adorned with statues of gods and heroes. Prodigious canals were dug through each ring and roofed over, making them subterranean and allowing swift, direct passage by even the largest ships to every part of Atlantis on a moment's notice. On the southwest outer coast of the land ring were two separate, gigantic, underground docks, constructed to service several large warships at a time, yet completely invisible to all but the initiated. Military as well as civilian considerations inspired these huge engineering feats; their creators feared revenge from any of a dozen conquered enemy lands.

The inner, smaller land ring was occupied by the splendid temples, private homes, and offices of the empire's high priests, scientists, artists, engineers, and elite warriors. Their buildings were among the finest in the empire, second only to those of the imperial family. Some were built with one color of stone; others tastefully combined different colors, for the whole island was rich in a variety of natural building materials. The spiritual and intellectual elite lived in monumental structures, as luxurious as they were comfortable, with hot and cold running water, sunlit courtyards, and flowery balconies. Every building was filled with statues large and small; murals depicting mythic scenes enlivened the walls, and multicolored mosaics covered the floors. In contrast to the tumult of the military land ring, this inner haven behind the flashing orichalcum wall rang with the sounds of artisans, choral singing, and music of all kinds, from lone flute players to choruses of harpists. In sacred groves and dark, solemn temples, the inner ring was home to numerous religions, cults both light and dark, where a quiet struggle was being waged between priests and sorcerers.

THE TEMPLE OF POSEIDON

Shorter bridges and canals identical to those that spanned the outer rings connected the inner to a central island, home of the emperor and his family, a household guard, retinues of servants, and the most extraordinary architectural and spiritual feature of Atlantis, the Temple of Poseidon. Titanically broad and proportionate in height, the exterior surfaces of the immense, white-stone building were completely covered in molded sheets of silver, which contrasted with gilt, sculpted figures of the god and his divine attendants mounted in the temple's pediment.

During the day, light was admitted into the cavernous interior through a few narrow windows, hardly more than slits, near the ceiling, itself a miracle of carved ivory picked out with geometric designs of gold, silver, and orichalcum. In the dim silence heavy with an unseen presence reared the alabaster colossus of Poseidon, a statue so gargantuan that his lordly head practically brushed the roof of the building high above. He was portrayed standing in his monstrous nautilus shell chariot, all gleaming mother-of-pearl worked with flowing sheets of orichalcum and gold leaf. The chariot was drawn by a team of winged horses sculpted in white stone; they represented the foaming waves that roll before the progress of the god.

Completely surrounding Poseidon were one hundred smaller statues, rendered in gray stone, of golden boys riding the arching backs of dolphins. These were the Nereids, acolytes of a mystery school particularly sacred to the sea god. The entire monument rested on a raised circular platform, itself surrounded by a pool of clear water, making it yet another island, the smallest, holiest and most central on Atlantis. Before Poseidon, fronting the circular pool, stood a massive altar depicting in sculpted relief his divine character and exploits. Privileged seers came here to scry the future.

The temple was a veritable storehouse of sacred statuary. Monumental representations of the original queens and kings lined the circular interior, yet the building was far too enormous to be cluttered.

The first such statue was Atlas, who gave his name to the great sacred mountain and the island itself. The capital, too, derived its name from him: Atlantis, "Daughter of Atlas." In addition, there were many other statues dedicated by private persons of great wealth, both native Atlanteans and those who came from the far corners of the Empire. The temple dazzled with a profusion of molded orichalcum covering the walls, climbing the pillars, and even spreading across the floor. For nighttime ceremonies, it shimmered in the flames of burning tripods like dreams of the Otherworld.

Immediately behind the temple was a sacred grove with a large and verdant pasture. Here the sacred bulls were given free reign and nurtured by priestly attendants until chosen for sacrifice in the island's most important ceremonies. Although close, the Temple of Poseidon did not stand at the absolute center of the island. That position was reserved for a much smaller shrine, one of particular sacredness to the island's inhabitants. It was here that Poseidon lay with a mortal native, Kleito, to beget the empire's royal lineage. The holy precinct was enclosed by a wall of gold and entry was forbidden to all but the high priests, who lay seasonal offerings from the ten allied kingdoms on a sacrificial altar stone that resembled a great egg. This was the original Omphalos, the "Navel of the World," center of the oldest mystery religion on the island, if not on Earth, with roots going back unknown millennia to the days when men lived in caves. The altar stone was originally molten rock ejected from the mouth of Mount Atlas. After it had cooled, the stone was retrieved and venerated for its special powers and significance.

THE IMPERIAL PALACE

Not far from the acropolis was the palace of the emperor. While certainly magnificent, it did not sprawl in gaudy splendor, but was a tasteful synthesis of monumental simplicity. The palace served not only as the emperor's home, but also as his imperial base of operations and reception hall for important guests from other parts of the empire and beyond. It was surrounded by a large courtyard that stretched up to its gates with trimmed hedges running down on either side. It contained a four-acre orchard of pear, apple, orange, lemon, pomegranate, and fig trees.

At the other end of the leafy enclosure was a vineyard, complete with wooden racks for drying hundreds of grapes at a time, vats for trodding upon them, and every kind of facility the most skilled vintner could require. Nearby an extensive vegetable garden was laid out in long rows watered by two natural springs. The emperors' wife and daughters cultivated gardens of their own. Many varieties of flowers flourished in the island's extraordinarily fertile, volcanic soil. Several small fountains bubbled near the corners of the shrubbery and occasional statues of nature gods and goddesses lent an unobtrusive sanctity to the quadrangle. Fantastically plumed birds of iridescent orange and yellow with incredibly long tails cried out strange songs as they winged among the tree tops, and bees zigzagged across the flower beds. This embracing courtyard full of life and color created a serene setting for the royal residence.

The palace's high, bronze-sheeted walls were topped with a line of blue tiles that ran under a gently slanting red roof. The main entrance was a high, ornate affair of silver-sculpted greatness enfolding a pair of huge doors embedded with plates of incised gold. On either side of the threshold stood life-sized statues of two dogs, one gold, the other silver. More than symbolic guardians, they represented the solar, male principle and the lunar, female principle, respectively, of an ancient canine cult associated with the island's earliest kings. This grand entrance opened into a spacious hall. At its center stood a long table of dark, superbly carved hardwood with several dozen high-backed chairs of the same material and draped with cloth covers beautifully woven by the women of the royal household.

Gold, life-sized statues of heroic youths in the glory of their nakedness bore torches throughout the reception hall. Here feasts, entertainments, consular meetings, and other secular conferences took place. Beyond was the throne room, where the emperor, in all the power and glory of his supreme office, held sway over an imperial enterprise unmatched in scope and influence by any empire before and few after. Atlantis was the queen of an ocean she was mighty enough to name after herself. She sat at the center of an imperial web that spread from Asia Minor in the east, where her army fought in the Trojan War, across the sea in the distant west to the shores of the Opposite Continent.

THE ISLE OF THE BLESSED

Beyond the magnificence of the triple-walled capital, a far-flung, rectangular plain, fruitful and eternally green, was irrigated by an ingenious, extensive water system by communities of industrious, prosperous farmers. The whole island was studded with precipitous mountains, which embraced Atlantis on all sides up to the sea, sheltering the capital with an impregnable defense against the strong winds that often dashed against their flanks. There were pleasant meadows and many freshwater lakes, some of the larger ones bordered by small villages. The countryside was a temperate beauty of wooded valleys and high mountains, whose peaks sent down meandering streams of pure water for towns and private estates.

The Atlantean land abounded with a profusion of animal life. Some, like the large herds of horses bred for the battlefield, the plow, the wealthy man's chariot, and the racetrack, were imported from the European mainland. Others were native to the island, some, curiously so. Foremost among them were the elephants, evolved descendants of extinct mastodons who crossed over the long-sunken land bridges from North Africa unguessed millennia before. The island was a paradise for birds, which flocked in fabulous varieties from both sides of the ocean. Apiaries buzzed with honey production and the entire island was a cornucopia of various fruits, nuts, maize, wheat, barley, grapes, meat and milk. Warmed by an almost tropical sun but forever freshened by ocean breezes, it was no wonder even later generations of foreigners would remember this place as the Isle of the Blessed.

Large, thick forests supplied the island's flourishing lumber trade, an important part of the empire's aggressive naval programs. Fine, resilient wood was always in demand to keep the imperial sailors and marines afloat. But one tree no woodsman would dare threaten with his ax. This was the Tree of Life, ancient and alive when primitive hunters, following animal herds across long-ago collapsed land-bridges from the Eastern Continent, first arrived in the island. Under its huge, gnarled branches, priests and followers of the primeval religion gathered to perform their rites of spring with golden sickle and severed mistletoe and to tap its holy Dragon's Blood for healing purposes. Its lower limbs were hung with tinkling effigies, most notably the orichalcum cutout of a seven-humped serpent disgorging an oval, the Cosmic Egg, from its jaws. The primeval mystery cult of Atlantis, it still had followers long after the rise of rival religions, even into the last days of the Atlantean imperial period.

Natural hot, tepid, and cold springs were converted into numerous baths. There were baths within the palace for the royal family, huge affairs of smooth marble, glistering ivory and bright bronze. The private baths of the aristocracy were nearly as opulent, while the public baths might have graced a king's private chambers in any other land. There were even elaborate baths for horses decorated with motifs of Leukippe, the primeval Queen of Atlantis. Huge baths, more like ponds, were installed for laboring elephants and sacred bulls. The wonderful result of these extensive ablutions was a high level of national hygiene with a parallel rise in the general health of the population.

And over this fortunate isle loomed the world-pillar of Mount Atlas, its frowning summit often obscured by cloud. From time to time there had been rumblings from deep within his bowels. Occasionally his obscured face glowered, casting an eerie, roseate light over the entire city and much of the island. And sometimes the towers of his capital swayed precariously, while the ground itself quivered beneath the anxious Atlanteans' feet. But these things were no more than the god reminding his people that he was still alive.

To the sage priests gathered beneath the time weary branches of the Tree of Life, the Dragon Tree, they meant much more. They were *ostenta*—portents and admonitions. Skilled observers of the heavens learned of impending doom and endeavored to share their knowledge with the emperor. Their observation of a celestial threat seemed to be confirmed by numerous other portents reported from all over the empire. Had the Emperor noticed the unusual quiet in his sacred grove? That was because the birds were gone. Weeks ago, they began flying away in all directions, never to return. In the absence of their songs, an ominous silence descended over the entire island. Other animals were behaving strangely, too. Some elephants had become unmanageable and broke away from their keepers. Horses reared on their hind legs and refused to run the racetrack; goats no longer gave milk. The people themselves seemed possessed with a dreadful torpor, a mixture of fear for and resignation to some terrible event in the making.

The emperor listened to his priests with respect, but told them they had been wrong about such things before, and alarming his good subjects, especially during this time of uncertain war, would be disruptive. Besides, what were they supposed to do? Abandon

Atlantis, the most powerful kingdom the world had ever known, just because of a few unnatural events? If the threat they spoke of was so great, no precautions would be of any use, and so, good night to you! But even as the disappointed priests shuffled from his royal presence in the palatial reception hall, the emperor distractedly fingered a crystal pendent hanging from a slim golden chain around his neck. He was reminded of the expedition to the Delta Land of the east undertaken by his forefathers, who saved the world from catastrophe by installing a device with the help of native workers. But that was many centuries ago. The device had fallen into ruin and Atlantean scientists, more interested in the riches afforded their genius by materialism and militarism, could not repair it, even if they were allowed to work on it, which they were not. Tragically, the Egyptians who shared in the creation of the great instrument were now the enemies of Atlantis.

The emperor sat pensively on his throne. It was overlaid with his gold-embroidered, purple robe of state. He wondered if there really was a causal relationship between the morality of a people and the physical universe. The gods were the intermediators between man and chaos. If he angered them by failing to uphold their laws, would they in fact allow nature to fall on his civilization? Earth was once worshiped as the living mother of all life. Now, mining operations on a truly Atlantean scale were being dug into her flesh to excavate quantities of orichalcum so immense entire fleets of freighters were needed to carry them away. The greedy hands of several dozen kingdoms stretched out for the high-grade copper they would eagerly forge into the terrible weapons of war. It seemed a blasphemous cycle into which he and his predecessors had led the world, but the troubled monarch did not know how to escape it.

He ruminated, too, on the character of his own people, who had grown increasingly materialistic and careless in their respect to the forces which created them. Even homage to the Immortals was declining, unlike former times when the islanders' fathers and grandfathers, fleeing from the Trojan conflagration, cried unto heaven for rescue. Since then, not content with unchallenged sovereignty over an entire ocean and more of the world than other men even knew existed, the Atlanteans dwelt on thoughts of revenge against far-off Egypt for past defeat at the hands of the wily old pharaoh Merenptah.

FEARFUL OMENS

In the early morning of the day after his arrival, the captain of the freighter from Elasippos, together with his officers, was a guest of the emperor at the palace. They were joined by a few court officials and soldiers of the household guard. Their audience was not a particularly remarkable occasion, because Atlantis royalty maintained a long-standing tradition of personal accessibility to common people, on occasion. Besides, the foremost man of the empire was curious. The bronzes were displayed on the long table in the great hall, and the emperor, in an expansive mood, declared Elasippos craftsmen the finest in the world.

At this, his favorite hunting hound, which throughout the presentation slumbered unnoticed in a corner of the hall, started up with a panic-stricken howl and fled through an open door. The emperor attempted a feeble joke about his dog as art critic, and both captain and court responded with dutiful mirth. But outside, throughout the island of Atlantis, there were other animal omens observed far less lightheartedly by the priests. They gasped when they read the prophetic livers of sacred goats ritually sacrificed on the grand altar of Poseidon. The *auspicium* experts were no less appalled: Not a single uncaged bird remained on the island. All had flown away. And those kept as pets were now possessed of some panic. There were signs that even the common people, their thoughts generally on personal gain, were puzzled and dismayed to see.

Thousands of dead fish choked the canals, while the frightened trumpeting of elephants began to tell on the Atlanteans' nerves. Inexplicably, a heavy depression had hung over the populace for days, while strangely calm weather prevailed across the entire island. Most alarmed of all was the priest specifically delegated to observe the behavior of Mount Atlas from a shrine outside the city. The apparently supernatural apparitions at the summit of the mountain, thinly veiled in dense cloud and afflicted by incessant, weirdly thunderless displays of azure lightning, frightened him from his observation post.

No, the *ostenta* were not good. They had been predicted many months before by the chief astrologer. This high priest had sailed away weeks ago after his prognostications were received with official indifference. Now they were coming to life in the Elasippos bronzes still displayed before the emperor. The cups and statuettes were rattling and tinkling of their own accord, while a massive candelabrum of translucent seashells swayed pendulum-like on its gilt chain, extinguishing some of its flickering flames and alternately extending and shortening shadows cast from the company standing below. "Earthquake," the emperor explained the obvious without concern. But his guests were breathless and silent. "We have them often enough. Just the gods jealous of our attention." This time his assembled subjects could not smile. The floor bowed noticeably up and down beneath their feet, and even the emperor's royal composure began to crumble. One bronze, then another, fell tinkling from its place and clattered along the swaying floor. No one stooped to pick them up.

IT BEGINS

"Your Majesty!" The priest charged with observing Mount Atlas hurled himself unannounced into the imperial presence. "The mountain is distorted with a ghastly bulge on its southeastern slope! It is pregnant with horrible danger, Lord! We must abandon this place at once!"

"Get up!" the emperor hoarsely demanded. He nervously fingered the clear crystal talisman hung about his neck, but any further speech stuck in his throat. Now there were screams of men and women from somewhere in the palace, followed suddenly by the heavy sound of falling masonry. His wife and their daughters, alarmed but self-controlled, clustered around the emperor.

"This way," he ordered at last, and the company followed him out of the hall and through the sacred grove, its fountains abruptly dry. The ground moved beneath them, making passage difficult, but no one stumbled. They heard the sound of thunder. Unlike that of a storm, it did not die away, but sustained itself in a dreadful monotone. The emperor led the small party to a pair of moderately sized vessels, his yachts, berthed in the small canal leading to the Temple of Poseidon, the reflection of its towering roof distorted in the water rippling with subterranean energies. "Captain, take command," the emperor ordered, while everyone frantically piled into the long, narrow boats and he assigned which men would crew which vessel. "I'll take the helm," he volunteered. His slender, white-hulled yacht with its gilt-appointed details was not capacious. "Throw all this overboard!" he shouted, as he joined the others in rapidly tearing out the costly purple canopy from amidships. Without a word, but keenly aware of its significance, he up-ended the thronelike seat into the water already lashed with waves.

The Elasippos captain called out the count to his men at the oars and orders to his emperor leaning grimly on the stern rudder. Desperation whipped the volunteer oarsmen to physical exertions greater than any galley master could have wrung from them, and the imperial yacht attained a speed never reached during all the leisurely cruises of better days, its sister ship bearing the emperor's family close behind. The boats sped like arrows away from the central island of palace and temple, then parallel to the inner land ring, its splendid homes and fabulous temples shaking to rubble before their eyes.

The morning daylight was altered by degrees as an enormous cloud of coal-black ash spread rapidly and monstrously across the sky. The empress pulled a purple, shell-embroidered shawl over her shoulder against the sudden chill. A darkening shadow accompanied by jolting sounds of a noise more than thunder was falling over her homeland. She noticed there were many other craft afloat around them, and she could identify at least some of their owners by the sails.

Suddenly, there was a terrific thunderclap, as though lightning had struck the mast. Then a hesitating silence, followed a few minutes later by a thick firestorm that descended all around them with a deafening roar. Thousands of flaming stones, some as large as boulders, fell in a splashing, clattering barrage. "Make for the canal!" the emperor yelled once at the oarsmen, then turned to repeat his command to the captain of the craft close behind. The roofed canal that cut through the middle land ring was only a few strokes away, and both vessels glided into the subterranean slip before being hit by volcanic artillery. But their long passage through the dark was frightening. Numerous oil lamps designed to burn perpetually had been extinguished and both captains had to steer by the just-adequate bow and stern lanterns of their yachts. Unnerving, too, were the monstrous, incomprehensible sounds that echoed through the tunnel. But the progress of the boats was at least unhampered by any other craft.

VENGEANCE OF THE GODS

When they finally reached the end of the canal, the Elasippos captain brought the yacht to a halt. He stretched to look outside. The heavenly bombardment appeared to have stopped. Other seismic activity had also quieted. "Let's go!" His voice echoed powerfully all along the tunnel, and the rowers bent to their oars. The spectacle that greeted them was appalling and almost shattered their self-control. The waters were littered with dozens of broken, burning boats and ships. Not one had escaped unscathed. The few that remained afloat were burning out of control, their sails evaporating into flames like crisp leaves in a gardener's fire.

Charred debris was everywhere, including horribly mutilated corpses and the thrashing desperation of frightfully injured survivors. They screamed for help as the already overcrowded yachts flew by with no hint of rescue. The empress and her daughters wept, but the grim men at the oars rowed on in silence. As her ashen-faced husband turned to look at his wife, some movement on the shore of the outer land ring swiftly falling astern distracted him. The once highly trained horses, abandoned by their keepers, were aimlessly running about in panic-stricken herds. Their shrieks of terror were hardly less awful than the cries of drowning men.

Now a new dimension to the horror was unfolding itself. A thick cloud spread rapidly from the direction of Mount Atlas as though it would replace the blue heaven with a coal-black sky of on-rushing ash. Darkness was overtaking morning. The Elasippos captain skillfully maneuvered his boat around a chariot floating upside-down in the water. Both yachts made straight for a secret canal. All the others were hopelessly jammed with traffic. The royal channel, excavated many years before as a contingency against just such an emergency, conveyed the emperor and his improvised crews out of the last water ring. Its surface suddenly frothed with seismic agitation again.

The men took brief shifts at the oars, resting just long enough to catch their breath. But even their frenzied rowing could not obscure the continuous thunder that seemed to resonate from both earth and sky. Their work was made all the more laborious by the ash that began to descend like a heavy, gray vapor. They coughed and spit and daubed their eyes on their forearms, but plied the oars without missing a beat. As they pulled for the outer wall, the emperor observed a peculiar white streak trailing from behind his yacht. For a moment, he was perplexed. Then he realized that the channel water was boiling the paint from her planks. Keeping the realization to himself and hoping those in the boat behind would not notice, he wondered how much longer he could expect the disintegrating pitch to hold the hull together. The air grew colder as the incessantly thundering clouds belching from Mount Atlas cast a pall of deepening darkness over the world.

A lifetime of horror had passed since the emperor and his company first shoved off from the central island, but they finally reached the main harbor on the southern coast. Docks and quays were crowded with masses of terrified, shouting people. Some of them were fighting hysterically among themselves. The rowers grimly laid to their oars, and at first no one on shore seemed to regard the small, beautiful boats making for the swelling, open sea. Then a shout of recognition went up from the densely thronged mob. The shout was repeated, louder and by more voices. The crowd made its desperation heard above the volcanic drumming of Mount Atlas and across the widening distance as the royal yachts pulled farther away with every determined stroke of the oars. The cry rose louder still to become a chant, an improvised lament from thousands of throats calling in unison to their departing emperor. They saw him at the stern, a tiny figure raising his right hand high over his head, more a gesture of benediction than farewell, his eyes nearly blind with ash and tears. There was no condemnation in their common voice, only a tragic mixture of sorrow, resignation, and homage.

In a terrible moment, from the direction of erupting Atlas, a cloud the size of a black mountain sped low over the city, completely enveloping it, enfolding in its heavy billows even the harbor with its masses of people, who were instantly silenced. Moments later, a great surge of wind, accompanied by a detonation of thunder, dispelled the monstrous cloud and pushed the boats away from Atlantis at an unnatural velocity. The vessels fairly flew over the disturbed waves, but their sails, though strained to the limits of their linen fabric, held. The wind passed almost as quickly as it had overtaken them, and the Elasippos captain again felt himself in control of the yacht.

He noticed that many vessels of every size and description were likewise fleeing across the uncertain ocean. Some were already far over the horizon. Their captains, having read the portents of doom days or even months ago, heeded the signs and departed the doomed capital. A collective moan of horror floated across the widening distance of water, and the emperor turned to behold one of the multistoried watchtowers tear from its high wall and topple headlong into the crowds flocking around its base for shelter. The men beheld his face and wept openly.

THE WORLD IN FLAMES

"Look at the god!" someone yelled suddenly. The peak of Mount Atlas was transformed into a colossal pillar of light, burning the sky. Showers of fiery boulders by the thousands rained like dislodged stars onto the defenseless city. Torrents of incandescent lava slid down the mountain's slopes, rapidly engulfing splendid temples and private homes. Only then did the thunder of a terrific blast reverberate over and through the men in the royal yacht, now far out at sea, rattling her boards and drumming terror into their chests. Their beautiful homeland, the birthplace of civilization, was dying before their streaming eyes.

Avalanches of molten rock incinerated the fields and turned the rivers of pure water into steam. The huge, angry mouth of Mount Atlas continued to vomit cascades of liquid fire down its sides in all directions, incinerating forests with a speed no animal could outrun. At the mere approach of these blinding rivers, huge villas and even whole villages exploded into flames.

The sacred mountain was beset by convulsions. In tormented Atlantis, the accumulated greatness of centuries was being shaken to fragments; the city possessed by screaming madness. Atlanteans perished by the thousands, buried under the buildings in which they sought shelter, mercilessly pelted by barrages of flaming stones as they fled through the streets, gasping out their lives in the incandescent air. Elephants, horses, and humans threw themselves headlong into the rings of water where they were boiled alive.

On the central island, the forsaken Temple of Poseidon was illuminated with a ghastly glow reflected by its silvery exterior. Inside, a red haze pervaded the darkness. A sudden series of powerful shocks split the floor in quarters, and the standing colossus lurched over, crashing through the temple wall, which began to collapse around the fallen sea god. Nearby, the consecrated precinct where Poseidon and Kleito conceived a line of Atlantean kings, the Omphalos shrine remained upright but empty. Warned in advance of what was to come, its priestly caretakers spirited away the blessed stone, the Cosmic Egg, to relocate the Navel of the World to another site in some distant land.

DEATH THROES

By nightfall, the emperor, his dominion abruptly shrunk to two boatloads of exhausted refugees, still leaned at the tiller. His eyes were fixed on the island burning evermore fiercely in the retreating west, garishly illuminating the oil-black sea for miles around. The unreal scene was punctuated from time to time by bursts of volcanic thunder that echoed far out over the ocean, muffled by distance. "It is the god calling me back," he mused, "cursing me." He looked at the vessel hardly more than an arm's length away. In it sat his wife, silent and numbed by terror, the torn fragment of a sail, not her imperial robe, draped about her shoulders. But it seemed to him that she still bore herself as the empress. Regarding her in her natural dignity, he felt mixed extremes of pride and pity. Closely clustered in her lap were their little girls, sleeping with frowns on their fair faces.

At least the seas were calm, unusually so, and the voyage to Elasippos was otherwise routine. "Elasippos!" The awful irony of the captain's return trip to his home on the Eastern Continent was too much to consider. Only two days ago, he had voyaged to Atlantis with a simple cargo of bronzes in a common freighter. Now he was returning in command of the imperial yacht with the emperor himself minding the tiller! He felt lucky, no, *blessed* to have survived the worst holocaust humans had ever seen. He was filled with remorse for the crew he left behind, for his lost ship. But what were those compared to a city, an island full of death, the destruction of a civilization? The island had experienced earthquakes before, ones that had damaged the city. And an occasional outburst from Mount Atlas was known to have burned homes and even a village now and then. But *this!*

No one had expected anything of such magnitude. Exhausted by his own struggle for survival, his mind dwelled on thoughts of home, not far ahead. What a tale he had to tell! His family and friends would never believe it. In a few hours, the rising sun would lay a golden path across the face of the sea for them to follow. For now, he could only steer by the faroff, flickering glow of burning Atlantis falling astern. Ash clouds completely obscured the night sky, and even at this distance, everyone on board tasted the persistent acridness of sulfur on their tongues.

Most of the passengers, save the captain and his distressed emperor, were dozing when the relative darkness was suddenly transformed into something brighter than daylight. It was as though a new, more powerful sun had just thrust itself into the west. As abruptly as the brilliance appeared, it winked out, leaving everyone in blackness. As their eyes began to adjust again to the night, they heard the sound of a new, faraway thunder sustained on a single note. It steadily gathered volume until it seemed to fill the world. A shock wave traveling rapidly out of the darkness struck the two small vessels with such force their boards rattled violently and the emperor was afraid they would fly apart. It shook awake his daughters, who began crying. Theirs was the only sound as the ocean

TWO

Where Is Atlantis?

Civilization exists by geological consent, subject to
change without notice.
Will Durant

Plato reported that Atlantis was the chief city on a large island "beyond the Pillars of Heracles," known in our time as the Straits of Gibraltar. It sank "in a single day and night" of seismic upheavals. For more than two thousand years, investigators have wondered if such an event could have actually occurred in the location he described. Many insist it could not, and went on to search other parts of the world. But if one follows Plato's story, the expanse he indicated offers some intriguing possibilities.

The Mid-Atlantic Ridge is a ragged seam, a cleft in the floor of the Atlantic Ocean stretching from the Arctic Circle to an area at the same latitude as the tip of South America. It is a gash in the sea bottom created by the opposing motion of eastward- and westward-bound continental plates. As the drift continues, magma forced up from the Earth's molten interior rises and undersea mountains are created. Sometimes the mountains are so large that their peaks break the surface to become islands. Because the Mid-Atlantic Ridge is subject to contradictory forces, geologic violence, such as volcanic activity and tsunamis (destructive waves generated by submarine quakes), are common, in terms of geologic time.[1]

Iceland was born through just such activity in a massive undersea convulsion of rising, piling magma. As recently as November 1963, the island of Surtsey arose out of the North Atlantic depths off Iceland's southwest coast under a dramatic cloud of steam and lightning. Although it grew to only one and a quarter square miles, it peaked 560 feet above sea level. Two centuries before, British sailors discovered an uncharted Atlantic island and named it after their ship, the *Sabrina*. When they returned several months later with a party of hopeful settlers, the island had vanished beneath the waves.[2]

In 1447 Captain Alonso Leone discovered an island northwest of San Miguel, in the Azores. He christened it Asmaida, and the substantial island was settled by Portuguese colonists, who established farms and built towns and harbors. However, sometime before 1555, they were forced to evacuate the island, because it began to rapidly collapse into the sea after its hitherto dormant volcano erupted. The settlers escaped with their lives but little else. A small portion of the island remained above the surface and came to be known as Barenetha Rock. Some 260 years after the initial eruption, Barenetha vanished, and is today identified as the Milne Seamount.[3]

Nyey Island was discovered between Greenland and Iceland in 1783; it disappeared in 1830. The "pillar" island of Geir fuglasker (Great Auk Skerry) collapsed into the sea after less than a day of seismic violence. As recently as the mid-1960s a pair of islands rose and fell back beneath the surface of the North Atlantic. Before they disappeared, Syrtlingur towered 210 feet above sea level and Jolnir spread to fifteen square kilometers. These and similar examples imply an exceptionally active and unstable sea bottom, with ancient and recent histories of creating and reclaiming sometimes sizeable tracts of land within exceptionally short periods of time.[4]

Clearly, the existence and sudden disappearance of Atlantis is not outside the geological experience of the highly unstable Mid-Atlantic Ridge. In the late 1960s, soundings taken by research vessels such as the *Glomar Challenger* detected a sunken landmass roughly the size of modern Portugal, likewise somewhat rectangular, straddling a fault zone along the Mid-Atlantic Ridge. The Madeira and the Canary Islands may be its only surface remnants. The existence of a rather indefinitely shaped, large island under the surface of the mid-Atlantic is no speculation. In 1971, in the relatively shallow waters of the Vema fracture zone, dredgers from the University of Miami recovered limestone impregnated with granite; granite formations found beneath the sea are known as "continental rocks," because they are fragments of the landmasses to which they once belonged.[5]

FRAGMENTS OF A LOST CONTINENT

Over the next four years, geologists with Esso Petroleum and the University of Geneva examined the limestone-and-granite samples, which were shown to contain the remains of fossils that had formed when the limestone was less then thirty meters beneath the surface of the ocean. The slabs also showed traces of tidal action, indicating that the large island from which they came was once at sea level. Oxygen- and carbon-isotope ratios proved conclusively that the limestone had been recrystallized from a high- to low-magnesium form of calcite in the open air. A reporter for *New Scientist* observed that the limestone had been taken from the top of "a residual continental block left behind as the Atlantic spread out into an ocean."[6]

The presence of Mesozoic fossils in the retrieved limestone indicated the island was formed between 230 million and 65 million years ago, a long period during which the Eur-African and American continents were pulling away from one another. As they did, they left this continental fragment or block about midway between the Antilles in the west and the Guinea coast of Africa in the east. This subsurface remnant may be part of a larger sunken landmass or broken series of landmasses skirting the eastern flanks of the Mid-Atlantic Ridge as far north as a point parallel to the British Isles. When the continental island on the Vema fault sank is unknown. But vertical scratch lines along its flanks were made when it rose to stand above sea level. How long it remained dry land is uncertain. Nor do geologists know just when it sank to its present position. But the fact that the vertical scratches are still visible suggests it did not sink all that long ago; within the past 7,000 years is the oceanographers' best estimate.

In any case, the Canaries and Madeiras are also composed of continental rocks. Long ago, a landmass common to all the islands pulled away from the Eur-African continent by the opposing forces of plate tectonics, a process whereby the continents, resting on lithospheric plates, are pushed across the face of the Earth by subterranean forces in the planet's molten center. Over time, the Mesozoic continental fragment gradually succumbed to the encroachment of the sea until, perhaps as recently as 17,000 B.P. the island had entirely disappeared beneath the surface. Only the peaks of its tallest mountains still stand above the waves as the Azores, Madeiras, Canaries, and other groupings. While this Portugal-sized island pulled away from Eur-Africa, slender land bridges still connected the two separating landmasses. The verity of these bridges is beyond question.

On July 13, 1976, the internationally sponsored Deep Sea Drilling Project discovered a mountain range connecting the southernmost tip of Greenland with the European continent through Ireland and England. Both countries are the surviving remnants of that land bridge; the remainder sank four thousand feet beneath the sea. The Canaries were part of a different land bridge, according to submarine evidence showing that the seven distinct islands were originally contiguous. A land bridge connecting the Canary Islands of Fuerteventura with Lanzarote, the island nearest to Morocco, was discovered in relatively shallow depths after the Second World War.

As Wilhelm Schreiber writes, "The Atlas Mountain Range [in Morocco] marches toward the Atlantic Ocean and there breaks off quite abruptly. The legend of the doom of the island of Atlantis might therefore be based upon the natural catastrophe in which the end of the mountain chain was swallowed up."[7]

Such a physical connection between North Africa and the Atlantic islands must have existed until at least 17,000 years ago, as proved by the remains of Cro-Magnon men and women on Tenerife, the largest of the Canary Islands. These early humans were not seafarers, but hunters, who undoubtedly crossed the land bridge from Africa following herds of migrating game. Britain was still connected to Europe by a land bridge between Dover and Calais only five or six thousand years ago. The Atlantic island may have been linked to North Africa just as recently. But the Portugal-sized island was certainly inundated before the advent of what most would call civilization.

The facts of orogenesis (mountain building), plate tectonics, and continental drift show that geologic change on a continental scale is not rapid (at least in human terms). The rise and fall of seas and landmasses is counted in many hundreds of thousands or millions of years, not in "a single day and night." Sometimes this gradual change is evident in cases of relatively smaller areas, such as the Azore Islands, where today Flores is measurably sinking, while Corvo is simultaneously rising. They are being manipulated by the same deliberate yet observable geologic forces that once swallowed a much larger Atlantic island.[8]

EVIDENCE FROM THE BOTTOM OF THE SEA

Modern maps of the seafloor reveal that the present-day Atlantic islands off the coast of Africa sit on a plateau at the end of a sunken landmass connected to the southern Iberian coast. Known as the Azores-Gibraltar Ridge, it was a land bridge from the European continent to the large Atlantic island when it was still above water.

Oceanographers recognize a chain of sunken mountains extending from this ridge, linking the mid-Atlantic Ocean with the Iberian coast.

In deep-core drillings of the Azores, the fossil remains of freshwater algae as far down as 12,000 feet have been recovered, proof that the islands were once more than two miles above their present level. The otherwise inexplicable presence of freshwater algae at so great a depth confirms the findings of Dr. Maurice Ewing, professor of geology at Columbia University in 1949.

Sailing along the Mid-Atlantic Ridge in the vicinity of the Azores aboard a research vessel appropriately christened *Atlantis*, Dr. Ewing's expedition for the National Geographic Society obtained core samples from the ocean bottom more than two miles beneath the surface and far from any present-day beaches. He concluded that the retrieved specimens came from a former beach at sea level. The possibility of floating ice rafting the sand out from shore during early glacial periods was excluded, because the fine grains he recovered did not contain any fragments of larger, extraneous materials. Moreover, the nearest landfall was more than twelve hundred miles away. It was clear to Dr. Ewing that the beach sand could not have formed underwater, but rather along a shoreline that had been subject to untold centuries of wave action at sea level.[9]

While such material evidence has been confirmed over time, other "proofs" dredged up from the bottom of the Atlantic can be misleading. For the last one hundred years, virtually every author attempting to establish credible geology for Atlantis has repeated the story of a broken cable retrieved from the sea bottom near the Azores. Along with the cable came bits of the ocean floor, including basaltic glass splinters that could only have been formed in dry conditions. At least that was the scientific judgment in 1898, when these tachylite chips were embraced as confirmation of a sunken continent. Geologists have since learned that basaltic glass can be formed both in open air *and* underwater conditions, so the samples may or may not have formed when that part of the Atlantic was above water. The evidence here is no longer conclusive, and that people continue to use it to support arguments on behalf of a factual Atlantis shows how carefully one must discriminate among all the pertinent material available.[10]

To be sure, Atlantologists have a vast and growing body of verifiable evidence from which to choose in presenting their case for a former landmass in the mid-Atlantic. In 1963 Dr. Maria Klinova, sailing aboard the *Mikhail Lomonsov* for the Soviet Academy of Sciences, retrieved unusual rocks sixty miles north of the Azores from depths of more than six thousand feet. What made her find so interesting was that the specimens could only have been created in the atmospheric pressures available on dry land. The Soviet discovery tends to show that the tachylites found sixty-five years before were formed above sea level after all. Klinova's research was preceded by that of Stockholm's Riks Museum in 1957. Dr. Rene Malaise announced that members of the Swedish Deep Sea Expedition recovered fossilized freshwater diatoms from nearly two miles beneath the mid-Atlantic. The diatoms, small algae, were seventeen thousand years old, thus coinciding with one date for the final submergence of a Portugal-sized island in the Atlantic.[11]

These retrievals were not isolated freak specimens. Malaise's colleague, the noted paleobotanist R. W. Kolbe, cataloged more than sixty exclusively freshwater diatom species taken from eight-thousand-foot depths 578 miles from the west coast of Africa, in an underwater region known as the Sierra Leone Ridge. Moreover, all were discovered beneath a layer of marine sediment, perhaps volcanic debris deposited within the past ten thousand years. The species belonged to a wide variety of groups, some of which thrived in nutrient-rich habitats, others in nutrient-poor ones.

The broad diversity of organisms indicates that they flourished in large numbers for a long period in a large, dry-land environment. Their very abundance seemed to prove that freshwater lakes once existed on an island in the middle of the Atlantic Ocean. Critics were not convinced, however, and argued that the diatoms had been carried out to sea from Africa by powerful currents. Kolbe replied, "If ever we should accept the faint possibility of a turbidity current flowing from the African coast and dumping its load of freshwater diatoms at a distance of 930 kilometers from the coast, it remains to be explained how it was possible for this current not only to carry its load such a distance, but, at the same time, to climb uphill more than 1,000 meters before dumping the load on top of a submarine hill."[12]

OFFICIAL RESISTANCE TO ATLANTIS

Swedish scientists also found the silicified remains of terrestrial plants one and a half miles beneath the ocean surface. Their ship, the *Albatross*, sailed around the world for two years, surveying the depths of all the oceans. But only in the mid-Atlantic did they find organic evidence for a submerged landmass of the kind retrieved from the Sierra Leone Ridge. One might imagine that this magnificent achievement of the Swedish Deep-Sea Expedition would have have galvanized public interest with the exciting discoveries of its researchers and inspired the entire scientific community to a renewed search for the Atlantean fountainhead of earthly civilization. Instead, establishment scientists shrugged with indifference, then turned away to browbeat Atlantologists with harebrained theories of a Cretan Atlantis, examined below.

Tragically, to date no one has followed up on the wealth of indisputable evidence gathered by Dr. Malaise and his colleagues. It rests quietly in the Riks Museum, a trove of precious data, an oceanographic treasure map that might lead a future Atlantis-hunter to the greatest archaeological discovery of all time. But, for most salaried experts, any allusion to "the A-word" is politically incorrect.

Special credit is due when one of their number, fed up with the deplorable state of modern scientific opinion in these matters, breaks his silence to voice the obvious. One such hero was Dr. Kenneth Landes, chairman of the Department of Geology at the University of Michigan. In his annual Sigma Xi address to the Virginia Polytechnic Institute of 1958, during the height of his colleagues' attacks on Dr. Malaise, Landes asked emphatically, "Can we, as seekers after the truth, shut our eyes any longer to the obvious fact that large areas of the seafloor have sunk vertical distances measured in miles? Why not accept this, and devote the cerebral horsepower now being wasted on futile attempts to explain away the truth to finding out the mechanism which produces these drastic drops of the ocean bottom?"[13]

Anyone aware of the dogmatic climate of modern scientific institutions can appreciate just how courageous Dr. Landes's remarks were. Opinions voiced in favor of a factual Atlantis, the possibility of overseas visitors to the Americas before Columbus, or any theory contrary to generally accepted hypotheses will ruin the professional careers of such independent thinkers and deny them access to the scholarly publications in which they would otherwise present findings for discussion among their fellow researchers. To cite but one of numerous examples, professional investigators at the Oasis Oil Company in 1972 found convincing evidence to show that, in Pliocene times (about 5 million years ago), the Mediterranean Sea was thousands of feet below its present level. Apparently, making such a painstaking discovery was not as difficult as publishing it. According to *Scientific American*, "They could not get their manuscript published in a scientific journal, since no one would accept such an outrageous interpretation." Tragically, today's academic scholars are as resistant to unpopular ideas as the scientific authorities from whom Leonardo da Vinci was forced to hide his research.[14]

A REALISTIC SCALE FOR THE DESTRUCTION

Despite the reluctance of many scholars to consider the evidence, it would seem that the best geological data available point to the one-time existence of a mid-Atlantic continental island that stood above sea level for several million years until geologic upheavals initiated a prolonged process of subsidence. In the words of Dr. Ewing, in his *National Geographic* article "New Discoveries in the Mid-Atlantic Ridge" (May 1949), the ridge contains "many layers of volcanic ash."

The original Atlantic island connecting the Azores with Madeira and the Canaries was joined to Eur-Africa by trailing, elongated land bridges and positioned above an area of particularly intense seismic unrest, which was undoubtedly responsible for its eventual submergence. The larger part of its surface area probably sank over a protracted period of time. But the gradual settling of this large landmass over the deep, eternal fires of the Mid-Atlantic Ridge could have made the island's future subsidence a far more explosive affair.[15]

The forces that took millions of years to sink a continental landmass, once concentrated, could sink a single, volcanic island in a matter of hours. The cataclysmic result of such inconceivable pressures brought to bear on so tiny a focal point would be comparable to a major nuclear event. The longer the molten forces of the Mid-Atlantic Ridge accumulated inside and beneath Mount Atlas, the more potent the pressures that would eventually vent themselves in an eruption. This would result in the most explosive kind of volcano, one known as a composite. It is formed when lava and rock debris are forced violently from a central vent. The best documented example of a composite was Anak Volcano on the island of Krakatoa, in the Sundra Strait, between Java and Sumatra. In 1883, Anak detonated with the explosive magnitude of more than two hundred twenty-megaton atomic bombs.

Its fourteen-hundred-foot summit was literally vaporized, and the event excavated a hole at the bottom of the Pacific Ocean some nineteen hundred feet deep at one end, while ejecting six-foot-long boulders twenty-five miles into the atmosphere. The 150-foot-high wave it created swept across the face of the ocean for hundreds of miles from the blast center, drowning thirty-six thousand people. Dr. Ewing reported finding the scars of a similar catastrophe in the general vicinity of Plato's Atlantis: "Running south parallel to the Ridge, we crossed the Hirondelle Deep on the Azores' platform, the base of the islands, where our fathometer showed a great hole dropping down to 1,809 fathoms [10,804 feet], as if a volcano had caved in there at some time in the past."[16]

Whether or not this collapsed volcanic island is actually the site of lost Atlantis only a well-equipped underwater expedition may be able to determine. The Hirondelle Deep's collapsed mountain is another possible location for the lost island. Both sites meet the essential qualifications for such an identification, in that they were both above sea level in the general vicinity of Plato's lost city before being sunk by a natural catastrophe.

LIVING TESTIMONY

There are, additionally, examples of curious natural phenomena that suggest the former existence of a large island in the Atlantic Ocean. Every three or four years, hundreds of thousands of European lemmings (Lemmus lemmus) head away from the Norwegian coasts, swimming far out into the Atlantic Ocean, where they thrash about in a panicky search for dry land, before drowning. The small rodents do not begin this strange journey in packs, but usually head out individually, joining with others until their numbers grow into a large mass. Overpopulation and the unavailability of local food resources have been rejected as the cause of this phenomenon; animal experts do not understand why the self-destructive migrations take place.

But it is the singular *manner* in which this process occurs that points to something special in their migratory pattern. Lemmings have a natural aversion to water and hesitate to enter it. When confronted by rivers or lakes, they will swim only if seriously threatened and will otherwise move along the shore or bank. Their mass migrations into the ocean dramatically contradict everything known about the creatures.

Animal behaviorists recognize that lemmings seek land crossings whenever possible and tend to follow paths made by humans or other creatures. Could their suicidal instinct be a persistent behavioral pattern set thousands of years ago, when some land bridge, long since vanished, connected the Norwegian coast to an island in the Atlantic? Three other lemming genera *(Dicrostonyx, Myopus,* and *Synaptomys),* whose habitats have no conjectured geographical relationship to such an island, do not participate in migratory mass suicides.[17]

Nor are these the only animals with self-destructive instincts that lead them in the direction of the mid-Atlantic. Some species of Norwegian birds, especially hawks and falcons, fly far out over the sea, circle empty stretches of water, and then fall exhausted to the surface. Facing the sunken Atlantic island on the other side of the ocean, the Catopsila butterflies of Guiana behave in much the same fashion, although the males do not circle aimlessly before a final plunge. Instead, they have been observed diving straight into the waves. Coincidentally, the sunken landmass discovered in the vicinity of the Vema Fracture Zone by University of Miami geologists in 1971 lies in the position targeted by the Catopsila, many generations of which doubtlessly visited the dry land before it disappeared. Their persistent instinctual relationship with the former island means that it must have been above sea level in the recent geologic past, possible only a few thousand years ago.[18]

The strong migratory instinct of the Sargasso eel leads tens of thousands to their deaths in an area of the Atlantic closer to what was perhaps the northwest coastline of a now-sunken landmass below the Azores. Interestingly, the migrations of the Norwegian lemmings and birds and those of Guiana's Catopsila and the Sargasso eels cross in the same general mid-Atlantic position.

Nostophilia is a term animal behaviorists use to describe the apparent instinct of certain birds, insects, and other creatures to migrate very great distances.[19] Does some behavioral memory of a large, lost island that for countless generations sheltered and nurtured birds and other animals still survive in the evolutionary memories and compelling instincts of their descendants?

The geological and biological evidence tends to support the story of an Atlantean catastrophe. While it has been established that a landmass large enough to pass for the fabled kingdom does in fact lie under the area of ocean assigned to it by legend, proof of its submergence at least during the Middle or Upper Neolithic Periods (in other words, at a time when man could have occupied the island with something more than the rudiments of early society) cannot yet be confirmed. Still, the known history and observable activity of the Mid-Atlantic Ridge perfectly suit the area of ocean described by Plato as the setting for Atlantis. There are the otherwise unaccountable suicidal migrations of vastly different species of animals from widely separated quadrants, converging on empty seas in the same general vicinity as the large, former landmass lying in the traditional location of Plato's island.

These considerations cannot unequivocally establish the existence of Atlantis. But when two sciences as different from each other as geology and biology reach similar conclusions, the credibility factor climbs to a new level. And if, as I hope to show, the biological and geological evidence is further supported by history, archaeology, comparative mythology, and other sciences, then probability may yield to certainty.

ATLAS ARISES

Pulled between the eastward-migrating Eur-African continent and the westward-migrating American continent, the deep forces of the Earth may indeed have opened up to annihilate an island perched over the resulting rift. And something very much like a continent did, after all, make up the first Atlantic landmass. The Canary Basin, together with the Iberian Abyssal Plain of the West European Basin, was dry land (although probably not contiguous) some twenty-nine hundred miles long by fifteen hundred miles wide across at its widest point. Kenneth Caroli, a noted Atlantologist and feature writer for *Ancient American* magazine, wrote, "This may be the size which the island remnants now cover, but it is very unlikely to ever have been one, large landmass. If anything, it probably resembled strings of spaghetti straggling across the surface of the ocean, or long rent pieces of fabric from a garment."

But that was long before the evolution of humanity. Nevertheless, its protracted submergence must have begun with its birth, because the same forces of continental drift that created this mid-Atlantic territory also undermined its foundation in the tearing ocean bottom. The Atlantic landmass undoubtedly underwent many cataclysmic convulsions that caused ever greater areas of dry land to sink, until the one-time continent shrank to cover an area smaller than present-day Portugal; perhaps the area identified by University of Miami geologists and researchers aboard vessels such as the *Glomar Challenger* and *Atlantis*.

Plate tectonic theory began to be accepted in the late 1960s. The theory can be used to explain not only the existence of an Atlantic continental fragment, but also its eventual subsidence and final volcanic destruction: As the Eur-African and American continents moved away from each other and the seafloor spread, the continents trailed extended land bridges to Morocco, Portugal, and other parts of Europe. As the continents continued to pull away from a common center, great cracks were torn into the spreading seafloor, thereby creating an elongated zone of seismic instability perpetually irritated by forces parting the continents.

The Atlantic continent rested over this rift, which poked volca-

nic holes into the land above to release up-welling magma. The rift
could not indefinitely support an entire landmass of this size, and,
over time, more and more of it fell into the sea, resulting in an
island smaller than Portugal. This, too, began to collapse, leaving
behind only the peaks of the island's highest mountains standing
above sea level. These became the Atlas, Canary, and Madeira Islands—all of them volcanically active and seismically unstable.
Much later, in historic times, accumulating pressures were too much
for the relatively tiny vent of Atlas to contain, and the island
suffered an annihilation comparable to that of Krakatoa or a major
nuclear explosion.[20]

The Atlantis cataclysm was no geologic anomaly, but rather
among the most spectacular of its kind. There were others. On
November 24, 1934, the Associated Press reported the sinking of an
island off Trinidad, in the British West Indies, during a single day
and night, recalling Plato's account of Atlantis. This and similar
examples combine to portray the mid-Atlantic as the credible setting for a natural disaster comparable to the one described by the
Greek philosopher.

WAS ATLANTIS A LITTLE GREEK ISLAND?

Although Atlantis has been generally associated by most investigators with the Atlantic Ocean, as a preponderance of the evidence
suggests, fringe theorists have occasionally assigned the island to
other locations, some of them quite bizarre, for almost always
ulterior reasons. The latest of these eccentric interpretations gained
some acceptance among professional archaeologists and historians,
probably because it did not disturb their bias against transoceanic
voyages in pre-Classical times. The theory belonged to K. T. Frost, a
pre–World War I writer for the *Journal of Hellenic Studies*, who moved
Atlantis from the Atlantic Ocean to the Mediterranean island of
Crete. Since then, his hypothesis has been expanded by (perhaps

not surprisingly) many Greek scholars (including Galanopoulas, Marinatos, and others) to include the Aegean island of Santorini, known in ancient times as Thera.

Their advocacy of a Greek Atlantis was the latest in an unfortunate, chauvinist tendency on the part of some Atlantologists to associate their own national backgrounds with the lost civilization. For the German pastor Jurgen Spanuth, Atlantis was Heligoland, an island in the North Sea off the German coast. Henrietta Mertz, a name still honored in diffusionist circles, believed the pre-Columbian earthworks in her native United States were the ruins of Atlantis. At least one Swedish investigator said it was in Sweden, another one, British, wrote it was in England, and a recent Canadian Atlantologist, and a capable one, writes it lies in the sea off Labrador.

Such extrascientific motivations for conveniently finding Plato's island in the investigator's own homeland have not done the search much credit. But the motives currently driving professional scholars of all nationalities (especially, these days, the Americans) to insist that Crete or its neighboring island and Atlantis are one and the same are more harmful. It is, therefore, important to understand why they want to explain away Atlantis in what has come to be known as the Minoan Hypothesis.

The island of Thera was part of the Minoan commercial empire, and excavations on Santorini uncovered an early, advanced civilization that once flourished there. The small island was actually a volcanic mountain that erupted in much the same way as Anak on Krakatoa did; the island quite literally plunged into the sea. A two-hundred-foot-tall wall of water swept over Crete and wreaked havoc among its coastal ports, while accompanying earthquakes badly damaged the inland capital, Knossos. The Minoans were so disrupted by this natural disaster that they could not organize an effective resistance to Mycenaean aggression, and their civilization disappeared, absorbed in part by Greek invaders. Seizing upon these events more than a thousand years before his time, Plato modeled

Atlantis directly after either Crete or Thera, or both, an analogy for his ideal state.

Thera is only a fraction of the size of Plato's Atlantis, lies in the Aegean Sea instead of the Atlantic Ocean he specified, and was destroyed seventy-eight hundred years after the destruction described in the *Dialogues*. These apparent discrepancies are handily dismissed by some scholars who assume that Plato's account is inflated by a factor of ten either deliberately by Plato himself, to make for a grander tale, or by translators, who misread the original version of the Atlantis story, written in Egyptian.

There are similarities between the Atlantean culture described in Plato's narrative and what archaeologists know about Minoan civilization in the eastern Mediterranean. For example, bulls were part of ritual ceremonies on ancient Crete, just as they were in Plato's Atlantis. Both Atlanteans and Minoans built great palaces and powerful cities, operated thalassocracies (or sea powers), practiced a pillar cult, traded in precious metals, and had elephants roaming about. Eumelos, cited by Plato in the *Kritias* as the first Atlantean king after Atlas, is echoed on the Minoan island of Melos. Eumelos is, in fact, mentioned on an archaic Greek inscription at Thera. Even the concentric arrangement of the Atlantean capital, as described by Plato, may to this day be seen in the waters of Santorini Bay.

The Minoan theorists argue that only in the Aegean Sea have relatively small tracts of land ever suddenly disappeared beneath the water's surface. One such example is the city of Helice, in the Gulf of Corinth. They rule out the Atlantic Ocean and the Azores, because supposedly no islands in the area are known to have sunk during the past seventy-two thousand years. The numerous flood legends, particularly the Babylonian Epic of Gilgamesh, are cited as literary evidence of Thera's destruction.

It is true that, like Atlantis, Thera was a volcanic island and the people that lived on it part of an advanced thalassocracy that vanished after the island's primary mountain exploded and sank into the sea. But move beyond this general comparison and the Minoan Hypothesis begins to unravel. Thera was a minor Minoan colony, a small outpost, not its capital, as the *Dialogues* have described Atlantis. Mycenaean influences from the Greek mainland did supplant Minoan culture on Crete, but the transition appears to have been largely, if not entirely, nonviolent, certainly nothing resembling the scope of Plato's Atlanto-Athenian war that raged across the Mediterranean World.

The Minoans never made a move to occupy Italy or Libya, nor did they threaten to invade Egypt, as the Atlanteans were supposed to have done. From everything scholars have been able to learn about them, the Minoans were an extremely un-warlike people more interested in commercial than military conquests, while the Atlanteans are portrayed as aggressively bellicose. As a foremost writer on the subject concludes, "Thera's candidacy as Atlantis rests largely on its cataclysmic destruction alone, while Plato's story had far more to do with a war between two antagonistic peoples than with the disaster that later overwhelmed them both."[21]

A Case of Mistaken Identity

The Minoans operated a dynamic navy to combat piracy and keep open the routes of international trade, but their Cretan cities were not ringed by high walls or battlements of any kind; compare unfortified Knossos or Phaistos with the armed towers and ramparts surrounding Atlantis. Moreover, these leading Minoan cities were laid out in the architectural canon of the square grid, unlike the concentric circles upon which Atlantis was built.

Some theorists claimed to have actually seen such a concentric, circular arrangement underwater, in the bay created when Thera's volcanic mountain collapsed into the sea.[22] But Dorothy B. Vitaliano, a prominent geologist specializing in volcanology with the U.S. Geological Survey, reports that the subsurface topography at Santorini "was not in existence before the Bronze Age eruption of the volcano; it has been created by subsequent activity which built up the Kameni Islands in the middle of the bay, to which a substantial amount of land was added as recently as 1926. Any traces of the precollapse topography would long since have been buried beneath the pile of lava whose highest portions emerge to form these islands."[23] Clearly, a recent geological feature has been mistaken for an ancient city. Structures designed in concentric circles prevailed, not in the Mediterranean, but in the Atlantic, as found in the Canary Island's circular temples and Britain's Stonehenge.

Caroli points out that "the Atlantean capital lay on a substantial plain surrounded by high mountains on a large island. Thera does not fit this description. The Cretans and Therans did not plate floors, walls and columns with metal, as Plato says the Atlanteans did. Plato's description of Poseidon's temple implies a structure with metal-covered walls, decorative pinnacles and at least two pillars, which were metal-plated. All this sounds like a Bronze Age Phoenician temple. The votive offerings do, as well. The massive statue of Poseidon is more reminiscent of Egyptian or Classical Greek sculpture. The statues of kings and queens are likewise more Egyptian or even Etruscan. None of this resembles anything belonging to the Minoans, who did not plate their public buildings with metal, had no inscribed pillars, nor sculpt colossal statues in the round."[24]

The huge Temple of Poseidon described by Plato as the centerpiece of Atlantean civilization is entirely un-Cretan, because the Minoans conducted their worship in sacred caves and at hilltop sanctuaries, not in public temples. They revered a variety of deities, foremost among them being the Earth Mother, the Goddess of the Hunt, and the God of Beasts. Nothing suggesting a Poseidon- or Atlas-like figure seems to have occurred to them.

Atlantis featured interconnecting canals and lay close to the sea; Phaistos and Knossos are inland and have no canals. The canal and irrigation systems Plato ascribed to Atlantis were immense and complex, on a grand scale similar to those constructed by the Egyptians, the Sumerians, the Chinese, the Maya, and the pre-Inca Chimu. Carthage, Tyre, and even the Aztec capital, Tenochtitlán, feature gigantic waterworks fundamentally similar to those attributed to Atlantis; nothing of the kind existed at Knossos or any other Minoan city. Neither Knossos nor Phaistos had harbors, because the lightweight Minoan ships could be hauled up on a beach, unlike the oceangoing Atlantean ships, which required the deepwater ports mentioned in the *Kritias*. In any case, the harbor arrangement described by Plato would not have been possible in the eastern Mediterranean Sea, because the main channel would have been fouled without the ebb and flow of the tides that do occur "beyond the Pillars of Heracles." This point alone is sufficient to prove that Plato was describing a location in the Atlantic Ocean, not the Aegean Sea.

Melos, the Minoan island associated by some scholars with King Eumelos of Plato's *Dialogues,* is so tiny it could never have supported the capital of a large kingdom. The *Kritias* states that Eumelos ruled over a region close to the Pillars of Heracles called Gades, today's Cadiz, on the Atlantic coast of Spain. That much in Plato is quite certain. It takes quite a stretch of the imagination, to say nothing of the facts, to relocate Eumelos in the Aegean. Although it is the only name mentioned in the *Dialogues* that does indeed appear in the eastern Mediterranean, no other Atlantean king finds a correspondence in that part of the world.

Atlantean names do abound throughout Atlantic Europe, North Africa, the Canaries, even in Mexico and Colombia. Parallels can be drawn between Eremon, an early Irish king who survived a great flood, and Euaemon, an Atlantean king mentioned in the *Kritias*. The Atlantes, inhabitants of coastal Morocco, were described by Diodorus Siculus and Herodotus. Teugueste, a pre-conquest province on the Canary Island of Lanzarote, sounds similar to Taegaete, an Atlantide, or Daughter of Atlas in Greek myth. Aztlan was the Aztecs' ancestral island in the east. The name of Musaeus, an Atlantean king documented by Plato finds an echo in the Muyscas Indians of Colombia, who happen to have a flood legend in their mythology.

Reducto ad absurdum

The Minoan theorists argue that when Plato wrote of Atlantis lying beyond the Pillars of Heracles, he did not mean the island was in the Atlantic Ocean, but actually outside the Straits of Melea, off the Greek Peloponnesus; this area, they claim, not the Straits of Gibraltar, must have been the genuine Pillars of Heracles.[25] Aside from their failure to produce a single shred of evidence suggesting that the Straits of Melea were the original Pillars of Heracles, the Atlanteans were supposed to have conquered Italy and Libya and threatened Egypt and Greece, all of which Plato described as located "within" the Pillars of Heracles, a geographical impossibility if he meant the Straits of Melea. He does, after all, describe Atlantis as "Atlantykos nesos," the "*Atlantic* island." Additionally, in the *Odyssey* (I, 53), Homer portrays Atlas as "the guardian of the Pillars of Heracles," which unequivocally puts the first king of Atlantis outside of the Aegean, which Homer describes as lying far to the east of Atlas. As Caroli explains, "There are no straits between Egypt and Crete or Thera, and none ever known to have been called 'the Pillars of Heracles.'"[26]

The island of Atlantis was supposed to be rich in precious metals; Crete and Thera have few. The Atlanteans operated heavy, three-man chariots; the Minoans preferred lighter, one- or two-man chariots.

A tenfold error in translating the original Egyptian into Greek seems unlikely when one looks at Egyptian numerals for 100 and 1,000. As the noted British researcher, Andrew Collins, points out, "Those Egyptologists who have taken time to examine the problem assert that no such confusion could have occurred. The hieroglyphs used to denote the numerical values of one hundred and a thousand are visually quite different. Solon, the Athenian law-giver who heard the story of Atlantis related by temple priests at the Nile Delta around 550 B.C., or anyone else for that matter, could not have made such a mistake."[27] Then there is the self-evident fact that Crete did not sink into the sea, as Atlantis was alleged to have done. Thera's volcanic mountain did collapse, but its island survives to this day; in the *Kritias*, both city and island were utterly destroyed. Proponents of an Aegean Atlantis might just as well claim any one of a half dozen other underwater sites. The submerged Sanctuary of Apollo at Halieis, in southern Greece, or the drowned island of the Pharos Lighthouse, one of the Seven Wonders of the Ancient World, off Egyptian shores of Alexandria, seem no less eligible than Thera.

That rituals involving bulls were practiced by both Atlantean and Minoan civilizations proves nothing, because the animal was similarly venerated in mainland Greece, Egypt, Assyria, the Hittite Empire, Iberia, across western Europe as far back as Neolithic and Paleolithic times. Another creature plays its own part in the comparison. The *Kritias* reports that there were elephants on the island of Atlas. A "pygmy elephant" did indeed inhabit Crete, but it became extinct around 7000 B.C.E., a full thousand years before the first humans arrived and four millennia before the beginning of Minoan civilization. No elephants ever set foot on Thera. Craftsmen on both islands worked in ivory, all of it imported from Africa.

Plato's brief but important mention of elephants on Atlantis simultaneously establishes the veracity of his narrative and confirms the near-Atlantic location of his sunken kingdom. A 1967 issue of *Science* magazine reported the discovery of mastodon and mammoth teeth from the Atlantic Continental Shelf two to three hundred miles off the Portuguese coast. Numerous specimens were recovered from at least forty different underwater sites along the Azores-Gibraltar Ridge, some from depths of 360 feet. The teeth were found in submerged shorelines, peat deposits, sand banks caused by surface waves crashing against a beach, and depressions that formerly contained freshwater lagoons. These features prove that the area was formerly dry land.

The *Science* writer concluded, "Evidently, elephants and other large mammals ranged this region during the glacial stage of low sea level of the last 25,000 years."[28] Moreover, elephants are known to have inhabited the northwestern shores of present-day Morocco, which faces the location of Atlantis and is at the junction of a vanished land bridge that led out into the ocean as late as the twelfth century B.C.E. Both Plato and Homer wrote that the Atlanteans worked in great quantities of ivory, fashioning ornately carved ceilings from this precious medium. The presence of a native population of elephants on Atlas Island would have been a ready source of the material. These two apparently unrelated points in the *Dialogues*—the existence of elephants on Atlantis and the Atlanteans generous use of ivory—are evidence that herds of such animals existed, which seems to be confirmed by deep-sea finds. Unless he read it in an authentic document describing Atlantis, Plato could have never guessed that elephants once inhabited an area of the world presently covered by the ocean.

An Ocean of Sunken Islands

There are many examples to refute Minoan theorists, who claim that no sizeable landmasses have sunk into the Atlantic Ocean. The Fernando Noronha Islands were points of contention between Great Britain and Portugal until they sank after one week of seismic activity in 1931.[29] Nor was Atlantis the only island-city to have gone under the Atlantic. The Janonius Map of 1649 identified Usedom, formerly a famous market, which was swallowed up by the waves of the sea. The same island was mentioned five centuries earlier by the Arab cartographer, Edrisi. Actually, the town in question, Vineta, was located on the northwest corner of the island of Usedom, which was near Rugen Island in the North Sea. Its five thousand inhabitants were engaged in a flourishing trade with Germans, Slavs, Arabs, and, lastly, Christianized Vikings from Denmark. The Vikings sacked the place in 1098, after which Vineta was abandoned and, over the next two hundred years, slid into the sea. By 1304 it had entirely disappeared, although coins and numerous minor artifacts are still being dredged up in its vicinity.

Vineta is the sunken civilization mistaken by Spanuth for Atlantis, the submergence of which predated Usedom's by several thousand years.[30] The North Frisian island of Rungholt, near the island of Suedfall, although not as large as Usedom, was likewise once inhabited before it sank about the same time as Rungholt. It partially reemerged around 1310 C.E. Incredibly, plow furrows left by early-fourteenth-century Rungholt farmers were still visible and examined in the late-nineteenth-century by the noted archaeologist, Andreas Busch. In its heyday, Rungholt merchants carried on a lively commerce with Hamburg and Flanders, as documented in trade records preserved at Ghent.

Of course, none of these islands were Atlantis, but they do demonstrate that an Atlantean event was by no means beyond the geologic purview of the Atlantic Ocean. Islands large and small have been swallowed up, sometimes in a matter of days or hours. The destruction of the Jamaican city of Port Royal was similar to the destruction of Plato's metropolis. Its similarity to Plato's metropolis is nothing short of uncanny. Like his ancient capital, Port Royal was a capital of power and sin, a harbor town whose sea-roving captains were not unacquainted with piracy.

By the end of the seventeenth century, Port Royal's captains and residents had amassed fortunes through both trade and privateering, while their city sparkled with ostentatious opulence. The place was fabled from Britain to India for its prosperity, influence, and degeneracy. At the zenith of this joyful decadence, a series of tremendously powerful earthquakes struck the island. At precisely 11:43 on the morning of June 7, 1692, the entire city, including its spacious harbor, collapsed into the sea. More than eight hectares of the island disappeared beneath the waves, and two of its mountains were moved nearly a quarter of a mile.

The catastrophe lasted just three minutes, during which two thousand persons were killed. Over the next three centuries, the port was increasingly regarded as legendary, until most historians doubted such a place ever existed. It was not until the 1960s that modern underwater search equipment discovered Port Royal on the floor of the Caribbean Sea. Incredibly, many buildings remain standing and hundreds of artifacts are still being recovered, including a watch that stopped at exactly the same moment as the earthquake struck, verifying the time of the disaster.[31] It took less than three hundred years for historians to divest Port Royal of its reality and consign it to the realm of legend. The doubters and debunkers have had much longer to dismiss Atlantis. But more advanced versions of the technology that found Port Royal will some day do the same for Plato's lost island.

A Labyrinth of Misinformation

The flood legend common to the Epic of Gilgamesh, the Old Testament, and early myths cannot have resulted from the destruction of Thera, because the deluge myth prominent in Middle Eastern civilization traces back to Sumerian origins, predating the downfall of Minoan Crete by more than a thousand years. Furthermore, the Greek tradition of Theras, the mythic founder of Thera, shares no elements in common with Plato's story, nor hints of anything remotely Atlantean.

The Minoan Hypothesis was so much in vogue among archaeologists during the 1970s that the famed oceanographer Jacques Cousteau spent a great deal of time and energy, plus nearly $2 million provided by the Monaco government to search the depths around Santorini. Thus lured by a fashionable theory designed to dismiss Plato, not explain him, Cousteau's research turned up nothing resembling Atlantis. But even before his expeditions, proponents of the Minoan Hypothesis began to lose ground among their colleagues.

R. W. Hutchinson, an authority on the Ancient Aegean, concluded, "It is clear, however, that Plato himself did not identify Atlantis with Crete, and if he used folklore referring to Minoan Crete he was quite unconscious of any connection between them."[32] The modern translator of the *Dialogues* for Penguin Books, Desmond Lee, regards Plato's story of Atlantis as the earliest known example of science fiction, but rejects the Minoan Hypothesis: "I really don't believe that the Atlantic mud is the quicksands of Syrtes (in the Aegean); nor do Frost's other details convince. There may indeed be a Minoan cup showing a bull caught in a net [the Vapheio Cup, a Minoan artifact discovered in a Mycenaean context on mainland Greece]; but I can see no real connection between Plato's rather complex ritual and what we know of the bull of Minos. . . . any hunt for correspondence of detail between Atlantis and Minoan Crete is a wild goose chase."[33]

While at first glance and from a distance the Minoan Hypothesis may appear tenable, it begins to disintegrate the closer one approaches. Almost point for point, an Aegean Atlantis does not match Plato's straightforward account and is uniformly contradicted by the evidence of geology, history, and comparative mythology. As a last-ditch effort to save something of their excuse for a Cretan interpretation, its advocates claim that Plato merely used the general outline of events at Thera as a vague, historical framework on which to present his notion of a consummate culture in the fictionalized guise of Atlantis.

But here, too, they err, because, as Lee points out, the *Dialogues* define Atlantis as the enemy of Plato's idealized state. So often has it been repeated that he invented Atlantis to exemplify his ideal society, that this misconception is even repeated by the publisher on the back cover of Lee's own translation! In any case, the ideal city Plato does describe, Megaera, is square, not circular.

But only one piece of evidence is required to invalidate the Minoan Hypothesis in a single stroke. The cornerstone on which its supporters depend is the date for the collapse of Thera's volcano into the sea, because it was this disaster, they argue, that brought down Minoan civilization in 1485 B.C.E. The havoc wreaked by tsunamis that crashed along the shores of ancient Crete and the earthquakes that toppled her cities was compounded by Greek armies who took advantage of the natural catastrophe to wage war on the disorganized Minoans, plunging them into a dark age from which they never emerged.

Geologists have discovered the pivotal eruption date through evidence in ice-cores. Caroli explains that

> ice cores reveal "acidity peaks" at the times of major eruptions, because ash falls on the ice caps and affects their chemistry. Long cores by hollow pipes used as drills (some hundreds of feet in length) taken from both Greenland and Antarctica have been examined to determine the past climate of the Earth. By analyzing the chemistry of these cores, "acidity peaks" can be found, many of these visible to the naked eye as dark streaks in the ice made by the ash that fell long ago. Some of these cores have annual layers, like tree rings, or sedimentary glacial deposits at lake bottoms. These can and have been counted back for thousands of years. The oldest of these "long cores" was drilled in 1963 at Camp Century, in north central Greenland. For years, it was the only core that went back far enough into the past and had been studied in sufficient detail to potentially reveal the timing of Thera's eruption.[34]

The date arrived at was 1390 B.C.E., plus or minus 50 years, too late and somewhat "incomplete" for the Minoan theorists, who reworked the ice-core data with complementary radio-carbon dating. Sixteen years after the Camp Century drilling, more accurate procedures were applied at Dye 3, in southern Greenland. In Caroli's words,

There was a prominent acidity peak at 1645 +/– 7 B.C., with an outside variable of 1645 +/– 20. Thus, the very incompleteness of that section of the Camp Century core was seen as partial confirmation of a seventeeth-century date for the eruption.

Then the dendrochronologists stepped in. Study of tree rings in the American Southwest revealed abnormally narrow growth rings at 1626–29 B.C. Irish, English, and German tree rings were found to show a similar pattern. Tree rings from a log removed from a Chinese bog and Greek and Turkish tree-ring data also confirm an early 1600 B.C. eruption.

American, Asian, and European tree rings support a 1620 B.C. date. A majority of the Theran radio-carbon data also supports this date (once corrected). The ice-core data lend still more support. Furthermore, Kevin Pang has noted Chinese descriptions of what could be dust-veil phenomena from a major eruption near the time that the Shang Dynasty came to power. Pang used astronomical retrocalculations to date the Shang Dynasty to 1625 to 1575 B.C. The Thera eruption dates are supported by Pang's research; the accuracy of his calculations are in turn bolstered by the proposed dates for Thera eruption.[35]

The Demise of a Theory

It is now understood that Thera erupted between 1623 and 1628 B.C.E., almost one hundred and fifty years earlier than the Minoan theorists initially believed. The significance of this discrepancy renders their entire hypothesis invalid, because Minoan civilization did not disappear in the wake of a natural disaster. "By all indications," Caroli points out,

> the Minoans not only survived the eruption, but reached their peak *after* it. There was no dark age or loss of literacy following the eruption, as Plato describes in his work. He repeatedly indicates that literacy was lost in the Aegean following the Atlantean cataclysm. That is not true after Thera's eruption. If anything, literacy expanded in the Mycenaean era, as Linear B

writing is far more commonly found in Crete than the earlier
Linear A. Some scholars claim that Linear B is at least slightly
more advanced and refined as a tool for communication than
any of the prior Aegean types of writing. Crete remained popu-
lous and prosperous for over 400 years following the Theran
event.[36]

Late Minoan Ib pottery, with its distinctive marine motifs, represented the artistic height of Cretan culture, which was reached years
following the Thera disaster. Robert Drews, a Princeton scholar specializing in Bronze Age studies, reported that Crete's economic and
cultural life did not drastically decline after 1400 B.C.E.[37] Even A.
Kanta, an Establishment researcher who accepts the orthodox dating
for Thera around 1485 B.C.E., admitted that Minoan civilization at
this time was still "prosperous and enterprising."[38] In the most thorough survey of Ib Cretan pottery undertaken, Philip Betancourt
found that the thirteenth century B.C.E. represented "the golden age
of the Minoan ceramic industry."[39]

Proponents of an Aegean Atlantis call upon Egyptian history for
corroboration, but here, too, they find contradiction to their asser-
tion that Minoan Civilization was shattered by Thera's eruption.
Pharaoh Amenhotep III dispatched an embassy to the cities of Crete
and found them still occupied nearly one hundred years after their
supposed destruction. The Egyptian record was confirmed in the
late 1970s when excavations around Knossos revealed evidence for
final occupation by the Minoans in 1380 B.C.E., a hundred years later
than even the original, incorrect date for the eruption of Thera.[40]

Caroli's assessment seems conclusive: "And so the Minoan Hypothesis is left with no war, no maritime civilization destroyed by
catastrophe, the wrong kind of disaster, the wrong date and no
comparable dark age as a result. What does that leave us? To my
mind, not much."[41]

The Minoan Hypothesis is primarily advocated as a self-serving cop-out by conventional scholars who cannot tolerate the slightest consideration of ancient man's capabilities for transoceanic travel, and regard any other discussion of Atlantis as the worst heresy. Too long haunted by the specter of Plato's lost island, they have stopped fighting Atlantis and embraced it by turning its story inside out in order to support their own entrenched prejudices. They threw out most of the details found in the *Dialogues*, transplanted Atlantis from the Atlantic Ocean to the Aegean Sea, shrank its capital down to an obscure island, reduced its transatlantic empire to a corner of the eastern Mediterranean, adjusted the story to fit their own in-valid chronology, inverted Atlantis from Plato's original enemy state into his ideal state, and changed the Atlanteans into Cretans.

They are thus guilty of doing precisely that for which they have always condemned Atlantologists: making the facts conform to a preconceived theory. Plato disguised Crete/Thera as "Atlantis" and that is all you need to know. Case closed. Thus neatly packaged for public consumption, Atlantis-as-Minos may be reassuring to intol-erant professionals who have long wished to rid themselves of the Atlantis Problem without endangering the credibility of scientific dogma in these matters. But theirs is, nonetheless, a degraded, falsified portrait that bears scant resemblance to the original pre-sented in the *Dialogues*. The puny material contrived to support such a feeble theory is dwarfed by abundant evidence establishing the existence of Atlantis in the ocean to which it gave its name—the Atlantic.

ATLANTIS IN THE BAHAMAS?

Opposite the Minoan theorists, geographically as well as theoreti-cally, are some leading Atlantologists who believe the lost island lies in the Bahamas. A far westerly location was not seriously considered until the late sixties, when, in 1967, an underwater feature was discovered off the northern point of Bimini, a small island fifty-five miles east of Miami. The huge, square-cut blocks running in two straight, divergent lines across the ocean floor for about nineteen hundred feet, was found only nineteen feet beneath the surface and suggested a paved road to early investigators. The site was instantly dismissed by professional critics as nothing more than beach rock. They claimed the limestone had formed while being washed over by waves seventeen thousand years ago. It was no different, they said, than other natural formations known all over the world. Had the Bimini Road been found on dry land in Peru, Bolivia, or Mexico, the university-trained debunkers would have readily accepted it as man-made. But because they are opposed to the idea of such structures popping up outside the parameters of conventional archaeology, especially if those places happen to be under water, the site was declared "natural."

However, geologists point out that, during the close of the Pleistocene epoch, waves couldn't have reached what is now referred to as the Bimini Road, because it stood too high above sea level. The structure was not covered by the ocean until approximately 2800 B.C.E., emerged again roughly thirteen hundred years later, and remained above water until circa 960 B.C.E.

Even though the doubters' supposition was invalidated by core drillings taken from the site in the mid-1980s, skeptics still choose to ignore anything that postdated their pronouncement and continue to define the structure as a work of nature, not man.[42] Subsequent core samples revealed fragments of micrite, which does not occur in beach rock. In 1995 divers at the site recovered granite, which is not native to the Bahamas; the state of Georgia, hundreds of miles away, is the closest source.[43] Moreover, stones found adjacent to each other in the Bimini Road sometimes contain different geological components, such as aragonite in one and calcite in its next nearest neighbor, unlike the chemical uniformity found in naturally occurring beach rock.

As even a casual snorkeler will observe, the stones that make up the Bimini Road are not at all the same as the very real beach rock found in shallow waters off Bimini's western shore. The Road's stones are massive, square-cut, pillowlike blocks fitted together, sometimes placed one atop another. The Road terminates in a completely unnatural J.[44] About two miles away, the beach rock occurs in roughly squarish flakes that are by no means nicely fitted together nor stacked on top of each other, but often overlap at their edges like a bad set of teeth as they curve parallel to the shore.

The demonstrable fact that the Road runs diagonal to Bimini's former, ancient shoreline is really all the evidence needed to prove beyond question that it is man-made, because it would have been impossible for such an orientation to have formed naturally in situ. The naturally occurring beach rock on the island is comprised of a single layer, compared to three and four layers of stone in the Road. Beach rock is only a few inches thick; the Road's blocks are several *feet* thick. Comparison between Bimini's west-side beach rock and the north-point rock that makes up the Road leaves no doubt that they were not created by the same forces. The Road also contains several angular keystones with notches that fit into tenons, a prehistoric building style encountered among the Andean walls of Cuzco, Sacsahuaman, and Machu Picchu. The Road's resemblance to these structures is in some respects remarkable. Even more remarkable is the Bimini Road's similarity to the massive walls of Lixus in Morocco.

Many of the modern inhabitants of Bimini are direct descendants of West African blacks who were brought to the island three centuries ago by Spanish slavetraders. Older residents have testified that the Road as it appears today is only a fraction of what it was as recently as the 1920s. When they were children, they could see waves breaking over its uppermost stones during low tide. Their recollection tallies with early-twentieth-century navigation charts, which warned of an unspecified, subsurface hazard just north of Bimini.

In 1997 I accompanied William Donato, president of the Atlantis Organization, on an underwater survey at Moselle Shoals, a site that lies 20 feet beneath the surface about three miles northeast of Bimini. There we found dozens of rectangular stone columns, averaging 8 feet long, 3 feet wide, and weighing about 4 tons each. They resembled the tumbled remains of a monumental edifice thrown into the sea by some geologic violence. At the site's southern edge was a sunken trawler, perhaps 150 feet long. Several of the large columns lay on top of the wreck, and had crushed its boiler, smashing the starboard side. The vessel had apparently been engaged in hoisting the massive stones from Moselle Shoals when one broke through her hull and sank her. The boat must have been part of the salvage operations said to have been conducted around 1930. Before the Depression, Florida salvage operators allegedly removed all but the bottom course of the Road and transported the huge blocks to build facilities in Miami harbor. Traveling just fifty-five miles to harvest blocks from Bimini made economic sense, because good construction stone is rare in Florida.

The Lucayan Indians, a branch of the Arawak, inhabited Bimini before the Spaniards arrived in the sixteenth century and supplanted the native population with black slaves. The Lucayans referred to their island as "the Place of the Walls." No wall-like structures of any kind were found on land, so the ancient name is highly evocative of the massive stone formation that lies under water just off-shore. They also claimed that the Bahamas were once part of a much larger landmass that was overcome by "the arms of the sea."

The structure at Bimini is not actually a road, but it could be the remains of a quay, breakwater, or other harbor facility of some kind that was originally an elongated oval. Such an interpretation is given some support by the feature's position at the northern end of the island, because a ship casting off from this location would sail directly into a North American current that would take it along the Eastern Seaboard as far north as the Gulf of Maine, before swinging sharply east to head directly for the Azore Islands and Europe beyond. Moreover, the Lucayans also called Bimini "the Place of the Wreath" or Crown, which may refer to the structure's circular configuration. Their name for the island, in their own tongue, was Guanahani. Although its specific meaning in Lucayan has been lost, the name handily translates into "Island of Men " in the language of the Guanches, the aboriginal inhabitants of the Canary Islands almost directly across the Atlantic Ocean from the Bahamas.

The philological origins of "Bimini" are obscure. It may be the contraction of a Spanish word for "half," which, however, doesn't make a great deal of sense. Curiously, the word "bimini" corresponds to the Egyptian word *baminini*, "homage to [ini] the soul of [ba] Min [Min]." Min was the Ancient Egyptian god of travelers, who appealed to him for guidance and protection whenever they set out on long journeys. Appropriately, Min was also the patron of roads. Could the island have been known to Egyptian seafarers, their first landfall after long transatlantic voyages? Egyptian dynastic civilization began in 3100 B.C.E. While the road stood above water at that time, only three hundred years later it was submerged.

An Egyptian provenance is supported by a similar breakwater at the harbor at Alexandria, on the Nile Delta, probably built during the New Kingdom (1550 to 1070 B.C.E.), and certainly restored in Ptolemaic times (323 to 30 B.C.E.). The Egyptian breakwater had roughly the same length as the Bimini structure, and likewise terminated in a J shape. Does this striking physical resemblance mean that Egyptians built the Bimini Road, or were the Egyptians and Bahamanians alike recipients of a construction technology the Atlanteans brought to both sides of the world?

The Bimini Hypothesis

While the man-made, ancient origins of the Bimini structure are well established, some Atlantologists have gone further and assert that the Road marks the location of Plato's sunken civilization, chiefly because:

1. It is under water in the Atlantic Ocean.

2. It was built on the large scale associated with Atlantean construction.

3. It stood above the surface of the sea during the period defined by Plato in a literal reading of his account.

4. From it, both other islands and the "Opposite Continent" (that is, America) could be easily reached.

5. Bimini has mineral springs, as did Atlantis.

6. During the tenth millennium B.C.E., defined by Plato as the period during which Atlantis reached the apogee of its greatness, the sea around the Bahamas Bank was lower than at present, revealing enough dry land to support a kingdom and its capital city.

While these points are certainly valid, they fall far short of establishing Bimini as the lost Atlantis, at least in its final, late Bronze Age phase. As with the Minoan Hypothesis, a Bahamian explanation appears sound at first glance, but disintegrates on closer inspection. Researchers of the Bimini site have included respected investigators such as Manson Valentine, who first described the Bimini Road as a man-made structure in 1968 and was one of the most brilliant American scientists of the twentieth century; Dimitri Rebikoff, undersea explorer with a worldwide reputation; Dr. David Zink, who probably did more than anyone to establish the site's authenticity; Charles Berlitz, an internationally recognized name in linguistics; and William Donato, president and founder of the California-based Atlantis Organization and currently the leading authority on the Bimini enigma, who continues to organize professional expeditions to the underwater structure. These gentlemen are formidable researchers who have spent thousands of hours and dollars out of their own pockets for on-site investigations. Without disparaging their important achievements, the facts nonetheless rule out the Bahamas as the likely site of Atlantis.

Even if the Bahama islands were restored to their tenth millennium B.C.E. extent, we would see none of the high mountains nor fertile plains that Plato described as being in Atlantis. Nor any of the red, white, and black volcanic stones he said were used as building materials. Nor any veins of precious metals from its limestone substrate. Missing are the lakes and meadows of the Atlantean island. The Bahamas have always been far too arid and its soil too poor to support large forests or rich agriculture. According to Caroli, "The location and topography of Bimini and the Bahama Banks conform in almost no way with Plato's description, save that it [the Road] lies in the Atlantic Ocean and is now underwater."[45]

While diving into an underwater cavern near the Bahamian island of Andros, Jacques Cousteau found stalactites and stalagmites. They could only have been formed when the cavern was above water. But the depths at which he found the cavern, in excess of 160 feet, mean the stalactites and stalagmites were formed hundreds of thousands of years before the present time, given what we know about sea-level fluctuations. Few entertain the notion that a civilization such as that described in the *Dialogues* could have flourished so long ago. The very idea of elephants or horses on Bimini is plainly absurd. Despite years of aerial surveys, scuba dives, and sonar searches, no trace of the Temple of Poseidon, palaces, towers or any of the largest architectural features associated with Atlantis have been found, even though the seas of the Bahama Banks are so shallow that downed aircraft may be easily seen with the naked eye. The waters beyond the banks are certainly very deep, but sonar readings here, too, are inconclusive at best. There is no evidence of either Atlantis's concentric layout or of its huge canals anywhere in the Bahamas, unless the features are suggested by a subjective interpretation of the islands themselves, a configuration even many determined Atlantologists fail to see.

A Bimini Atlantis renders impossible any chance of an Atlanto-Athenian War or military operations against Egypt. Perhaps most important of all, evidence of a natural catastrophe that destroyed everything "in a single day and night" is absent. The covering and uncovering of the Bimini Road represented gradual fluctuations in sea level, not a single cataclysmic upheaval. And, like Thera and Crete, Bimini is still dry land. It did not disappear into the sea. Finally, when Plato said that Atlantis was "beyond the Pillars of Heracles," could he have really meant that it lay thousands of miles from the Straits of Gibraltar?

The massive stone structure off the northern point of Bimini is certainly the work of a great maritime civilization. It might very well have been built by the Atlanteans, who took advantage of the island's freshwater springs and fortuitous location in the North American current to construct a harbor for their ships with rich cargoes of high-grade copper returning from America—Plato's "Opposite Continent"— to their homeland strategically placed at the entrance of the Mediterranean.

Members of Dr. David Zink's Poseidia Expeditions to the Bimini structure in the 1970s believed that in its layout they traced a recurring pattern of the Sacred Numerals (five and six) Plato said were incorporated by the Atlanteans in their architecture.[46] If so, then the relationship between the Road and Atlantis draws much closer. Caroli, who personally investigated the site, concludes, "Though unlikely to be Atlantis, it could still relate to the activities of the people Plato called 'Atlanteans.'" The discovery and ongoing investigation of the Road comprise one of the great scientific adventures of the twenty-first century. And if Bimini is not exactly Atlantis, it may nonetheless be the site of the first example of Atlantean civilization to be found and recognized as such since the island's destruction.

ATLANTIS IN CUBA?

On May 14, 2001, Paulina Zelitsky, the Russian-born president of Advanced Digital Communications, a commercial oceanographic corporation, was aboard her research vessel, the *Ulises,* plying the waters off the northwestern coast of Cuba. She had been hired by the Castro government to find valuable mineral deposits in Cuban waters. Her company was well equipped for the assignment with satellite-integrated seafloor positioning systems, high-precision side-scan double-frequency sonar, and remotely operated vehicles (ROVs) that could transmit television images from far beneath the surface of the Caribbean.

Watching one of the monitors scanning the ocean bottom, Zelitsky was startled to see what appeared to be the sonar image of a stone building sitting under 2,200 feet of water. She ordered the *Ulises* to come about, and a concerted examination of the unusual target was made with all the high-tech instruments aboard. Their results were shared with directors of Cuba's National Science Institute. Additional passes over the deeply sunken site supposedly revealed a megalithic structure reminiscent of Britain's Stonehenge, except only that the Cuban example appeared to be partially coated with metal sheeting and a proto-Greek or Etruscan-like inscription.

Remarkably, only two years before, Andrew Collins, a British author, identified Cuba with the lost island of Atlantis. At this writing, research is still proceeding to confirm the archaeological provenance of the Cuban underwater site. If its artificial identity is indeed established, some difficult questions will have to be answered. For example, how could a man-made structure arrive, apparently intact, nearly a half mile beneath the surface of the ocean? Sea-level rises have not undergone fluctuations great enough to sink anything that deep since the Age of the Dinosaurs, more than 65 million years ago. And it is hard to comprehend a seismic event that would gently drop a building without destroying it before hitting

2,200 feet below. Until these problems are convincingly solved, Atlantologists are cautious in their enthusiasm.

But if, after all, the Cuban target is an ancient structure, it may indeed be Atlantean. Zelitsky's description of walls sheeted in some kind of metal are straight from Plato's *Kritias*. Even so, the underwater site is in the wrong location for his Atlantis, because the Caribbean was too far removed for the Atlanteans to have waged their war of conquest against Europe and Egypt. Zelitsky's find appears similar to the Bimini Road: the remains of an Atlantean outpost in the Americas. And both structures may have arrived at their watery positions due to the same series of natural catastrophes that destroyed so much of the ancient world, including Atlantis, around 1200 B.C.E.

Too little is so far known about the Cuban find to make any final determinations. It nonetheless merits further investigation and implies that something of potentially dramatic significance may be discovered. In any case, Cuba in the context of Atlantis is unworkable, except as a colonial outpost. ("Has Atlantis been Found in the Caribbean?" by Linda Moulton-Howe, in her "regular column" on "Coast-to-Coast with Art Bell," broadcast 19 November 2001, www.artbell.com).

LIKELIEST LOCATIONS FOR ATLANTIS

If the sunken capital may not be found in the Bahamas or the Aegean, where should we search for it? Plato tells us Atlantis lay "beyond the Pillars of Heracles," a general enough description, but his implication would seem to be just directly beyond the Straits of Gibraltar. Strabo, the first-century Roman geographer and historian, quoted his Greek predecessor, Eratosthenes, as locating Atlantis due west from Tartessos, modern day Huelva, in southern Spain.

This position not only fits Plato's description better than most, it is also near the focal point of one of the most geodynamic areas in the Atlantic Ocean. If Atlantis was indeed located in the so-called near ocean, directly out from Gibraltar, it perched precariously at the tailend of a seismic whipcord known as the Oceanographic Fracture Zone. Part of the unstable fault boundary line between the grinding movements of the Eurasian and African plates, all the geologic forces traveling outward from the Mid-Atlantic Ridge would have gathered exponentially accumulating energy until they climaxed at this fault's endpoint. If the destruction of Atlantis did indeed occur, it must have happened here. Appropriately, the area is also known for its shallows; in some places, the seafloor is less than 200 feet below the water's surface.

The Atlantis catastrophe may have been so widespread that it hindered passage from the Mediterranean into the Atlantic. Plato reported that after the island sank the area was impassable because of resulting shoals and an abundance of volcanic debris. Are the shallows at the terminus of the Oceanographic Fracture Zone the settled remains of that massive volcanic eruption?

About fifty years before he wrote the *Timaeus* and *Kritias*, the geographer Seylax of Caryanda described in *Periplus* the ocean "beyond the Pillars of Heracles, where the parts of the sea are no longer navigable because of shoals of mud and seaweed."[47] Plato's most famous student, Aristotle, mentioned the same conditions in *Meteorologica*.[48] So did another contemporary, the Phoenician admiral Himilco, during his voyage around Iberia to Britain.[49]

The Roman author and administrator Pliny the Younger mentioned numerous sandbanks immediately outside the Pillars of Heracles even as late as the Imperial Period, circa 100 C.E.[50] The Roman biologist Claudius Aelian who lived one hundred years later, reported that ships were forbidden by law to remain among the Pillars of Heracles beyond a fixed amount of time, on account of dangerous subsurface obstructions.[51] His contemporary, Philo Judaeus, wrote of Atlantis, "becoming sea, not indeed navigable, but full of gulfs and eddies."[52] Plutarch described the seas just beyond the Pillars of Heracles as "difficult of passage and muddy through the great number of currents, and these currents issue out of the great land [sunken Atlantis], and shoals are formed by them, and the sea becomes clogged and full of earth, by which it had the appearance of being solid."[53]

This testimony from so many classical scholars provides a persuasive argument for a major geologic event in the area of ocean described as the location for Atlantis. As late as the twelfth century A.D., the noted Arab geographer Edrisi told of a ship of "Magrurin," Moorish sailors from Lisbon, who had been forced to alter course for the Canary Islands after encountering an impassable stretch of shallow ocean outside the Straits of Gibraltar.[54]

More recent eruptions have disrupted ocean travel. In 1783, a submarine volcano rose thirty miles from Iceland and vomited huge masses of pumice that spread over a 150-mile radius; no ship could make headway through it.[55] The 1815 eruption of Sumbawa Island spewed forth so much volcanic debris that only the largest ships were able to cut through the clogged waters.[56]

Swedish Nobel Prize winner Svante Arrhenius described the aftermath of the final eruption of Anak Volcano in Krakatoa: "large stones containing innumerable bubbles, pumice stones, float on the sea and are slowly ground to sand by the waves. The amount of the floating pumice stone is such that it is often dangerous or interferes with ships." The heavier ash that settled in the immediate area of Krakatoa turned into a thick sea of mud that bonded the floating pumice in a kind of viscous soup, a hazard to navigation in the Java Straits that remained for years.[57]

In the late twentieth century, when the 120-foot-high island of Jolnir collapsed into the mid-Atlantic, it left far-spreading shoals 60 to 120 feet below the surface.

A similar situation on a far grander scale occurred in the Atlantic Ocean outside the Straits of Gibraltar after the island of Atlas suffered a natural catastrophe. Destruction wrought by the eruption of Mount Atlas was so vast it transformed the seas around it for some three millennia thereafter. Even today, the area most likely to be the location of ancient Atlantis is known to the Portuguese as particularly good fishing grounds because of its shallows.

ATLANTIS NO "LOST CONTINENT"

None of the ancient sources, including Plato, describe the drowned civilization as belonging to a continent. Nor do the classic Atlantologists, such as Ignatius Donnelly and Lewis Spence, characterize it as anything more than a large island. Just when and by what means "the lost continent" entered public domain is difficult to determine. Perhaps Helena Blavatski and her fellow Theosophists were the first, proposing a continental Atlantis during the nineteenth century. In any case, the popularity of this notion is important, because it continues to undermine consideration of Atlantis by serious investigators. Oceanographers using ever-more advanced underwater instruments began to put to rest the possibility of a true continent in the Atlantic in the 1950s.

As Caroli points out, "The Atlantic crust is too thin to support even a mini-continental platform."[58] And Francis Hitching of London's Royal Archaeological Institute reduces the findings of modern geology to a few words: "The steep sides of the Mid-Atlantic Ridge, similar to the Rockies or the Alps, make it impossible for a lost continent to have existed there."[59] Plato's description of Atlantis is usually translated as "larger than Libya and Asia combined." But the word he uses is *mezon,* which means "greater," not "larger." Did he mean, then, that Atlantis was more powerful than all the kingdoms of Libya and Asia put together, or that it was as geographically as large as the modern equivalent of Turkey combined with coastal North Africa from the Egyptian border to Tunisia?

Even if Atlantis was a landmass of this size, it would still have been far smaller than a continent. True, an island about the area of Portugal did occupy the mid-Atlantic in the past, but it vanished long before Plato or any civilized human being knew about such a place. The *Dialogues'* description of Atlantis as "greater" than Libya and Asia was a peculiar choice for a Greek. Caroli believes it represents internal evidence that tends to confirm that the account originated in Egypt after all, just as Plato said it did.

The Egyptians were bounded by traditional enemies in both the east and west. They referred to the various peoples of Libya as the *Libbu* or the *Temehu*. The Hittites, Trojans, Assyrians, Israelites, Hyksos, and so forth, who inhabited the Near East from the Sinai through Anatolia, were lumped together as simply "the Asians." The Egyptians conceived of their foreign opponents in terms of race and population, not as people residing in nations with clearly defined borders. It was natural for an Egyptian to think of Libya and Asia when discussing his enemies. It was not for a Greek. Very probably, this Libyan-Asian analogy that appears in the *Dialogues* was translated verbatim from the original Egyptian source. If this was so, then further credibility is added to the Atlantis story as handed down by Plato.

It can then be assumed that the original Egyptian version did not imply that Atlantis was geographically larger than the indefinite territories occupied by Libyans and "Asians," but more powerful than these kingdoms combined. Even if we assume Plato was making geographical comparisons, in his time Libya was a thin strip of territory running along the Mediterranean shores of North Africa between the Algerian and Egyptian borders. "Asia" vaguely comprised the western half of Turkey. Combined, these regions would have resulted in a landmass roughly the size of Spain, but nothing the dimensions of a continent.

A TALE OF ANCIENT ESPIONAGE

Caroli cites additional internal evidence that implies the story as heard by Solon from the Egyptian priest was something more than a simple history. The *Kritias* discusses the Atlanteans' dispositions, types and numbers of their warships, infantry and chariotry, their distribution of manpower, how funding for naval and army expenditures was raised; lists various kinds and numbers of weapons, provides a general layout of the city's defenses, describes the system of alliances with other kingdoms, and the Atlanteans' operations in western Italy and Libya, and so forth. The account's preoccupation with military details suggests it was based on the report of an Egyptian spy who personally visited Atlantis on a covert intelligence mission. The Atlantean Empire did, after all, go to war against Egypt, and there must have been a period of tensions before the outbreak of hostilities.

Indeed, the famous peace treaty concluded between Pharaoh Ramses II and the Hittite Emperor Muwatalis, agreed upon in 1283 B.C.E. after the Battle of Kadesh, in Syria, specifically mentions the "Sea Peoples" as a common threat against which both men pledged to defend their peoples. Maria Settegast, one of the most erudite writers on the subject, affirms that the main thrust of Plato's story is the war between Atlantis and Athens. Caroli's supposition that the *Timaeus* and *Kritias* were based on an intelligence report, while unprovable, is not that far-fetched. But harder evidence must be sought on the ocean floor.

Where in past years all that Atlantologists had to go on were simple observations and uncertain theories, underwater technology is now unfolding a true panorama of the sea and its mysteries based on a rapidly accumulating database. And while this new technology establishes beyond question that nothing resembling a continent existed in the Atlantic before the advent of ancient civilizations, it just as surely demonstrates the feasibility of an island large enough to support a community and its geologic destruction. One must be careful that this theoretical island conforms to the geologic parameters of all the other midocean islands, because it was subject to the same forces that created and, in some cases, destroyed them. In estimating its credible dimensions, Gran Canaria, off the North African coast, is a good reference. This island nearly matches Plato's description of Atlantis in essential particulars. It is nearly circular in shape, dominated by a central volcano (the 6,400-foot, dormant Los Pechos), which is surrounded by other high mountains that slope in a broad plain toward Las Palmas, the capital, a port city on the sea.

Gran Canaria's climate is temperate year-round, its soil is fertile, fruit grows in profusion, forests provide abundant timber, and freshwater springs are plentiful. When the Spaniards arrived in the fifteenth century, they found it inhabited by the Guanches, a native people who preserved oral traditions of Atlantis, chiseled petroglyphs of the image of Atlas, and built ceremonial enclosures of concentric rings of stone in the Atlantean style. The island also experiences violent seismic activity from time to time. If Los Pechos should ever erupt with the explosive magnitude of Krakatoa, Gran Canaria would be decimated.

THE MECHANISM OF ANNIHILATION

Thus far I have attempted to establish that Atlantis was located on a large island in the Atlantic Ocean about 250 miles west of Gibraltar astride an unstable fault zone. Such a conclusion is archtraditional, because it confirms Plato's original story with modern evidence. It is contrary to the conclusions of some of my fellow Atlantologists, who either argue that Atlantis was a continent or, at any rate, a much larger island in the Bahamas, or insist it was a much smaller island in the Aegean. The truth seems to lie at some middle ground, most likely, in the Mid-Atlantic Ridge. Until the remnants of the sunken island are actually found and explored, investigators can only speculate about the precise manner of its destruction.

But enough is known concerning submarine geology to limit the options for destruction. If the island of Atlantis was the size and configuration of Gran Canaria, an eruption the magnitude of that which occurred on Thera could obliterate more than half the island, but the rest would remain, albeit in severely mutilated form. Santorini survived, by no means intact, but it did not completely sink into the sea, as Plato described for Atlantis. Other Atlantic islands, such as Sabrina, totally vanished beneath the waves.

What distinguishes these two kinds of destructions? If a volcanic outburst, no matter how powerful, erupts vertically, the force of the blast will travel directly upward and downward, thereby confining its zone of devastation. However, if the blast occurs horizontally, the area affected is far greater. The 1980 eruption of Washington's Mount Saint Helens is a case in point. Its vertical vent was too narrow to contain the eruption, which blew out one whole side of the mountain with infamous results. The area of devastation was prodigious. Yet, Mount Saint Helens is a moderate volcano. The effect of a Thera or Krakatoa exploding in its place would have been several times more cataclysmic.

Lateral eruptions occur in the following manner. In the magma chamber (a gargantuan hollow within the base of the volcano), pressures build and seek their escape. Sometimes the lava dome above the chamber is too heavy or the vent through it is too small to allow the pressure to release vertically. The pressure inside the chamber then generates powerful seismic shocks, which cause landslides. The mountainside thins, less material contains the internal forces, and they burst laterally out of the volcano. Volcanologists call this a Pelean eruption, after Mount Pelée, which exploded laterally in May 1902, killing thirty-thousand inhabitants on the island of Martinique. Mount Saint Helens exploded in a similar fashion.

Now, if instead of having been surrounded by forests on dry land, let us suppose that Mount Saint Helens was an island with all but one-quarter of its mass underwater. The lateral blast that opened the entire mountainside in one stroke would have allowed an inconceivably monstrous portion of the sea to rush into the magma chamber. Millions of tons of water spilling into the superheated chamber would continually transform into steam. The rapidly increasing weight of the in-pouring sea combined with pressures confined within the magma chamber would result in the collapse of the lava dome (its weight dislodged to implode upon itself) and the violent subduction of the entire mountain, at least those parts of it above the eruption. Thus, Mount Saint Helens, had it been an island instead of on dry land, would have sunk (more accurately, been sucked or pulled) beneath the surface of the ocean. This, in fact, is what happened when the Anak volcano erupted at 5:30 in the morning on August 27, 1883.

According to Emily and Per Ola D'Aulaire, who sailed to Sunda Strait, the site of the blast, the earth burst open far beneath the volcano's base, allowing several million tons of sea water to gush into its interior.[60] The water was instantly transformed into super-heated steam and detonated through the island. After the explosion, most of the island surface slumped into the sea. More than three-fifths of its land area sank beneath the Indian Ocean. Krakatoa would have been lost entirely had Anak's eruption been more than a partially lateral blast.

ATLANTIS AS GEOLOGIC REALITY

That the island of Atlantis succumbed to a volcanic event is a reasonable assumption, given the geologic character of the mid-Atlantic. But Plato nowhere in his *Dialogues* mentions the word "volcano." He writes that Atlas and its city were "overwhelmed by earthquakes."[61] It is possible, although far less likely, that seismic forces alone were responsible for the destruction. Port Royal was sunk by an earthquake, and islands such as Sabrina, Nyey, Geir fuglasker, Syrtlingur, and Jolnir did not submerge through overt volcanic action. But an earthquake would not have produced the great masses of pumice the *Kritias* reports floated outside the Pillars of Heracles.

Even so, Plato left his story of Atlantis unfinished. Just as he is about to describe the nature of its destruction, the narrative breaks off. He put it aside, temporarily it seems, to complete *The Laws*, which also discuss the Atlantean flood. Plato appears to have intended combining the *Timaeus, Kritias,* and *The Laws* in a trilogy, a philosophical history of the world, drawing moral examples from actual events, of which the account of Atlantis was one. But he died before the project could be realized. Computer analysis of his collected works indicates the three *Dialogues* were, in fact, written at the end of his life.

Despite his unfinished narrative, the great Athenian thinker left us tantalizing clues that describe what really happened. The testimony of modern oceanography and geology presented here represent the highlights of all the scientific materials that credibly argue on behalf of an Atlantean catastrophe.

The weight of evidence compels us to conclude that Atlantis was (at least in its final phase) an island about the size, geology, and topography of Gran Canaria and situated approximately 250 miles west of the Straits of Gibraltar. It collapsed into the sea following a Pelean eruption of its foremost volcano. Today its remnants lie a thousand feet or less beneath the ocean's surface, among the seamounts located between the Mid-Atlantic Ridge and the western coasts of Portugal and Morocco. This much science can tell us. But precisely when did the catastrophe take place and what triggered it?

THREE

The Queen of Legends

Like you, I am also convinced that it is incautious to brush
away the Greek legends obtained in Egypt about
a sunken island which they called Atlantis.
Dr. Thor Heyerdahl,
in correspondence with the author
May 3, 1984

If Atlantis was really destroyed by a huge disaster that affected all humanity, where are the ancient records for such a cataclysmic event? What proof from ancient sources do we have that such a place ever existed in the first place? Before we can even begin to discuss the Atlantean drama, we must have some historical support for its existence.

The earliest more or less complete account of Atlantis and its destruction was set down by Plato sometime before 350 B.C.E., many centuries after the imperial capital's demise. He wrote that Atlantis was the chief city of a far-flung empire that dominated much of the world from an island in the Atlantic Ocean outside the Pillars of Heracles, known today as the Straits of Gibraltar. Its people rose to great heights of civilized splendor and mineral wealth, primarily through their abilities as sailors and miners.

For most of their history, the Atlanteans were virtuous, but with material abundance came decadence, and they engaged in military aggression. Initially successful in their conquest of Mediterranean lands as far as Italy and Libya, the Atlanteans seriously threatened Egypt and the people of the Aegean before they were finally defeated by Greek forces that drove them back to their oceanic capital. While the invaders were in full retreat, their entire island home was suddenly obliterated by a natural catastrophe that sank it beneath the sea after "a single day and night" of geologic violence.

Although Plato repeats throughout the *Dialogues* that his narrative was not fable but the truth, modern critics insist he was writing myth, not history. But what is a myth? Is it just a story, a kind of folktale of no real importance, save to preach some primitive morality in the guise of an entertaining fable? Certainly the majority of professional historians regard myth as such. The oral traditions of a people preserved over countless generations count for little or nothing among most salaried experts, who deal only in the hard evidence of physical excavation. Myth is too vague, too open to interpretation, they argue, for much use. For them, it is fiction or at best an echo of some past event distorted over time by innumerable re-tellings into unrecognizable shapes. This materialistic mind-set has dominated scientific thinking for most of the twentieth century and represents a tragic arrogance. It demeans the rich legacies of whole peoples by dismissing them as irrelevant, and results in a myopic view of history that shuts out potentially vital evidence.

Happily, the long-entrenched dogma of materialist scholars is being rendered progressively obsolete by a new generation of historians brought up on the lifework of Joseph Campbell. It was this man, more than anyone, who promoted myth as something far grander than mere fable or folkish fiction. In his many insightful books and engaging lectures, he showed how any myth that continues to be retold over the course of centuries must be saying something of continuing importance. Taking his cue from Carl Gustav Jung, the great Swiss psychologist, Campbell showed that myths are of two fundamental types: the subconscious and the historical. Both he and Jung demonstrated how the survival of particular themes among various peoples separated by vast differences in geography and cultural sophistication mean that a "collective unconscious" of all humans is expressing itself through myth. In other words, the universality of myth is a poetic manifestation of dreams common to all human beings.

BURNING THE MEMORY OF MANKIND

The historical myth is never a bloodless report fit for some bureaucrat's archives, but an event of essential importance rendered through drama as a means of perpetuating its existence. How may a society without a written language preserve those instances of its past that are deemed supremely important, if not in myth? Writing is no guarantee of permanence: Written materials are perishable. Records are lost, libraries go up in smoke, even letters engraved in stone erode.

Thousands of medical and other scientific scrolls were burned by Cyrus the Great when his Persian hordes sacked the temples at Thebes and Memphis in 525 B.C.E. Later, led by Darius I, the Persians struck the Psistratus in Athens. All the literary works of ancient Greece, save only the poems of Homer, were lost. The Greeks revenged themselves when Alexander the Great sacked Persepolis, destroying twelve thousand volumes of the Magi, written on ox hides in gold. An estimated half a million scrolls, the written knowledge of Phoenicia, were lost when the Athenaeum was burned during the fall of Carthage in 146 B.C.E. While on campaign in Gaul, Julius Caesar ordered the Bibractic Druid College, which contained thousands of written records on such subjects as medicine, philosophy, chemistry, and astronomy, razed to the ground.

According to Augustus Le Plongeon, the father of Maya archaeology,

> With the advent and ascendency of the Christian Church, the
> remembrance of the existence of such lands [Atlantis] that still
> lingered among students, as that of the Egyptian and Greek
> civilizations, was utterly obliterated from the mind of the people.
> If we are to believe Tertullian and other ecclesiastical writers,
> the Christians, during the first centuries of the Christian era,
> held in abhorrence all arts and sciences, which, like literature,
> they attributed to the Muses, and therefore regarded as artifices
> of the devil. They consequently destroyed all vestiges of as well
> as all means of culture. They closed the academies of Athens,
> the schools of Alexandria; burned the libraries of the Serapion
> and other temples of learning, which contained the works of
> the philosophers and the records of their researches in all
> branches of human knowledge.[1]

The supreme act of anti-intellectualism took place when mobs
torched the Great Library of Alexandria, which housed more than a
million volumes. The written record of Western civilization literally
went up in flames. The few thousand manuscripts that survived were
eventually burned by invading Muslims, who believed that if the
books contained information already stated in the Holy Koran there
was no need to preserve them, and if they carried words contrary to
the Koran, they were heretical.

Much later, on the other side of the world, Bishop De Landa had
the Maya natives of Yucatan make a huge pile of their illustrated
books, hand-painted birch paper folded into equal sections, and set
them on fire. "They cried as though I had burned their children,"
the good bishop proudly reported to his superiors in Madrid.[2] The
Maya had accounts of ancestral origins on a great island in the
Atlantic Ocean; today only the myth remains. It is not a surprise,
then, that so little written source material about Atlantis is available.
What would any Atlantologist give to walk through the halls of the
Great Library at Alexandria or the Athenaeum of Carthage! Sadly,
those burned books shall never be read. All that is left are myths. But
they preserve history well. Encased in a shell of poetic imagery, they

float safely through time, while most written histories are reduced to ashes.

A tradition that has rooted itself in folk consciousness will exist as long as the people themselves continue, because the tradition has become an organic extension of their soul. A historical myth is, then, the preservation of a memory vital to the identity of a people in poetic form. That such memories continue to be revered millennia after the people to whom they belonged perished only proves the profound significance of the myth to subsequent generations.

Myth is neither fable nor falsehood, but the precise opposite: the enshrining of some important historical or psychological truth in the vehicle that best enables its preservation over time. As Robert Graves, one of the most important authors and mythologists of the twentieth century, wrote, "They are all grave records of ancient religious customs or events, and reliable enough as history, once their language is understood and allowance has been made for errors in translation, misunderstandings of absolute ritual and deliberate changes introduced for moral or political reasons."[3] It is the historian's or mythologist's task to carefully peel away the overlapping layers of poetic embellishment accreted through the years, thereby getting to the kernel of fact around which the myth formed.

The Atlantis Myth is neither exclusively psychological nor historic, but a combination of the two. At its center is an actual event, one so profoundly traumatic and universal in magnitude that it seared the memory of humankind to the core of our collective unconscious. The destruction of Atlantis is our most powerful species memory, because it was there that we first arose from savagery to civilization, achieved heights of material and spiritual greatness, then lost it all in a cataclysmic flash that annihilated a broad swath of humanity. A Dark Age of ignorance, a backslide into barbarism, draped itself over the world for five centuries thereafter. The historical Great Killing was transmuted through the agency of myth, which persists to this day, because it lives on in our subconscious.

Nothing else can account for a story that, unlike any other, has continued to haunt the imagination of every generation since. In fact, the Atlantis Controversy is more alive today than it has ever been, thanks to a growing number of competent, even brilliant researchers from many and diverse fields, whose conclusions lead them back inevitably to the perished motherland of civilization.

Time is running full circle. What began as an actual event, became transformed through myth, and degenerated into denial is rapidly gaining ground as historical fact. That such a cycle spans the past thirty-two centuries is entirely proper and comprehensible, since the technology necessary to positively identify the drowned city is only just beginning to come into existence. But even that most stupendous of all finds, when it comes, as it inevitably must and shall, would not convey the broad sweep of its human signifi-cance without the presence of at least some of its story, preserved for millennia in the myths of survivors on both sides of the terrible ocean that swallowed a civilization.

PLATO'S OTHER ACCOUNT OF ATLANTIS

The earliest complete version of the Atlantis story is contained in Plato's *Timaeus* and *Kritias*. These works have been exhaustively covered in many other studies and are both quoted and referred to throughout this one. However, his lesser known work, *The Laws*, is not often mentioned by Atlantologists and is quoted even less. It is a significant oversight, because *The Laws* is the only other Platonic text to deal specifically with the Atlantean catastrophe. Strangely, while most scholars condemn the *Timaeus* and *Kritias* together as an improbable fiction, they regard *The Laws* as veritable history. It is structured as a conversation between an Athenian, who seems to speak with Plato's own voice, a Cretan, and Clinias, a Spartan.

> *Athenian:* Then what view do you both take of the ancient legends? Is there any truth to them?

Clinias: What legends are you talking about?

Athenian: Those which recount recurring destructions of humanity by floods, epidemics or from a variety of causes, when only a few survivors are left behind.

Clinias: Oh, those stories are entirely credible to anyone.

Athenian: Well then, let us discuss one of those mass exterminations, the one that was brought about by the Great Deluge.[4]

Here, as throughout his story of Atlantis, Plato reiterates his insistence that the account is true. In a similar vein, he makes a clear reference to Solon, whose unfinished epic poem was the basis for the Atlantean Dialogues:

Athenian: Poets, you know, singing as they do under divine guidance, are among the inspired and so, with the help of their Graces and Muses, often hit upon true historical fact.[5]

The geologic destruction that overwhelmed Atlantis was not confined to the Atlantic Ocean, but, as a matter of historical record, spread beyond to the Aegean Sea and Asia Minor. Robert Drews, a noted scholar on this period, observed that settlements in Crete were hastily built high in the mountains to accommodate displaced populations. Commonly referred to by investigators as "cities of refuge," they included such places as Karphi, 2,800 feet above sea level, and Kastro, even more remote. Their inhabitants had been residents of beautiful, comfortable cities below, near the coasts. Virtually all of these cities were suddenly destroyed, their populations forced to flee for their lives. They repaired to rude, makeshift villages high in the cold mountains. Drews remarks, "For the building of towns in such appalling locations a powerful motivation must be imagined."[6] That motivation was mentioned by Plato first in *Timaeus* and later in *The Laws:*

When the gods purge the Earth, the herdsmen and shepherds escape into the mountains, but those living in the cities are swept into the sea. [7]

That the few who escaped the destruction were mountain shepherds, mere scanty embers of mankind left unextinguished in the high peaks. And we may assume that at such a time there was total destruction of the cities located in the lowlands and on the seacoasts. Certainly, they were still haunted, we may assume, by a terror of coming down from the mountains to the plains.[8]

The Laws describes a dark age, when civilization was supposed to have slipped back into ignorance and chaos following the destruction of Atlantis:

Athenian: At such a time there was a total destruction even of the cities in the lowlands and along the seacoasts.

Clinias: Doubtless, we can make that assumption.

Athenian: Additionally, all kinds of tools, weapons, implements and instruments were lost, together with any scientific discoveries that were known before the destruction. . . . The condition of mankind after this calamity was as follows—There was horrendous and far-flung extermination, but, after the waters retreated somewhat, large areas of exposed land were left unpopulated for the remaining survivors and their diminished animal stocks. For their drowned city, its constitution and laws, the very things we are discussing here, do you imagine that, putting it mildly, even the faintest memory of them was preserved?

Clinias: Surely not.

Athenian: Then we may conclude that the numerous generations of men who led such a diminished existence for mere survival were unskilled and ignorant in the various arts, by comparison with the age before the Deluge or with our own.[9]

This dark age cited by Plato did indeed bring down a heavy

curtain of ignorance on the Bronze Age, around 1200 B.C.E. Virtually all the deeds and accomplishments of Western civilization up until that time were forgotten or transformed into myth. Thucydides, the first historian of classical Greece, wrote that nothing of historical consequence took place before the Greek equivalent of the eighth century B.C.E. The four centuries of intellectual night that overwhelmed civilization witnessed a wholesale regression of society without parallel until the fall of the Roman Empire. Plato says that the deluge triggered this dark age and uses it to explain why only the faintest memory of the society that preceded it survived into his time. He hinted that the earlier society was a particularly advanced one when he wrote of the scientific discoveries that were lost in the destruction. Along with the technology of this vanished civilization, Plato says that important minerals were likewise lost.

> *Athenian:* For iron, copper and metallurgy in general were so annihilated by the Deluge that they were no longer available. . . . As a consequence, every art requiring iron, copper and like metals were lost at this time and for long years thereafter.[10]

This is a particularly revealing passage, because the Bronze Age did in fact come to a speedy conclusion when supplies of copper were suddenly shut off. (Bronze is made by combining tin and zinc with copper.) The high-quality metallurgy that typified the era virtually ceased to exist after the thirteenth century B.C.E. Coincidentally, the world's richest copper was excavated from Michigan's Upper Peninsula by unknown miners from 3000 to 1200 B.C.E., the opening and closing dates of the Old World Bronze Age. Most of the mined American copper, more than half a billion pounds, disappeared. Some investigators believe freighters shipped the precious mineral to Europe and the Near East, where it was used in the manufacture of tools and weapons. The higher the grade of copper, the better the bronze.[11]

Old World copper supplies were inferior in both quantity and quality. In between Old World and New, Plato tells us, were the Atlanteans, a people he describes as proficient in seamanship and copper mining. After they were annihilated, the secret of the Michigan mines died with them. Moreover, the island's destruction was so cataclysmic it prevented safe passage beyond the Mediterranean for centuries. Plato's statements in *The Laws* conform remarkably well with the historical record in both the Old and New Worlds.

Interestingly, Plato makes not the slightest comparison between Atlantis and Crete in this *Dialogue*. Had he felt there was any relationship at all, as the Minoan theorists insist there was, this particular section would have afforded him special opportunity to do so, because Clinias is a Cretan. In fact, Minos is mentioned at the beginning of Book I of *The Laws,* but there is no attempt to connect him to the story of Atlantis or the Deluge.

WHY PLATO'S STORY OF ATLANTIS IS TRUE

Toward the close of Book III of *The Laws*, Plato indicates that his intention, had he been allowed to complete his project, was to have used Atlantis as a historical parable to show the cyclical nature of civilization. That is why he was so insistent that Atlantis was a real place. He meant to demonstrate that societies go through cycles of birth, virtuous youth, and material fulfillment in maturity, the superfluity of which leads to decline and ends in destruction. Had Atlantis only been a fairy tale, his analogy would not have worked. In other words, the story had to be true in order for him to have made his point. As he wrote,

> *Athenian:* The spectacle of this Titanic saga which our ancient legends describe is re-enacted through time, as man returns to his former condition of misery.[12]

Plato's *Dialogues,* regarded by most archaeologists as entirely fabulous and allegorical, are not only our first complete source for the story of Atlantis, but comprise a fundamental bridge between history and myth. It is important for us, as we observe the interplay between fact and metaphor, to understand just how myths can serve as reliable time capsules of major events. The following examples, separated from each other by great differences in space, time, and culture, were selected as representative of the universal power of myth to accurately, however poetically, preserve historical phenomena in tact over the course of many centuries.

The Myth of Menes

The Ancient Egyptians told a story of Menes, their first dynastic pharaoh. One day, while he was out hunting, his dogs suddenly turned on him and chased him to the bank of the Nile. The desperate king saw a large crocodile sunning itself in the mud. "Oh, crocodile," Menes implored, "Let me ride upon your back as you ferry me across the water to the other side, and I promise you a city of your own in my new kingdom!" The beast replied, "Surely, Pharaoh, I will carry you away from harm, for I prophesy that you shall some day be the king of a united Egypt." With that, Menes stepped fearlessly upon the back of the huge reptile, which bore him safely across to the opposite bank. There, crocodile rallied his fellows to the king's defense, and they joined him in battle against the rebellious hounds. After their victory, Menes kept his promise and raised a great city in the *nome* or governorship of the crocodiles, where the creatures would be honored by people from all over Egypt.

This was the story told by the priests of the sacred city of Shedet, known to the Greeks as Crocodilopolis. It was here that a sacred crocodile was provided with its own artificial lake, around which it lazily swam, adorned with crystal gems and golden earrings and bracelets, attended by caretakers entrusted with its well-being. When it died, its body was mummified and a new crocodile took its place. The myth, repeated into Roman times, by then already dated back

more than three thousand years to just before the political unifica-
tion of the Nile Valley.[13] While the real identity of Menes is still
uncertain, some of the various nomes of predynastic Egypt, symbolized by dogs (undoubtedly meant in a disparaging way), did indeed
resist the king, who endeavored to forge them into a single state. It
is also known that the image of a crocodile was the totem of a Lower
Nile nomarch who sided with Menes, and whose reward for loyalty
was the founding of Shedat.

In another version, Pharaoh Amenemhet III was identified with
the mythic king. Interestingly, his daughter was Sebeknefru, who
became queen after his son's early death. Her name is derived from
the loyal crocodile-god. She was the first of a number of monarchs
who incorporated the name of the god in their royal names and
titles. Amenemhet was a late twelfth-dynasty ruler; he lived seventeen hundred years before the Greek historian, Diodorus Siculus,
recorded the myth in his *Bibliotheca historica*.[14] In either case, the
crocodile's very early Egyptian allegory demonstrates how a forma-
tive political act of the distant past was preserved over thousands of
years in the vehicle of myth.

The Finn-men

Stories in Scotland and Ireland tell of the Finn-men, creatures that
assumed the shapes of marine animals and came ashore transformed
into seals. The myth was generally regarded as a fantasy by persons
residing outside the coastal areas, until a kayak (now at the Aber-
deen Museum) was found beached in 1685. Subsequent investigation proved that Greenland Eskimos had infrequently and furtively
put in along the northern shores of the British Isles for unknown
centuries. The Eskimos always wore sealskin clothing, which made
them appear as the metamorphic Finn-men. Stripped of fanciful
elaboration, which inevitably accretes any oral tradition with time,
the Scotch-Irish myth, like so many others, was constructed over
the centuries on a very real historic basis.[15]

The Myth of the Meteor

During the late sixteenth century, Europeans first encountered a rimmed, bowl-shaped pit 4,000 feet across among the rolling plains of Arizona's Canyon Diablo region. Much later named the Barringer Crater, after the family that stills owns the land on which it sits, the formation is open to the general public. Lying 19 miles west of Winslow, the feature is 570 feet deep, enough to engulf a 60-story building: if the Washington Monument were placed on the crater floor, its apex would be level with the ground above. More than 2.4 miles in circumference, the crater could accommodate twenty football fields.

Native Hopi and Zuni said that the crater had been created when God threw a flaming demon out of heaven. The resultant crash so frightened men they behaved themselves, at least for a few generations. The great hole in the world was and is revered by the Indians as a sacred site and a reminder to conform with God's will.

Mythologists who recorded the Native American tale of Barringer Crater concluded that the Hopi and Zuni had witnessed a meteor fall that resulted in the astrobleme. They noted that the Indians told early Spaniards who visited the area that the depression had been made by the fallen devil. Hence its name, Diablo Canyon. These investigators were belittled as fanciful interpreters by professional astronomers, who refused to admit that the site had been caused by a celestial event. As far back as 1891, G. K. Gilbert pronounced that the crater was an extinct volcano. His verdict stood as dogma for the next seventy years, even though his personal visit to the site was hardly more than a cursory look around. Gilbert was, after all, the chief geologist of the U.S. Geological Survey, and his word was law.

Not until 1960 was the crater's meteoric origin established beyond question, when studies of silica in the area showed that the mineral had been modified by the kind of high pressures only exerted by a meteor impact. They also found a profusion of nickel-iron debris, some individual pieces weighing up to 1,400 pounds, within a one-hundred-mile radius of the crater. A rocky matrix that includes nickel and iron is the material of which most meteors are composed. Researchers who collected thousands of tons of sand-grain-sized droplets determined they condensed from a gigantic cloud of metallic vapor that shot up high into the air over the meteor strike.

Since the true nature of the astrobleme has been recognized, the dramatic details of its formation have finally come to light. The crater was caused by a nickel-iron meteor about 150 feet across, weighing 100,000 tons and traveling at nearly 45,000 miles per hour, or 25 miles per second. It struck the earth with an explosive force in excess of twenty million tons of TNT, equivalent to a 4 or 5 megaton atomic bomb, and displaced over 300 million tons of rock in a matter of seconds. Some of the stones thrown thousands of feet from the impact center weighed in excess of 5,000 tons. The blast excavated a crater 700 feet deep, ejecting 175 million tons of limestone and sandstone over a distance of more than a mile. Intense pressures generated underground by the meteorite's impact transformed small concentrations of graphite into microscopic diamonds.[16]

This powerful event seemed to have been documented in native tribal myths long before scientists came to their own, similar conclusions. Even so, the critics of myth insisted the Indians or their ancestors could not have possibly witnessed the meteor fall that produced Barringer Crater, because the impact took place 50,000 years ago; in other words, about 30,000 years before human beings arrived in Arizona. In 1981, however, material from the crater's rim was subjected to a new dating process, using the radioactive decay of potassium isotopes into argon isotopes as a kind of clock. When the impact melted them, the "clock" was restarted, as it were, because the gaseous argon trapped within the rim was allowed to escape. Measurement of the amount of argon formed through radioactive decay thereby dates the rock to the last time it was molten. The isotopes recovered from Meteor Crater and subjected to the argon dating process proved that the meteorite struck Arizona only 2,700 years ago.[17] At that time, the Hopi and Zuni (or, at any rate, their immediate ancestors) did indeed inhabit the vicinity of the crater and were, therefore, probably eyewitnesses to the impact.

The Navajo, who live in the same area, regard the location as taboo, because they believe anything touched by lightning (the cause, they believe, of the crater), is profane. Their interpretation was inspired by the scorched quality of the local rock, not from any tribal memory. The Navajo were relative newcomers to Arizona, arriving about 600 years ago from the Pacific Northwest,[18] and, consequently, could not have seen the meteor fall. The Hopi and Zuni, whose shared myth is an obvious preservation of an actual event, trace their roots deep into the prehistory of the American Southwest, and therefore would have witnessed the cataclysm. This disparity between the Hopi-Zuni tradition and the Navajo demonstrates the essentially genuine character of historical myth. What the Hopi and Zuni have known for the past twenty-seven centuries took modern experts ninety years to confirm.

Black Birds

Far from Arizona, the Tlingit people of Alaska and the Pacific Northwest relied entirely upon oral tradition to preserve their history. At the turn of the nineteenth century, G. T. Emmons, an American anthropologist, was studying Tlingit myth.[19] He was surprised to find an accurate, highly detailed account of the tribe's first contact with a modern European, the French navigator, La Perouse, who visited them in 1786. Although their myth described the Frenchman's ships as gigantic black birds with white wings, the poetical quality of the tradition was transparent enough to allow for a thorough reconstruction of an actual event of great importance to the Tlingit.

The four examples presented were chosen because they represent the types of myths that form the Atlantis memory in the collective consciousness of humanity. The Egyptian story of Menes or Amen-emhet and the crocodile shows that a seminal history of nation-building may be as well preserved in myth as an insect in amber. Scotch-Irish tales of the elusive Finn-men demonstrate how encounters with representatives of radically alien cultures are mythically encapsulated. The Hopi-Zuni poetization of an extraordinary natural event and the Tlingits' tribal memory of their meeting with technologically superior culture bearers prove that myth does indeed perpetuate the recollection of significant occurrences in the history of a people for many hundreds, even thousands, of years. And these four types of myths are precisely the kinds of worldwide myths that have preserved the portrait of Atlantis in all its original colors.

The myths describing Atlantis and its destruction are far-flung, yet so consistently complementary and explicatory that they provide wonderful proof for the existence of the drowned civilization. Atlantis has been eternalized in the folkish consciousness of diverse peoples separated by thousands of miles and disparate cultural levels. Used in conjunction with complementary archaeological and geologic evidence, myth takes the form of a powerfully persuasive argument on behalf of historical Atlantis.

FOUR

The Fire from Heaven

*I confess for a long time I had regarded all this [myths per-
taining to Atlantis] as pure fables to the day when, better in-
structed in Oriental languages, I judged that
all these legends must be, after all, only
the development of a great truth.*
Athanasius Kircher, Oedipus a Egyptiacus

The one great myth of the world is the story of the Deluge. It is the
common heritage of all humanity. The variety of cultures that
define one people from another are cut across by something far
grander than legend, a planetwide experience of such high drama
that it resounds in the folk traditions of each continent. The Deluge
was the supremely powerful event that touched every ancestry, so
comprehensive in its horror that it lives on, a universal nightmare
in our collective unconscious, spanning the millennia from that
time to this.

The story of the Deluge did not originate in nor is it confined to
Genesis. The Old Testament rendition is just one of the more than
five hundred versions known around the world. The story is told by
the Inuit peoples above the Arctic Circle and the Patagonians of
Tierra del Fuego, at the bottom of South America; by the Sami of

Finland and the Maori of Polynesia. It was known to the Hopi
Indians of Arizona and the Greeks of Plato's day.

The scholars Le Haye and Morris collected and statistically
analyzed 215 variants of the Deluge story from as many cultures.[1]
They found that in 88 percent of them a family favored by a divinity
survives; 77 percent feature a huge vessel as the means of escape; 67
percent include the survival of the family's animals; 66 percent
describe the Deluge as the result of human wickedness; in 66 percent
the hero of the tale was forewarned by divine intervention. In an
undetermined but high percentage (perhaps as much as 75 percent)
the Great Flood was regarded as the event from which a survivor
emerged to found a new society. In a similarly high percentage, each
culture that preserves the report claims descent from the Deluge's
hero. Virtually all the known flood accounts are interconnected by
common themes, which, collectively, tell essentially the same story.
It is amazing that the Berbers of Morocco and the Chinook Indians
of British Columbia repeat a fundamentally shared tradition.

These global similarities are not due to Christian missionaries
who spread the word of the Bible to various parts of the world. The
renowned anthropologist and geographer, Dr. Richard Andree,
proved that 62 of a random 86 flood stories he collected from
Europe, Africa, Polynesia, America, Australia, and Asia were not
affected by Noah's story in Genesis.[2] No less significantly, the remainder of those native accounts that bore traces of biblical influence were known independent of and previous to contact with the
missionaries, who molded the indigenous myths to conform with
Christian teaching.

A remarkable case in point was illustrated when the first Spanish
missionaries began to preach among the Mixtec Indians. Native to
the northern and western regions of Oaxaca, the Mixtecs, although
today nominally Christian, never abandoned their old deities and
still revere Tlaloc, the Atlantean rain god. Archaeologists believe
their culture provides a particularly valuable insight into Meso-

america's deepest past, because the Mixtecs may have been related to the Olmecs, the earliest of Mexican civilizations, beginning at Vera Cruz and Monte Alban around 1500 B.C.E. When the Spaniards began to teach the Mixtecs about the Old Testament flood, the Indians responded with instant recognition: "Yes, that is the story of Nata and his woman, Nana, who came to our ancestors on a great raft over the Sunrise Sea after their home in the Old Red Land went under the water!" The Mixtec tale predated the Christians' sixteenth century arrival by perhaps three thousand years, given the Indians' links with the 1500 B.C.E. Olmecs.[3]

Virtually all the flood myths preserved by native peoples throughout the Americas and the Pacific portray the deluge hero as tall, fair-complected, and bearded.[4, 5] He is usually depicted as red-haired, from Red Horn of Wisconsin's Winnebagos (Ho Chunk) and Con-Tiki-Viracocha in Peru, to Tane in Polynesia.[6, 7] The majority of the North American myths describe him as crossing the Atlantic Ocean from the east. Conversely, European, African, and Near Eastern flood legends speak of his arrival from the West over the same ocean.[8]

"THE WORLD, TOO SAUCY WITH THE GODS, INCENSES THEM TO SEND DESTRUCTION"

James E. Strickling correlated his own set of specifics based on the percentages discovered by Le Haye and Morris.[9] A trained professional in the fields of statistics and industrial quality control, Strickling found that the possibility of themes common to worldwide stories of the Great Flood could have been independently invented was so far beyond statistical probability that such motifs could only come from a single, common source. They all originated, he concluded, in the universal memory of some catastrophic experience.

That universal memory was suspected by the pioneering naturalist, Alexander von Humbolt, as long ago as the mid-nineteenth century: "The belief in a great deluge is not confined to one nation, singly. It makes part of a system of historical tradition, of which we find scattered notions among the Maypures of the great cataracts; among the Indians of the Rio Erevato which runs into the Caura; and among all the tribes of the Orinoco." He believed that this "historical tradition" was not exclusive to the natives of South America, but had its origins "in a firmly rooted racial memory common to all men."[10]

A disturbing theme runs through many worldwide accounts of the Deluge. Some investigators find it difficult to accept, if only because the destruction of Atlantis was itself such an all-encompassing geologic event. The notion that one cataclysm could be sparked by an even greater catastrophe seems to them far-fetched. In 1785 G. R. Corli, a famous French astronomer, was the first scientist to conclude that the fragment of a passing comet collided with Earth to destroy Atlantis.

The earliest thorough investigation of the Atlantis Problem was begun nearly one hundred years later by the father of Atlantology, Ignatius Donnelly. His second book on the subject, *Ragnarok, Age of Fire and Gravel*, argued at length that the island civilization had been annihilated by a comet's collision with the Earth.[11] At a time when established scientists ridiculed the very idea of "stones which fall from the sky," his speculation was roundly dismissed as untenable fantasy. He was supported by only a few contemporary thinkers, including the Russian physicist Sergi Basinsky who argued that a serious meteor impact with the Earth was powerful enough to be responsible for the destruction of Atlantis and the simultaneous rise of Australia.

In the 1920s and '30s, Donnelly's theory was revived and supported by the cosmologist Martin Hoerbiger whose "Cosmic Ice" paradigm theorized that the Atlantean disaster was the result of an impact by a cometary fragment of frozen debris. The German's ideas were internationally condemned for political reasons, although his views were still cited as late as 1990 by many astronomers to explain the Tunguska Event of eighty-two years before, when "cosmic ice" from the comet Encke allegedly exploded above the Siberian tundra.

Hoerbiger's British contemporary, Comyns Beaumont, an influential publisher of scientific books, independently came to similar conclusions. Following the World War II era, Hoerbiger was championed by another well-known British researcher, H. S. Bellamy. Meanwhile, Beaumont's work formed the basis for Immanuel Velikovsky's famous *Worlds in Collision*,[12] which elaborated on the possibility that a celestial impact was responsible for the sudden demise of a pre-Flood civilization.

Intriguing or even as plausible as these "catastrophists" argued, their proof was largely inferential and circumstantial. But the extraterrestrial theory began to assume persuasive material evidence in 1964, when a former German rocket scientist, Otto Muck, wrote of a huge trail of impact craters across South Carolina pointing toward a pair of deep-sea holes in the ocean floor. They were caused by a small asteroid, he argued, that split in half and set off a geologic chain reaction that traveled the length of the Mid-Atlantic Ridge to the destruction of Atlantis.

Dr. Muck's impressive academic credentials as the inventor of, among other things, the submarine snorkel, lent his theory much professional authority. A veteran of Werner von Braun's guided-missile research team at Peenemünde, he owned more than two thousand patents at the time of his death in 1965. His *The Secret of Atlantis*[13] set something of a precedent and encouraged other university scholars to come forward with their own findings. They included the world's foremost authority on Halley's Comet, Dr. M. M. Kamiensky, a member of the Polish Academy of Sciences; Professor N. Bonev, one of the twentieth century's leading astronomers at the University of Sofia, in Bulgaria; and Jack Hills, of the prestigious Los Alamos National Laboratory.[14] They publicly stated their beliefs that Atlantis was destroyed by an extraterrestrial impact or series of impacts, a conclusion shared by the leading Atlantologist of the post–World War II era, Edgerton Sykes.[15]

PLATO HINTS AT A CELESTIAL CATASTROPHE

Thousands of years before a few modern scientists reluctantly began to admit the possibility of Atlantis and its demise through some cosmic event, mythic traditions from around the world graphically described a celestial holocaust so devastating its consequences were felt by the entire planet. This universal myth is by no means unique and usually cannot be separated from the more than five hundred known flood legends. In many of them it is an integral, central part of the story, cited as the immediate cause of the Deluge. Reconstructing all these traditions would require its own book. For the purposes of this investigation, recounting representative examples from various lands and peoples affected by the cataclysm should provide a revealing glimpse into the past.

An extraterrestrial cause for the Deluge was strongly alluded to in Plato's unfinished description of Atlantis, the prime source for information about the sunken civilization. In the *Kritias*, the last lines before the destruction read

> And the god of gods, Zeus, who reigns through the law, and who sees all things, when he saw the degenerate state of this otherwise admirable stock, determined to punish them and reduce their numbers in order to discipline them. He therefore called together his fellow immortals at his glorious dwelling place, which is located at the center of the cosmos and looks out over the entire universe of transformation, and, after they appeared before him, addressed them with these words.[16]

The narrative breaks off just as doom is about to be pronounced on Atlantis, but the first appearance of Zeus, wielder of the thunderbolt, at this important juncture can only mean that the catastrophe that followed must have been celestial in nature. And from the language Plato uses, it is clear that Zeus meant to take a direct hand in chastising the Atlanteans. Had he not been so personally dedicated to their punishment, he would have summoned a lesser god to carry out his orders. Atlantis was overwhelmed by a deluge, so its complete destruction was accomplished though the cooperation of Poseidon, god of the sea, and Zeus, ruler of the heavens. Plato's inclusion of Sky Father as the originator of the catastrophe can only mean it was brought about through a cosmic event.

Ovid, Rome's greatest poet in the early years of the empire, felt obliged, in his famous *Metamorphoses,* to briefly complete Plato's account (using the Latin names Jupiter and Neptune for Zeus and Poseidon).

> There was such wickedness once on Earth that Justice fled to heaven, and the king of the gods determined to make an end of the race of men. Jupiter's anger was not confined to his province of the sky. Neptune, his sea-blue brother, sent the waves to help him. Neptune smote the Earth with his trident and the Earth shivered and shook. Soon there was no telling land from sea. Beneath the water the sea nymphs, the Nereids, were suddenly staring in amazement at forests, buildings and cities. Nearly all men perished by water, and those who escaped the water, having no food, died of hunger.[17]

Ovid chose to employ some of the same elements found in the *Kritias,* including the degenerate condition of mankind as the moral cause of the catastrophe, employment of the sea god who created Atlantis, even his Nereid attendants. Smiting the world with his trident is an obvious poetic analogy for seismic activity. But the celestial aspect of the cataclysm is left to Jupiter, whose "anger was not confined to his province of the sky."

A GREEK COMMEMORATIVE CEREMONY OF THE ATLANTIS FLOOD

The other mythic characters passing through Plato's account, no matter how briefly, allude to the influence of the gods in the Atlantean cataclysm. Early in the *Timaeus,* he writes, "On the occasion when he [Solon] was drawing them [the Egyptian priests] on to speak of antiquity, he began to tell them about the most ancient things in our part of the world; about Phoroneus, who is called *the First,* and about Niobe, and after the Deluge, to tell the lives of Deucalion and Pyrrha."[18] Niobe, mentioned just once, was a granddaughter of Atlas and consequently belonged to the royal house of Atlantis. After the Deluge, she was turned to stone (a device used to describe the effects of some heaven-sent punishment), and covered by water for eternity.

Before her tragic transformation, she was the mother of Phoroneus, another figure cited in the narrative. Phoroneus's two sons were Atlantean culture bearers in the Aegean. The eldest, Pelasgus, led his followers, the Pelasgians, or "Sea Peoples," as the Greeks remembered them, to establish the first civilization on the Peloponnesus. His younger brother, Car, settled on the western shores of Asia Minor, where he became the eponymous founder of another sea people, the Carians. Their very name is connected with Atlantis: a caryatid is an architectural feature, a female figure supporting a lintel that usually represents the sky. It derives from "Caryea." Just as the statue provides support for a building, Atlas was conceived as a man upholding the heavens.

The historical reality of both Pelasgians and Carians is borne out by Egyptian records of the Twentieth Dynasty, which describe the Weshesh, or sea people of the Aegean, and by modern archaeologists, who regard the Pelasgians as the Bronze Age Mycenaeans, or their direct precursors. Returning to Phoroneus, Solon refers to him as "the First," because he was the earliest mortal king to reign after the Flood, which, according to Greek myth, was immediately preceded by a terrible conflagration in the sky.

A husband and wife, Deucalion and Pyrrha, mentioned in the *Dialogue,* escaped from the same Deluge. Of course, most academics dismiss their story as nothing more than a fable. The ancient Greeks did not. To commemorate the pair's survival, the Athenians held an annual three-day festival, the *Anthesteria*, named after the month (Anthesterion, late February or early March) in which it occurred. Deucalion and Pyrrha were traditionally honored on Friday the thirteenth. Is this the origin of our superstition? It is unclear whether the thirteenth of Anthesteria commemorates the arrival of Deucalion and Pyrrha in Greece or the actual date of the Deluge. In any case, the Anthesteria was a means of preserving historical information about the Great Flood.

Part of the festival involved sacrificing flour and honey into an earthquake fissure.[19] This aspect of the ceremonies seems particularly Atlantean, for why else include something of this nature in the commemoration of a flood?[20]

The Anthesteria largely honored Dionysus, the god of wine, and coincided with the maturation of the previous year's vintage and the beginning of spring. It was fitting that Deucalion was honored at this festival, because he sacrificed wine on Greek soil to thank the gods for his survival. Coincidentally, his name means "new wine sailor" *(deuco-halieus)*. The Anthesteria opened with libations to Dionysus from the freshly opened casks, an imitation of Deucalion's homage.

No less appropriate, the thirteenth, the day on which Deucalion and his wife were honored, also witnessed ceremonies for the dead, lending further credence to the persistence of our modern superstitions. These were the dead, killed in the Deluge, who were believed to live again through the mystery religion of Dionysus.

PHAETHON

In Greek myth, the Great Flood was supposedly triggered by a legendary figure who appears early in the *Timaeus*, Phaethon, illegitimate son of Helios, the god who drove the chariot of the sun across the heavens. Like a teenager demanding the keys to the family car, Phaethon forced his reluctant father to hand over the reins of his chariot and the youngster drove it into the morning.

Before long, however, he lost control of the powerful team of fiery horses. They careened among the constellations and dove down toward Earth, burning forests into deserts and setting cities aflame. Earth, humanity, and the very heavens were threatened with total destruction as the chariot was dragged back up toward the vault of the sky and down again over our imperiled planet.

Hearing the desperate prayers of Gaia, the goddess Mother Earth, Zeus hurled his thunderbolt at the delinquent charioteer. Set free from their burden, the horses raced back toward their stables in the western sky. But Phaethon fell on fire to Earth, his long hair turned to streaming flames; the remains of the broken chariot trailed in burning fragments behind him. This incandescent mass crashed into the sea, causing a great flood that overwhelmed much of the world and extinguished many of the fires sparked by the boy's wild ride.

No less a genius than Goethe was perhaps the first to write, in 1821, that the ancient tale spoke of a natural catastrophe.[21] But since the days of the Egyptian high priest featured in Plato's story of Atlantis, scholars have regarded Phaethon's story as the mythic account of a comet that collided with the Earth. The priest is quoted in the *Timaeus:*

> There have been and will be many different calamities to destroy mankind, the greatest of them by fire and water, lesser ones by countless other means. There is a story which even you have preserved, that once upon a time, Phaethon, the son of Helios, having yoked the steeds of his father's chariot, burnt up all that was upon the Earth, because he was not able to drive them in the path of his father, and was himself destroyed by a thunderbolt. Now, this has the form of a myth, but really signifies a derivation in their courses of the bodies moving around the Earth and the heavens, and a great conflagration recurring at long intervals of time.[22]

Plato's inclusion of Phaethon early in the narrative can only mean he intended to describe a celestial cause in his unfinished description of the Atlantis destruction.

The Shining One

That Phaethon was in fact a mythic representation of an actual cosmic event appears certain. In numerous ancient accounts, comets are almost invariably referred to as "hairy" or "long-haired," recalling the tragic hero's flaming tresses as he fell to Earth. *Phaethon* means "the Shining One" or "the Blazing Star." His story is best remembered in the later, Roman redaction, which had him crash into the Eridanus, usually considered to be today's Po River, which flows into the Adriatic. However, *Eridanus* means "great river," and was often linked to *Okeanus,* the "great river" that girdles the globe.

The myth's earliest version placed Phaethon's final plunge into the sea off the western coast of Ethiopia, squarely in the vicinity of Atlantis. (Until the turn of the first century B.C.E., "Ethiopia" referred to the Atlantic coasts of North Africa.) Even in early imperial times, Roman tourists visiting Egypt were mistakenly told that the colossus of Amenhotep III, in Thebes, depicted Memnon, the king of Ethiopia, which lay simultaneously in the far east and the distant west, so far had history forgotten its original location. The confusion arose through an apparent similarity between the name of the Egyptian and Ethiopian rulers. Memnon was the leader of ten thousand Ethiopians, who traveled from the west over a great distance to fight in the Trojan War. According to Quintas of Smyrna, he told his uncle, King Priam, how "the lily-like Hesperides raised me far away by the stream of Ocean."[23]

The Hesperides were Daughters of Atlas, *Atlantises,* who attended their father's sacred garden on a island in the western sea. After Memnon's death, another set of Atlantises, the Pleiades, were said to mourn him. Memnon's closest officers both bore Atlantean names, Alkyoneus and Klydon. The former bears the same name as the King of Scheria, the last monarch of Atlantis in Homer's *Odyssey;* the latter's name is the masculine version of Kleito, the mortal woman in Plato's *Kritias* who begot the lineage of Atlantean royalty. It seems clear that Memnon was the leader of forces dispatched from Atlantis to aid the Trojans. Their identity as "Ethiopians" was a Greek transliteration from an older name, probably something close to *At-i-ops.* This approximation of the original has a discernable Atlantean resemblance, and not only philologically. A nonliteral translation might be, "Serpents of At," or "Mountain Serpents," appropriately descriptive for a company of warriors.

With the rise of the kingdom of Mauretania, located in present-day Morocco, "Ethiopia" was moved to its present position between Sudan and Somalia. The earliest known version of the Phaethon myth was told by Hesiod in the eighth century B.C.E., when Ethiopia was still regarded as a coastal North African land.[24] The Greek mythologist undoubtedly recorded a myth with far older origins, but the important point here is that the scene of the fiery climax was originally set in the Atlantic Ocean. Even into late-imperial times, Roman scholars identified Ethiopia with a North African territory located in present-day Morocco. The early third-century historian Marcellus wrote a chronicle, only fragments of which survive, that told of human and natural events in the vicinity of Mauretania, then a Roman client kingdom located along the northwestern shores of Africa below the Pillars of Heracles.

His work, entitled *An Ethiopic History,* described the Guanche natives of Tenerife, largest of the Canary Islands. He wrote that they "preserved a recollection transmitted to them by their ancestors of the island of Atlantis, which was extremely large and, for a long time, held sway over all the islands in the Atlantic Ocean."[25] Here, Ethiopia is not only squarely placed on the Atlantic Ocean, but in proximity to Atlantis itself. Guenon concluded that "Ethiopia" was a post-cataclysmic name attached to Atlantis for some centuries after its destruction. Aithi-ops ("burnt faces") refers not to the negroes of East African, but suggests the physical after-effects wrought on the Atlantean survivors by the volcanic catastrophe.[26] Pliny the Elder left no doubt when he stated that Aethiopia was formerly called Atlantia!

The Dust-veil Event

Relying on ancient sources still available at the Great Library of Alexandria, Ovid recounted, "For in pitiable mourning his father hides his covered face and, if we are to believe what we are told, a day went by without the sun." After the tragedy, Helios drew a veil over his face, which had a dirty appearance. This is a poetic description of a phenomenon known to volcanologists and climatologists as a "dust-veil event," the presence of so much ash in the atmosphere following a major volcanic eruption or meteor collision that the sun's brightness is diminished and it appears "dirty." In fact, Ovid has Gaia cry out, "Such a quantity of ashes over my eyes, so much, too, over my features!" He writes that Jupiter intends to punish sinful humanity with "the fire from heaven," but, when he sees that the entire universe is in danger of destruction, changes his mind and turns the catastrophe into a Deluge. This is undoubtedly the destruction of Atlantis, indicated by his mention of its eponymous king: "Atlas himself is struggling, and can hardly bear the glowing heavens on his shoulders. . . . Great cities perish together with their fortifications and the flames turn whole nations into ashes."[27]

Cataclysm

Nonnos, a Greek poet of the fifth century, wrote that Zeus hurled a world conflagration at the Titans (Atlas, together with his nine Atlantean brothers), who were finally overwhelmed by the flood that ensued.[28] Lucretius, an earlier Roman authority, told of the Deluge that came as a consequence of Phaethon's crash, "The waters, according to the legend, rose over every mountain and engulfed many cities."[29] But Hesiod's description remains the most cataclysmic: "The life-giving Earth crashed around on fire. All the land seethed, as did Ocean's streams. The world and heaven embraced together in such a ruinous crash that the whole Earth was thrown into chaos, while the heavens from on high came hurling down."[30] Significantly, our "cataclysm" stems from *kataklysmos*, the Greek word, not for some general catastrophe, but specifically for "deluge." No less revealing, the word "disaster" is taken from a Greek word meaning "evil star." Could the very terminology employed to discuss the fate of Atlantis derive from words originally used to describe that destruction itself?

Writing on the Phaethon myth, the noted astronomers Clube and Napier conclude, "It seems very unlikely that this story is based on nothing. When the 'poetic' component is discarded, the core of the myth is essentially the same for all authors, and is the clear description of an impact. . . . [T]he Phaethon myth especially provides a link between a large impact, and a great conflagration followed by a great flood."[31] Victor Clube and Bill Napier are seconded by another leading astronomer, Rudolf Englehardt: "Therefore, we shall have to conclude from the sources that the fiery catastrophe that was interpreted as Phaethon's fall was really followed by a short-lived but extensive inundation which ended the lives of so many men that one could talk of a destruction of mankind."[32]

A century before, Ignatius Donnelly succinctly characterized Phaethon for his and future generations: "This is the story of the conflagration as treated by a civilized mind, explained by a myth, and decorated with the flowers and foliage of poetry. Divest this poem of the myth of Phaethon, and we have a very faithful tradition of the conflagration of the world caused by a comet."[33] Ovid himself certainly realized that the myth he retold was the poetic description of an astronomical event when he characterized Phaethon's descent as "a star falling from the otherwise serene sky."[34]

THE BIBLICAL ATLANTIS

Were the story of the sun god's reckless boy the only one to have survived into the present, there would still be sufficient evidence to conclude that the Atlantean world was brought to its violent end through a celestially triggered deluge. But given the magnitude of essentially identical accounts from hundreds of societies around the planet, that long ago catastrophe of catastrophes assumes a deeply disquieting sense of reality. Better known than Phaethon may be the Hebrew story of Noah. But far less famous are the Atlantis and cometary components in his myth.

Like the Atlanteans, Noah's generation is portrayed as unrepentently sinful and God determines to exterminate most of them. When Noah warns his neighbors of what to expect, they respond arrogantly: "What is this deluge? If it be a deluge of flame, we have asbestos, which is proof against fire. And if a deluge of water, we have sheets of metal to restrain any flood that may break from the Earth. However great this deluge, we are so tall that it cannot reach our necks." Here we encounter the same kind of foreshadowing found in the *Timaeus*, with suggestions of "a deluge of flame" followed by "a deluge of water." The sinners' "sheets of metal" implies the Atlanteans' powerful walls, generously emblazoned with precious metal. That island's "lofty character," as described by Plato, may have been what was meant when the citizenry said they were "so tall it cannot reach our necks," perhaps because mountaintops were regarded as places of refuge against such a calamity.[35]

The events that immediately preceded the Deluge appear to have been both seismic and celestial: "Earth shook, her foundations trembled, the sun darkened, lightning flashed, thunder pealed, and a deafening voice the like of which was never heard before, rolled across mountain and plain." Unprecedented earthquake activity was accompanied by a dust-veil event and celestial explosions. These effects are explained when God "opened Heaven's sluices by the removal of two Pleiades; thus allowing the Upper and Lower Water—the male and female elements of Tehom, which He had separated in the days of Creation—to re-unite and destroy the world in a cosmic embrace."[36]

In this passage it is apparent that although the Heavenly Father punished mankind chiefly through the agency of water, He also "rained fire on the evil-doers." The Pleiades constellation is associated with rain and floods among cultures as disparate as the ancient Hebrews of the Middle East and the Aztecs in Mexico. Yahweh throws a pair of "stars" (meteorites) from the Pleiades to begin the Deluge.[37] (Tehom is from the Babylonian goddess, Tiamat, personification of the primal chaos that reigned before the creation of the world.) More to the point of our investigation, the Pleiades are Atlantises, Daughters of Atlas. In Greek myth, one of their number, Electra, disappears after she sends her son, Dardanus, away from their homeland as it sinks into the sea.

Later in the Old Testament, the destruction of Atlantis is taken up again in the words of a survivor from that catastrophe. If God could save him from that worst of all disasters, He will protect him from any evil. The words of Psalm 18:7–16 graphically portray a blazing comet or meteor shower blasting open the sea depths: "Then the Earth did shake and quiver. The fountains of the mountains shook and spilled over because He was angry. His wrath streamed in billows of black smoke, and His face was all fire, from which coals fell. He bent the very heavens in coming down, while the darkness was under His feet. And He rode flying upon cherubim. He soared upon the very wings of the wind. He covered Himself in a cape of darkness. His vehicle was the darkness of waters and thick, dark clouds. Out of the blackness of this cloak rained hailstones, flaming coals. The Lord bellowed thunderously high in the heavens. Then the channels of the deep waters were seen and the foundations of the Earth laid bare. Yet, he rescued me out of the great waters."[38]

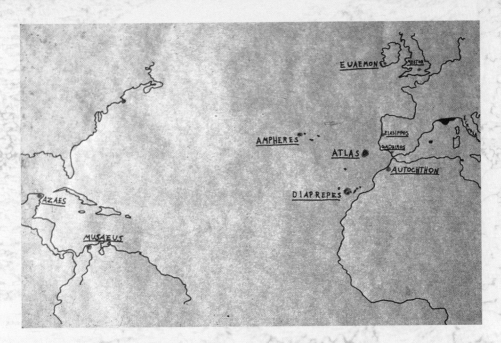

The Empire of Atlantis. Its kings, as provided in Plato's Dialogues, *correspond to specific geographical locations, and are the names of its colonies.*

A ruined Etruscan tower in the waters off Tarquinia. According to Plato, the Atlanteans occupied western Italy, where their direct descendants patterned Etruscan culture after the lost civilization of their seafaring ancestors.

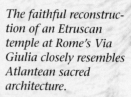

The faithful reconstruction of an Etruscan temple at Rome's Via Giulia closely resembles Atlantean sacred architecture.

A model of Queen Hatshepsut's funerary temple at Deir el-Bahri in west Thebes, Upper Egypt. The original was inspired by the construction her royal merchants observed during their major trading expedition around Africa, circa 1470 B.C., and preserves a glimpse into the monumental architectural style of Atlantis. (Rosicrucian Museum, San José, CA)

A dramatic monolith stands on the shore of Lanzarote, most easterly of the Canary Islands. While the inscription in an unknown language near its base is indecipherable, its design of concentric circles alternating five and six rings combines the sacred numerals and emblematic layout of Atlantis.

Atlantean-style architecture—defined by Plato as concentric, its rings interconnected by causeways—is still found on Tenerife, the largest of the Canary Islands, as shown in this Las Palmas Museum model.

Atlantean architecture identical to examples found on the other side of the world occur high in the Andes Mountains, at the pre-Inca ceremonial site of Sacsahuaman.

The oldest building in the world, Ireland's New Grange, is surrounded by folk traditions of culture bearers from a sunken kingdom.

Stonehenge conforms to the sacred numerical and concentric architectural canon of monumental Atlantean construction. Even the time parameters of Britain's foremost megalithic site parallel the rise and fall of Bronze Age Atlantis.

The concentric layout of Cuicuilco's pre-Aztec pyramid in the southern outskirts of Mexico City strongly suggest Atlantean influences supported by numerous native accounts of culture bearers arriving after the destruction of their homeland in the Atlantic Ocean.

A statuette of Tutankh-amun depicted as one of Pharaoh's ancestors, the Mesentiu, or "Harpooners," who arrived at the Nile Delta from the Distant West, where a natural catastrophe destroyed their island kingdom.

The Popul Vuh *("Book of Consul") reported that the ancestors of the Maya landed in eastern Mexico as refugees from a worldclass natural disaster that obliterated their homeland across the Atlantic Ocean.*

South Dakota's Bear Butte was chosen by Native American tribal elders as the site for their ceremonies memorializing the Great Flood. The butte resembles the island in the sea from which their ancestors arrived on the eastern shores of North America.

Minnesota's Jeffers Petroglyph Site displays some of North America's oldest rock art. Here, the Great Flood is depicted in a circle representing the sunken ancestral island. The horned giant follows a turtle, both carrying human survivors of the Deluge, to safety on the shores of a new continent where they will sire the Native American tribes.

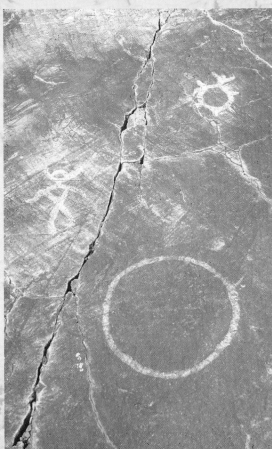

Karnak, in Luxor, Upper Egypt. On its walls, Ramses II inscribed the text of a nonaggression pact with his erstwhile Hittite enemies with whom he allied against the "Sea Peoples" of Atlantis.

This seventh-century B.C.E. funerary terra-cotta of an Etruscan couple evidences the oval faces, slightly slanted eyes, and red hair characteristic of their Atlantean ancestors.

A represetnation of Solon, Athens's great legislator, who learned the story of Atlantis firsthand from Egyptian temple priests. (Landmark Building, St. Paul, MN)

The entrance to Medinet Habu, a "Victory Temple" raised to honor Egypt's triumph over invaders from Atlantis.

Spain's Lady of Elche portrays a wealthy (royal?) woman belonging to the Atlantean colony of Gadeiros, today's Cadiz.

Lemmings commit mass suicide in their mad rush to the sea. Does some behavioral memory of lost Atlantis persist as a migrational instinct from the past?

Close-up of the Aztec Calendar Stone's central section shows (in square) the representation of an upturned bucket drowning a pyramid under a deluge. It signifies the catastrophic end of the fourth Sun, when a previous civilization was overwhelmed.

A portrayal of the destruction of Atlantis from the Acropolis of the Maya ceremonial center at Tikal, Guatemala. After discovering it in the early twentieth century, archaeologist Teobert Maler became an ardent Atlantologist.

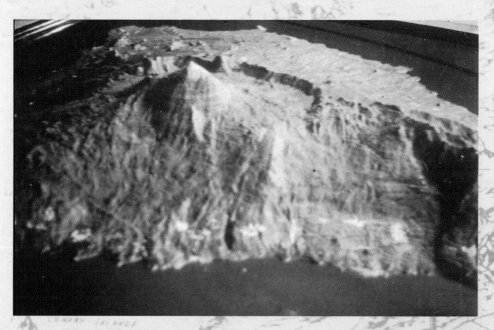

The island of Atlantis probably resembled this model of Tenerife, in the Canary Islands. (Las Palmas Museum)

The red (tufa), white (pumice), and black (lava) of Lanzarote, in the Canary Islands, were the Atlanteans' chief building materials, according to Plato.

A lateral volcanic eruption of the kind that may have destroyed Atlantis. (Photograph courtesy of the Oslo Natural and Geologic Museum)

A scene reminiscent of Atlantean survivors surveying the final moments of their obliterated homeland. An Icelandic mother and her children observe the Atlantis-like eruption and sinking of Surtsey in 1963. (Photograph courtesy of the Reykjavik Museum of Geology)

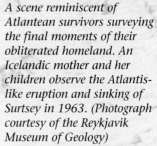

A meteorite the size of a semitrailer created this mile-wide crater in Arizona about 2,700 years ago. Less than a thousand years earlier, similar events, though on a larger scale, brought about the demise of Bronze Age Civilization, of which Atlantis was a part. (Photograph courtesy of The Meteor Crater Museum, Barringer, Arizona)

The Atlantis in Revelation

Genesis and Psalms do not contain the only biblical reference to the Atlantean catastrophe. *The Revelation of Saint John the Divine* offers perhaps the most vivid description of the destruction of Atlantis found in all the ancient source material. This last book of the New Testament is usually the least read and least understood, probably because it is an apocalyptic mix of visions, symbolism, and allegory. It was apparently composed by anonymous authors in the last quarter of the first century C.E., who relied upon the ancient texts and foreign traditions from which the Old Testament, particularly Genesis, Daniel and Ezekiel, are derived.

Revelation was written to preach moral lessons by way of historical examples, as were Plato's *Dialogues*. When John of Patmos rails against "the sinful city" and rejoices in its divine punishment, he is warning contemporary and future civilizations that God will judge them no less harshly. He calls the wicked city "Babylon," but the text's internal evidence reveals that it is not the same ancient metropolis whose ruins may still be seen near present-day al-Hillah, in Iraq. Bahb-Ilim, as this Near Eastern city was known by its inhabitants for a thousand years after its establishment during early in the first millennium B.C.E., was never on an island, never burned by a destructive comet, never vanished into the sea, all of which are described in *Revelation*.

The confusion is cleared up when one realizes that the name "Babylon" was not limited by biblical writers to the capital of the Babylonian Empire. As the famous biblical authority, the Reverend Bishop Fulton J. Sheen explained, in the New Testament "Babylon" is used for any great city.[39] When discussing a powerful capital, the biblical authors will refer to it as "a Babylon." In other words, they do not know the actual name of the city they portray. To them, the city was "a" Babylon, a splendid location, whose precise identity had been lost long before the moralists began writing, sometime around 175 C.E.

Caroli points out that "'Babylon' is not the sole name used in this context. In later years, 'Rome' was included. But other such names were 'Sodom,' 'Tyre,' and 'Egypt.' The reasons those names were so used by Hebrew and early Christian writers is rather obvious. Yet, if Revelations was really written at any time before the second century B.C., it cannot refer to Rome, because, by the Maccabean era, Rome was not yet involved in the Near East. Were the book the product of the third or fifth centuries B.C., a Roman analogy becomes still less likely."[40] Still, enough of the story survived for its authors to mold it into a spiritual allegory. And the "Babylon" they portray can only be the Atlantis described by Plato.

Bel-usur, also known by his Greek name of Berosus, translated the *Babyloniaca*, a three-volume work that continued the history and culture of his city into Greek. In it, he writes that the word "Babylon" was regularly employed by historians as both a descriptive title, and as the actual name of the city. There were, consequently, several "Babylons." In other words, it was common to describe one city by the name of another great and famous metropolis.

Most cogent to the Atlantean aspects of Revelations is the statement made by Berosus in *Babyloniaca* that the name "Babylon" was regularly used by his fellow Chaldean priests to signify an antediluvian city. That "first city," to use his words, could have been none other than Atlantis, as will become evident through the pertinent excerpts from Revelations.

> Come, I will show you the condemnation of the great harlot who sits upon many waters [Atlantis is feminine—daughter of Atlas. She sat at the center of a far-flung thalassocracy that spread over the North Atlantic Ocean.], with whom the kings of the Earth committed adultery, and the people of the Earth were drunk with the wine of her adultery. He [an angel] carried me away so I may behold a woman sitting upon a scarlet beast inscribed with blasphemous writing, and she had seven heads and ten horns. And this woman was adorned with purple and

scarlet [Plato wrote that the Atlanteans used rich purple raiment, especially for their kings.], and arrayed with gold and precious stones and pearls [The *Kritias* describes the walls and sacred and public buildings of Atlantis as having been profusely decorated with precious metals and stones.] Now, the seven "heads" of the woman were actually the seven hills on which she sat [Atlantis was supposed to have been mostly surrounded by hills and mountains.], and her ten horns were her ten kings. [The kings, Atlantis-like but entirely unlike the historical Babylon, arise from the sea. Plato wrote that there were ten kings of Atlantis, corresponding to the ten blood-related kingdoms.] And the woman you saw was that great city which dominates the kings of the Earth. (Rev. 17:1–2)

The merchants of the Earth grew wealthy through the power of her trade. [The Atlanteans controlled the copper trade, which made the Bronze Age possible.] Her iniquity rose to Heaven, where God knew of her sins. "Therefore," He said, "her plagues shall come in a single day." [Compare this with Plato's *Dialogues,* in which Zeus is offended by the degenerate Atlanteans, who perish "in a single day.") (Rev. 18:5)

And there appeared another sign in the heavens. And see, there was a great, fiery dragon with seven crowned heads and ten horns. [An obvious description of a great comet.] And its tail obscured a third of the stars, which began to fall toward Earth. (Rev. 12:3) The heavenly stars fell to Earth, even as the fig tree, shaken by mighty winds, wildly throws off its figs to the ground. And the very heavens themselves parted, like a scroll being unrolled, while all the mountains and islands were jolted from their proper places. And all the kings of the Earth, the statesmen and military commanders, the wealthy and powerful, as well as slaves and freedmen, hid in the caves and mountain clefts. (Rev. 12:6, 12:15)

And the angel took up his censer filled with fire and hurled it down to the Earth. [A meteor-fall.] And there came unnatural shouts and thunder, lightning and earthquake. And then followed hail and fire and water altogether pouring over the Earth. And a third of the Earth was scorched, while another third of all trees went up in flames and all the grass burned. A great fiery mountain fell into the ocean, and a third of the sea became bloody, because a third of the creatures that dwelt in the waters died, and a third of all ships at sea were destroyed. Then the second angel was heard, and a star fell from heaven, all aflame like a great lamp, and it descended upon a third of the Earth's rivers and also the fountains of its waters, destroying them. (Rev. 8:5–11)

And a mighty angel held up a rock like unto a great millstone, then threw it into the sea, declaring, "So shall that great city Babylon be overwhelmed with violence and nevermore shall be found at all!" (Rev. 18:24) There was a mighty earthquake the like of which had not occurred since man was created, so mighty an earthquake, so powerful. And the great city fell into three parts, and the cities of the other nations collapsed. And at that same hour occurred a great earthquake, in which a tenth part of the city fell, and the number of people killed was seven thousand. And all the islands vanished, and their mountains were gone. (Rev. 16:17–18)

And the kings of the Earth who committed adultery and lived sinfully with her will weep and mourn and wail over her when they see the smoke of her burning. Standing far away in fear of her torment, they cry, "Woe! Woe for that great city, Babylon, oh, that once-mighty city! For in a single hour you are doomed!" (Rev. 18:9)

And the sea-merchants of the Earth shall weep and mourn over her, because no one buys their goods any longer. Never again shall there be cargoes of gold and silver and the precious stones, and the pearls or fine linen and purple silks and scarlets, nor every kind of fragrant wood, nor all fine workmanship of ivory, nor the beautiful things made of costly wood, nor of brass, iron and marble. (Rev. 9:13)

And masters of all the ships with their passengers, together with the sailors, stood off afar, and cried when they beheld the smoke of her burning, wailing, "What city was like unto that great capital!" And they covered their hair with dust, weeping, "Woe! Woe, that great city, where all who had ships in the sea were made prosperous because of her preciousness! See, in but a single hour is she destroyed!" (Rev. 18:17–19)

Then the sun became black, like a hairy sackcloth, and the moon looked blood-stained. [Thick ash clouds would filter moonlight, giving it a "bloody" appearance.] And a third part of the sun was eclipsed and a third part of all stars and a third of the moon, and the day darkened. [A dust-veil event was the aftermath of the cataclysm.][41] (Rev. 6:12)

These excerpts from Revelation graphically describe the destruction of Atlantis. There is a similar description in the Old Testament book of Ezekiel, chapters 27 and 28. In that passage, the name "Tyre" replaces Atlantis, just as "Babylon" was substituted in Revelation. The actual city of Tyre was a seaport on the south coast of Lebanon throughout classical times, and survived into the end of the thirteenth century c.e. The city and destruction described in Ezekiel bear no physical resemblance to the historical Tyre, but do graphically depict the fate of Atlantis.

In the time when you shall be broken and sink in the depths of the sea, your merchandise and all your people in the midst of you shall fall. Behold, therefore, I will bring strangers upon you [the victorious Mycenaean Greeks of Plato's Atlanto-Athenian War], the mightiest of the nations [a title that in no way could have been applied to Tyre], and they shall draw their swords against the beauty of your wisdom, and they shall defile your glory. They shall bring you down to ruin, and you shall die the death of those who are slain in the midst of the seas. (Ezek. 27: 34–35, 28:7–8)

And I will destroy you, O sheltering cherub, from the midst of the stones of fire. [Cherubs or cherubim derive from the Hebrew *keruvim,* a winged servant of God who dwells in the highest heaven and does His bidding. The term here is a metaphor for a celestial phenomenon threatening destruction] Therefore I will bring forth a fire from the midst of you, and it shall devour you, and I will reduce you to ashes upon Earth in the sight of all those who see you. And those who know you among the people shall be astonished at you; you shall be brought to destruction, and you never shall be anymore. (Ezek. 28: 16, 28:18–19)

TWILIGHT OF THE GODS

Biblical descriptions of the cometary catastrophe are not the only such traditions. The Scandinavians had their own catastrophic tale. In the Norse poetic *Edda,* Odin, king of the gods, either perishes or vanishes in the Ragnarok, the final destruction of the world. This was a cosmic catastrophe with decidedly Atlantean overtones.

Hard is the world. Sensual sin grows huge. There are sword-ages, axe-ages. Shields are cleft in twain. Storm-ages, murder ages. [Here is the same moral cause, a degenerate civilization, for the coming disaster, as found in Plato and the Bible.] The Fenris-wolf advances with wide-open mouth. His upper jaw reaches to heaven and the lower is on the Earth. Fire flashes from his eyes and nostrils. The stars shall be hurled from heaven. [The approaching comet is mythologized as a celestial wolf, ravenous and deadly.] Already the stars were coming adrift from the sky and falling from the firmament. They were like swallows, weary from an over-long flight, who drop and sink into the waves.

Mountains dash together, heroes go the way to Hel and heaven is torn in half. The sun grows dark, the Earth sinks into the sea. The sea rushes over the Earth, for the Midgaard serpent writhes in giant rage and seeks to gain the land. But in this flood, Naglfar gets afloat. The giant Hrym is its steersman. [Naglfar was a spectral ship of gargantuan dimensions, composed entirely of dead men's fingernails. The vessel was a metaphor for world destruction and mass extinction. Hrym was a Norse combination of the Grim Reaper and Charon, the underworld ferryman in Greek myth.] Then happens that which will seem a great miracle, that the wolf devours the sun, and this will seem a great loss. [The darkening of the sun caused by a massive extrusion of ash into the atmosphere from the eruption of Mount Atlas and the effects of celestial collision is repeated.] The sunshine blackens in the summers thereafter, and the weather grows bad. When snow drives from all quarters, the frosts are so severe, the winds so keen, there is no joy in the sun. There are three such winters in succession without any intervening summer. [The climactic aftermath is convincingly described, and recalls Indonesia's Tambora eruption, which was so severe, the time of its detonation in 1815 was known as "the year without summer," because its ash clouds blocked out enough sunlight to cause a worldwide drop in temperature.][42]

Despite the carnage and difficult post-cataclysm conditions, there were two survivors, Lif and his wife, Lifthraser: "Neither the sea nor Surt's fire had harmed them, and they dwell on the plains of Ida, where Asgaard was before." The sagas imply several times that Asgaard, the abode of the gods, was not in the sky, but on a paradisiacal island in the Atlantic Ocean; its Atlantis identity seems all the clearer because of its sinking during Ragnarok. The "plains of Ida," which were said to be the remnants of sunken Asgaard, must be Tenerife in the Canary Islands. Its volcanic mountain, Teide, was known to its preconquest natives as Aide. These natives, the mysterious Guanches, were a racially European people who told their own story of Atlantis. They were exterminated by the Spanish in the sixteenth century.

When the *Eddas* were transcribed from oral tradition, the location in which Ragnarok took place was called Ginnungagap, the North Atlantic Ocean. At least one modern author writes that Asgaard was "adjacent" to Ginnungagap. Odin's blue cloak, his patronage of seafaring men and role as oceanic culture bearer are details that suggest his Atlantean identity. Perhaps, before it sank into oblivion, Asgaard *was* Atlantis, and only gradually, over centuries, transformed through myth into a position in the heavens. According to Donnelly, "The Scandinavian Olympus was probably Atlantis."[43]

The oldest known of the Norse myths date to circa 1200 B.C.E. and are found in the *Voelupsa* (transcribed from oral tradition in the thirteenth century). It describes a world-ending event of cosmic magnitude: "The sun turns black. Earth sinks into the sea. The hot stars down from heaven are hurled." The *Deluging of Gylfi,* which appeared later, tells of the same cataclysm in similar language: "The sun will go black, Earth sink into the sea, heaven be stripped of its bright stars. Smoke rages and fire, leaping the flame, licks heaven itself."[44]

ATLANTEAN ALBION

Britain's numerous flood traditions survived long after their semi-historical, legendary origins in Bronze Age antiquity were lost. Mythic details from widely scattered eras were melded together into national epics, such as the stories of Camelot. While King Arthur might be traced to an early medieval personage, Merlin's roots go back much earlier, to the pre-Christian Druids; some of the elements in his myth imply Neolithic elements. The majority of these long-standing traditions refer to England as "Albion," a name taken from the twin brother of Atlas, whose share of the Atlantean Empire was Britain.

The eighteenth-century English poet William Blake perpetuates this ancient tradition in his own epic, *America, a Prophesy:* "Albion's angel stood beside the stone of night, and saw the terror like a comet. The spectre glow'd his horrid length, staining the temple long with beams of blood. On those vast shady hills between America and Albion's shore, now barr'd out by the Atlantic sea, call'd Atlantean hills, because from their bright summits you may pass to the golden world, an ancient palace, archetype of mighty emperies, rears its immortal pinnacles." Blake associated the approach of a threatening comet, seen as far away as Britain, with the fate of Atlantis.

FROM LAPLAND TO AMERICA

North of Merlin's Britain and the Scandinavian bards who sang of Ragnarok, Laplanders of the remote Arctic Circle still tell of Jubmel, a terrible god of vengeance who wanted to punish all human beings for their wickedness. Their myth contains some of the most colorful description of a falling comet and the awful flood it spawned.

> The lord of heaven himself descended. His terrifying anger flashed with the red, blue and green of serpents, all on fire. Everyone went into hiding, while the children wept with fear. The god spoke in his anger, "I shall gather the sea together upon itself, form it into a towering wall of water and throw it against you wicked children of the Earth, exterminating you and all living things!" Foaming, crashing, rising to the sky rushed the wall of water over the sea, crushing everything in its path, until neither mountains nor highlands were revealed any longer by the sun, which could not shine in heaven. The groans of the dying filled the Earth, mankind's home, and dead bodies rolled about in the dark waters.[45]

If close comparisons between the Semitic Bible of the Near East with the Norse Eddas and Laplander myths of Northern Europe seem remarkable, how much more so are descriptions of the Atlantean flood encountered on the opposite side of the ocean among the native peoples of the Americas. While all tell essentially the same story, the details vary from version to version, suggesting that the accounts originated more or less independently from each other. There are far too many to repeat here, but a few representative examples should demonstrate how deeply and vividly a cataclysmic deluge etched itself into the folkish memory of virtually every Native American nation on the North American continent.

The Pima flood-hero, Suekha, escaped a mountainous tsunami

created when a colossal "lightning bolt" struck the sea. The Oklahoma Indians speak of a bright light suddenly appearing in the sky, "but it was mountain-high waves, rapidly coming nearer." Thereafter, "the Earth was plunged in darkness for a long time."[46]

Common to all tribes of the Upper Great Lakes on both sides of the U.S.–Canadian border is an ancestral myth that is still deeply revered as one of their most sacred oral traditions. It recounts a time when humans rose to greatness by living in harmony with God's law. But, after too many years of abundance, they grew selfish, corrupt, and abusive of Earth's natural bounty. At the height of their debauchery, a "bearded star" plummeted from the sky, falling into the Atlantic, where an island that saw the worst of human abuse was swallowed by the ocean. "All that was left of the humans' once powerful, developed area was one vast sea," which was whipped "into a seething mass of waves." A few survivors straggled to the remaining dry land, where they pledged themselves and their descendants to always remember the horrible flood as a warning against repeating the sins of the past.[47] Variations of the Great Lakes' tradition occur across the North American continent, from Florida to British Columbia.

The Apaches still refer to their ancestral homeland in the east with the evocative name of "the Isle of Flame." It was far across the Sunrise Sea, adorned with great buildings, canals, a fruitful plain, palaces and temples, a high, sacred mountain, and harbors for "big canoes" highly reminiscent of Plato's description of Atlantis. The myth goes on to explain that "the Fire-Dragon arose and their ancestors had to flee to the mountains far to the south."

In a remarkable comparison, the ancient Egyptians wrote of Aalu, the "Isle of Flame," a large island in the sea of the Distant West. It, too, was mountainous, with extensive canals, luxuriant crops and a palatial city surrounded by great walls decorated with precious metals. Aalu's earliest known reference appears in *The Destruction of Mankind*, a New Kingdom history (1299 B.C.E.) discovered in the tomb of Pharaoh Seti I, at Abydos, site of the Osireion, a subterranean monument to the Great Flood described in the account. Obviously, both the Apaches and Egyptians, although separated by thousands of years and miles, both both knew the same Isle of Flame, the volcanic island of Atlantis.

No less remarkably, the name the Maya used to describe their symbolic equivalent for the Aztec Aztlan was Alau, according to August Le Plongeon, the first man to excavate the Maya ruins of Yucatan.[48] Clearly, the Egyptian *Aalu* and the Maya *Alau* derived from a common source that impacted both peoples, however separated by distance and time.

The Chehalis Indians, neighbors of the Apaches, remember when "the whole Earth was on fire. Behind the fire came the water and flooded the whole Earth, even the mountains."

Native Americans Remember the Deluge

The idea that a comet caused the Great Flood is especially apparent in a myth common to many tribes north of the Rio Grande. The tale recounts that a god was sleeping in the sky next to a star that he was using as a camp fire when a demon pushed his head into the flames. The god, his long hair on fire, awoke in terror. Running about the heavens in a panic, he stumbled and fell to Earth. He ran about the forests and mountains, setting them ablaze, until the whole world was consumed in an awful conflagration.

As he ran, some of his hairs fell to the ground, where they took root and sprouted as tobacco. This plant alone survived the holocaust. Finally, he reached the ocean and jumped into the water to extinguish his fiery hair. In so doing, he produced an immense flood that covered the entire earth, and extinguished the fires the god had caused. Hence, tobacco came to be known as a sacred plant, used in ceremonies commemorating the Great Flood or to guarantee safe passage when crossing dangerous waters. In descriptions from around the world, throughout recorded history, comets are frequently referred to as "hairy."[49]

A typical variant of the Atlantean flood story is known to the Cherokee, Iroquoian people originally from the Great Lakes who migrated to eastern Tennessee and the western Carolinas. They preserved the story of Unadatsug, "the Group," stars known in the West as the Pleiades. It was from this constellation that a star with "a fiery tail" fell to Earth. At the impact site, a gigantic palm tree suddenly arose and the extinguished star changed into an old man who warned against a coming deluge. The palm tree is most likely a poetic description of the mushroom cloud that resulted from the meteorite impact.[50]

The Cherokee myth is remarkably similar to both the Greek story of Electra, the missing Pleiade whose fall presaged a flood, and the Hebrew deluge account, wherein Yahweh cast down a star from the Pleiades to initiate a catastrophe. From the Arctic Circle to Cape Horn, the Pleiades constellation was identified with a worldwide flood from which culture bearers survived to found new societies. The Seven Sisters were Atlantises, daughters of Atlas, and their widespread association with an ancestral deluge not only reinforces the reality of Plato's sunken civilization, but demonstrates that it played a seminal role in pre-Columbian American cultures.

That the Pleiades were identified with Atlas just as much in North America as they were in Europe is established by the Hopi Indian myth of Machito. Like Atlas, he "raised the firmament on his shoulders," then summoned seven maidens, who wove the moon into existence. Thereafter, they ascended into the heavens to form their constellation. "Machito appointed times and seasons and ways of the heavenly bodies. And the gods of the firmament have obeyed the injunctions of Machito from the day of their creation to the present." To the Greeks, Atlas was the inventor of astronomy and astrology. And both the Hopi and Greeks regarded the Pleiades as sisters.[51]

The Hopi deluge account is remarkably similar to the Norse version in the Eddas: "Mountains plunged into the sea with a great splash, seas and lakes sloshed over the land." Immediately afterward, the whole world "froze into solid ice."[52] The Hopi believe that the flood destroyed a Third Age of humanity remembered as the *Kurskursa*, a term that also refers to the copper- or bronze-tinged red color that comes with the sunrise. The Kurskursa was characterized as an extended period when great cities were built and men made far-flung war on each other until a catastrophe annihilated most of them and obliterated their capitals. Again, a strong echo of Plato's *Kritias* in Native American tradition.

Aztec priests used the rising of the Pleiades to mark the beginning of the new year; their appearance was identified with the Fourth Age, that which immediately precedes our own, the era of a world flood. Each fifty-two-week calendar began precisely when the Pleiades crossed the Fifth Cardinal Point (the zenith of heaven) at midnight in mid-November. The priests then repaired to the Hill of the Star, a hilltop on a peninsula jutting out into the very middle of a lake that surrounded the Aztec capital, Texcoco. In order to confirm his power, every new emperor was obliged, as part of his coronation duties, to observe the Pleiades at the same new year moment.[53]

The *Codex Fuenleal* relates how Tezcatlipocha was originally a sun-god. His name meant "Smoking Mirror," similar to the Greek's "Shining One," Phaethon. Tezcatlipocha was cast down from the sky by a spear thrown from the hand of Huitlipochtli, the god of war, just as Phaethon was struck down by Zeus's thunderbolt. Tezcatlipocha "descended into the water," but arose and transformed himself into a constellation—the same descent from the heavens and starry rebirth ascribed to Phaethon.[54] The *Codex Chimalpopca* describes an event similar to Plato's destruction of Atlantis, which occurred "in a single day and night": "The sky drew near to the Earth and in the space of a day all was drowned. . . . There suddenly arose mountains the color of fire."[55]

Another Aztec Phaeton was Piltzintli, the "Diving God," known for thousands of years to virtually every Mesoamerican society. Sculpted reliefs of him may be seen at the Maya ceremonial center of Tulum above the shore at Yucatan, and he is still worshiped throughout the Valley of Mexico in his Christian guise, Santo Niño de Atocha. He is portrayed as a male figure falling from the sky, his wild hair aflame and smoking, and accompanied by a representation of the sun. Piltzintli was regarded as the divine patron of mass migrations. The Aztecs believed he led their forebearers from an ancestral homeland, Aztlan, a great island in the Sunrise Sea, before it was overwhelmed by a catastrophic deluge. (The resemblance, philological and otherwise, between Aztlan and Atlantis is apparent.) As long ago as 1851, Arthur Schopenhauer wrote, "We find an even more striking agreement between many names, originally American, and those of European antiquity, for example between the Atlantis of Plato and Aztlan."[56] The Diving God's oceanic origins are emphasized by the gifts that his worshipers leave him— seashells—and the paved ceremonial road, or *scabe,* that leads from his temple at Tulum directly into the water.[57]

The allies of the Aztecs at the time of their conquest by the Spaniards in the sixteenth century were the people of Cholula, located about one hundred miles from the capital at Tenochtitlán (today's Mexico City). The outstanding feature of Cholula is its pyramid, originally about 220 feet high, and, at the base, nearly twice as wide as the Great Pyramid of Egypt. The massive structure was said to have been erected by "white giants" after a catastrophic deluge that lasted "during the day and during the night." At the summit of the Cholula pyramid once stood a temple (replaced, since the Spanish Conquest, by a church) enshrining a meteorite, "which had fallen from heaven, wrapped in a ball of flame." Before the pyramid was completed, "fire fell upon it, causing the death of its builders and the abandonment of the work."

The Nahuatl caption to an Aztec drawing of the Cholula temple read, "Nobles and lords, here you have your documents, the mirror of your past, the history of your ancestors, who, out of fear for a deluge, constructed this place of refuge or asylum for the possibility of the recurrence of such a calamity."[58] The earliest dates for its construction are to only the first century c.e., making it a contemporary of the similarly gargantuan monument at Teotihuacan, the Pyramid of the Sun (see chapter 5). Cholula means "Place of the Water Springs," and the pyramid may have been raised as a memorial to a deluge that occurred many centuries earlier. With its enshrined meteorite and related flood stories, the pyramid represents some of the most compelling evidence for an Atlantean cataclysm brought about by a celestial event. Maya civilization preceded that of the Aztecs, contemporary with the construction of the pyramid at Cholula.

Among the few original documents that survived the fires prepared by Christian missionaries was the *Popol Vuh*, translated in the early colonial period by a Maya fluent in Spanish. Written in Quiche, the language of the Guatemalan natives, it is the single most important source for information about the origins and history of the Maya. In describing the Deluge, the *Popol Vuh* recounts that the destructive god, Huracan, appeared as an immense fire in the heavens before he fell into the Eastern Sea, resulting in a world-ravaging flood: "It was ruin and destruction. There was a great din of fire above the heads of the people. The sea was opened up. It was a great inundation. The face of the Earth grew dark."[59]

Although the Popol Vuh is the most complete Maya document of its kind, it is not the only surviving example. The *Chilam Balam,* or "The Never-Forgotten Destruction," reads in part, "with one great, sudden rush of water, the Great Serpent was ravished from the heavens. And the Great Snake was torn from the sky, and skin and pieces of its bones fell to the Earth. The sky fell, and the Earth sank when the four Bacabs arose to bring about the destruction of the world. Then the waters rose in a terrible flood. And with the Great Serpent, the sky fell in, and the dry land sank into the sea. Finally, in one, last, curving green, watery blow, curled back and came all the ocean. The sky began to fall down with steam and fire, and then all of the dry land sank into the engulfing waters" (R. Cedric Leonard, Ph.D., *The Quest for Atlantis,* New York: Manor Books, 1979, pp. 111, 112). The Atlantean character of this tradition is underscored by the Bacabs. They were envisioned as men supporting the four quadrants of the heavens on their shoulders, just as Atlas held up the sky.

Following the catastrophe, the human survivors were given reassurance by the gods, whose wrath had been appeased: "And a rainbow appeared as a sign that the destruction was over, and a new age was to begin." Compare this detail from the *Chilam Balam* with the Old Testament story of Noah's flood: "Then He set a rainbow in the sky, saying: 'Whenever I bring rain clouds over the Earth, this shining bow will recall My promise!'"[60] The Mayan narrative concludes, "Then the Great Mother Ceiba was set up in the center as a record or memorial of the destruction of the world."[61] The ceiba is an enormous tree that flourishes in Guatemala, where it is still venerated as a sacred being associated with the Great Flood that washed ashore Middle America's first culture bearers, Itzamna and Ixchel. Perhaps the ceiba is connected in shared myth to the Cherokee legend cited earlier, wherein a gigantic palm tree appears at the location of the meteorite impact.

Itzamna was sometimes portrayed as a bearded old White Man, who, with his wife, Ixchel, the White Lady, arrived on the shores of Yucatan with the arts and sciences of a civilization that had been destroyed by a catastrophic flood across the Sunrise Sea. In Mayan codex and temple art Ixchel is depicted floating on water; nearby, a kind of valise is spilling its contents into the water, a symbol of material lost in the Deluge. The Itza Indians derived their name from Itzamna. They built a great observatory, El Caracol (the Snail, after its round shape) of Chichén Itzá, as a memorial to and replica of Itzamna's original temple on an island that had been destroyed by the Flood. Interestingly, although Itzamna was long known to have been the inventor of astronomy and astrology, as was Atlas, the use of El Caracol as an observatory was not established until the 1960s.

In other Maya sources the couple personified the Great Flood itself. The *Dresden Codex* climaxes, appropriately enough, with Itzamna as a huge, falling serpent spewing fire on the world. In this business he is accompanied by Ixchel, now portrayed, not as a survivor upon the waves, but as a ferocious woman with a sky-serpent for a headdress. She up-ends a vase to spill the waters of the Deluge upon Earth.[62]

An Atlantean El Dorado

Like Itzamna, the Andean Con-tiki-Viracocha was a white-skinned foreigner who brought civilization to South America after arriving in the wake of a terrible flood. He embodied both the beneficent culture bearer and the cataclysm itself, manifesting "his power by hurling the lightning on the hillsides and consuming the forests."[63] A Peruvian myth relates that the Andes were blasted open and their canyons formed when heaven made war with the world.[64]

Colombia, fronting the Atlantic Ocean, should be rich in traditions of the Atlantean flood. The resident Muysca Indians told the noted botanist Cieza de Leon and royal chronicler Father Anello Oliva, both of whom worked for decades among the Indians, of a tribe of "white giants" arriving in "big canoes" on the eastern shores of Colombia: "An angel appeared in a mass of fire from heaven and killed them all." The American anthropologist Adolph F. Bandelier concluded, "As for the manner in which the 'giants' came to be exterminated, it may be said that, while the natural phenomenon described in connection with their destruction seems to indicate the fall of a meteorite of unusual size, the possibility of some volcanic disturbance should not be excluded."[65] Both alternatives were, in fact, parts of the same cataclysm, one engendering the other—meteoritic collisions with the Earth produced widespread volcanic activity.

In the mountains behind Bogota, the Muyscas conducted ceremonies of royal initiation at Guatavita, a lake formed by a meteorite that struck the Andean highlands. Thousands of people assembled on the shore for the initiation of a new chieftain referred to as the "Gilded One." He was rowed out to the center of Guatavita. There his naked body was coated with resin and covered from head to toe in fine gold dust until he shone like a living statue under the noonday sun. This completed, he dove down into the lake, leaving a long trail of shimmering gold through the extraordinarily clear and bright blue water. Meanwhile, the appreciative Indians at the shore tossed in golden statues and other precious objects. Arising to the cheers of his subjects, he was wrapped in the royal azure robe of kingship for the first time.

The Atlantean connections to this ceremony become more apparent after reading the Orinoco Indians' deluge story, Catena-ma-noa, the Water of Noa. Noa's city was called "the Gilded One" (the same title as the Guatavita ceremony), the splendid capital of an island sunken beneath the ocean.[66] The Muyscas' newly installed king was identified with Noa's drowned city, as he dived into the center of the sacred crater lake. The gold dust that washed off his body signified the riches of the Gilded One lost at sea, while the royal initiate's blue robe recalls the azure raiment worn by the kings of Atlantis, as described by Plato.

The overtly Atlantean details associated with Guatavita are underscored by the origins of the site itself. The lake is an astrobleme, a crater caused by a fallen meteor, now filled with water. And while the date of its formation is uncertain, the fact that its impact was concurrent with cometary events involved in the Atlantis destruction is at strongly suggested by the oral and ceremonial traditions of the local populations. Lake Guatavita was recognized by the natives as a result of a celestial catastrophe, perhaps by a large fragment of meteoritic debris that accompanied the comet; hence, the ritual activity fraught with Atlantean overtones surrounding the location since prehistoric times.

Similar accounts occur in Venezuela among the Arawak Indians, who recalled the punishment meted out to their ancestors by the Great Spirit with "fires from heaven" followed by an overwhelming deluge rolling in from the sea.[67] Moving farther south along the Atlantic coast to Brazil, the Tupinamba worshiped Monan, the Ancient One, who, offended by the human beings he created, endeavored to exterminate them with first a terrible fire falling from the sky followed by a worldwide flood.

The Tupinamba account tells how "heaven burst and the fragments fell down and killed everything and everyone. Heaven and Earth exchanged places. Nothing that had life was left upon the Earth."[68] When queried by Spanish friars on the origins of this myth, the Tupinamba said their ancestors came from the "white island" of Caraiba, which, before it sank, lay beyond the sea in the east. (In another remarkable comparison, Hindu tradition recalled ancestral origins from sunken Attala, the "white island.")

The Mataco Indians of Argentina's Gran Chaco described "a black cloud" that covered the sky at the time of the Great Flood: "Lightning struck and thunder was heard. Yet the drops that fell were not like rain. They were like fire."[69] At the southern end of the continent, related traditions persist of a sinful humanity punished in the ancient past with celestial fire and a gigantic flood. Both the Yaman and Pehuenche tribes of Tierra del Fuego speak of such a time. The former claim the Deluge was started by a moon goddess, as did the Maya, Ixchel.[70]

EVIL STAR OVER ASIA AND THE PACIFIC

The same story moves west across the islands of the South Pacific and into Polynesia. It is known from Hawaii to Tahiti, beyond to Samoa and Micronesia, under differing names but all variations of a common theme. Typical is the Samoan version: "Then arose a terrible odor. The odor became smoke, which transformed into great black clouds. The sea rose suddenly, and, in a stupendous catastrophe of nature, the land sank into the sea." Virtually all humanity was blotted out of existence, save for a man and a woman who survived in a boat to land somewhere in the Samoan archipelago.[71] A Maori myth tells of a priest who prayed for salvation from a great celestial flame that threatened to incinerate the world. His prayers were answered with a colossal flood that extinguished all the fires but wiped out an ancient civilization, killing most of its inhabitants.[72] In Tahitian myth, Taaroa, the sky god, was so angry with humans for their disobedience to his will that he "overturned the world into the sea," drowning everything except a few *aurus*, or mountain peaks rising above the water. These became the islands of Tahiti.[73]

A Hawaiian version of the deluge story was told to Captain Cook by a native of the Kona Coast: "At that time, the Earth became hot, the heavens turned about, the sun was darkened at the time of the rise of the Pleiades. And the Earth came forth out of its debris."[74] The Hawaiians still speak of Nu'u, who loaded up family and animals on a large vessel in which they escaped a world flood caused by a monstrous tidal wave. Later, the sea god, Kane, set a rainbow in the cleared sky as a token of their survival. The biblical Noah, the Mixtec Nata, the Orinoco Noa, the North American Mandan Indians' Nu-Mohk-Muck-*a-nah* and the Hawaiian Nu'u, together with the rainbow-motif, demonstrate the validity of a shared cosmic experience.

For many Polynesians, the deluge story begins with the Rangi, spirits of the sky who made war against the storm god, Tawhiri-Matea. He, in turn, attacked Tangaroa, god of the sea. Coming to the defense of his brother, the god Ua-Roa, Long Rain, flooded the entire Earth.

In the Lake Taupo district of New Zealand, Rongo-mai was remembered as a war god who attacked the world in the guise of a comet. After bringing great destruction upon humankind, he transformed himself into a gigantic whale and then sank into the sea. The Australian Aborigines say that Yurlunggur, a colossal serpent in the sky, covered the entire Earth with a flood that drowned large tracks of land. He signaled an end to the catastrophe by twisting himself into a rainbow.[75]

Memory of the Atlantean cataclysm recurs throughout Asia. A variation of flood myths known in Viet Nam, Burma, and Laos is found in the northern Thailand story of the Thens, gods synonymous with the powers of heaven. When human beings refused to pay them homage, they drowned the world in a deluge from which only three families escaped, along with their livestock, via "a great raft with a house built on top of it." From these survivors, the earth was repopulated.[76] In the Mergui Archipelago, off the southern coast of Myanmar, the Selung natives tell how "the daughter of an evil spirit threw many rocks into the sea. Thereupon the waters rose and swallowed up all the land."[77]

Japan's Susa-no-wo was at once the god of the ocean and destruction. He battled a gigantic sky dragon who had devoured seven sisters and was about to dine on an eighth when he was slain by the hero. The dragon's blood gushed over the Earth, but the souls of the consumed maidens were freed to rise into the heavens.[78] In this Asian country, a world away from Ancient Greece, the stars are regarded as sisters connected with a cosmically induced deluge after it has done its worst. The great antiquity of these myths is emphasized by the appearance of the same theme among the Ainu, the aboriginal people of Japan, originally Caucasoids, whose presence on the islands goes back at least the fourth millennium B.C.E. They spoke of a flood that destroyed most of humanity.[79]

As recently as Marco Polo's visit to China, the Imperial Library featured a colossal encyclopedia alleged to contain all knowledge from ancient times to the fourteenth century, when additions were still being made. The 4,320-volume set included information about a time when Tien Ti, the Emperor of Heaven, China's equivalent to Zeus, attempted to wipe out sinful mankind with a worldwide deluge: "The planets altered their courses, the Earth fell to pieces and the waters in its bosom rushed upwards with violence and overflowed the Earth." Another god, Yeu, taking pity on the drowning humans, caused a giant turtle to rise up from the bottom of the ocean and transformed it into new land. (Remarkably, this version is identical to a creation myth repeated by virtually every tribe north of the Rio Grande. Native Americans refer almost universally to their continent as "Turtle Island" for the gigantic turtle that was raised up from the ocean by the Great Spirit for their salvation from the Deluge.)

Another Chinese text explains how "the pillars supporting the sky crumbled and the chains from which the Earth was suspended shivered to pieces. Sun, moon and stars poured down into the northwest, where the sky became low; rivers, seas and oceans rushed down to the southeast, where the Earth sank. A great conflagration burst out. Flood raged."[80]

"Peiroun! Peiroun!"

A legend from Taiwan describes Mauri-ga-sima, a large and opulent island kingdom of palaces and shrines. For many years, its inhabitants were virtuous. But in time they grew greedy, self-centered, and arrogant. Only Peiroun, the king, and his family remained kind and unselfish. One night he dreamt that a terrible flood would utterly destroy Mauri-ga-sima if the statues of In-fo-ni-woo and Awun turned red. These twin gods of creation and destruction were enshrined in their own temple. But the irreverent people mocked his dream. A particularly sinful man, thinking to play a hoax on Peiroun, stole into the temple after it was closed and daubed the faces of the statues with red paint. The next morning, the king saw the discolored figures, packed up his family with all their goods, warned his scoffing people they would drown if they did not leave their doomed island, then sailed to the southwestern shores of China. There he established that land's first dynasty. But even while his ship was carrying him away, Mauri-ga-sima suddenly vanished, taking all of its inhabitants to the bottom of the sea.

Blackett, quoting Kaempfer, reported, "At the present time [1883], particularly in the southern provinces, they [local Chinese fishermen] row out in boats as if to flee away, crying out—'Peiroun! Peiroun!'"[81] This account includes all of the Western myth and contains themes common to four continents, numerous peoples, and disparate cultures, from the twin gods of In-fo-ni-woo and Awun (the kings of Atlantis, as described by Plato, were twins), to the founding of new kingdoms following the destruction of an island civilization, to the gods' judgment on a people gone irreverent.

Comparison of this Taiwanese tale to similar accounts far removed from the China Seas is startling. An Egyptian variant of Atlantis is the Land of Punt, reigned over by King Parihu.[82] In an old French folktale, King Perion and his family were the only survivors of Amadis, their sunken realm, from which they arrived in Brittany to found a new dynasty.[83] There even appears to be a genuine philological correspondence between Amadis and Atlantis. When Hernán Cortés first saw Tenochtitlán, he compared it to Amadis, because the Aztecs' capital was surrounded by water and intersected by a canal system, all built after the style of their Atlantean ancestors. No less amazing is the enduring power of this story, as exemplified in the Breton legend, used by Jules Massenet for the basis of his opera, *Amadis*, premiered in Monte Carlo, in 1922. The Asian, Egyptian, and French traditions are so deeply rooted in prehistory one may conclude that these widely separated peoples were visited by members of a culture-bearing family (Peiroun-Parihu-Perion) from Atlantis, just as other Atlantean families named Noah-Noa-Nata-Nu'u arrived as survivors at different parts of the world.

India Remembers the Disaster

A deluge is described in several important Indian myths, but two in particular exemplify the cometary aspects of the Atlantean flood. The *Mahapralaya,* "Great Cataclysm," is among the oldest surviving Hindustani legends. In the story, the rapid approach of a comet is graphically portrayed:

> By the power of God there issued from the essence of Brahma [the sky] a being shaped like a boar, white and exceedingly small; this being, in the space of an hour, grew to the size of an elephant of the largest kind, and remained in the air. Suddenly [he] uttered a sound like the loudest thunder, and the echo reverberated and shook all the quarters of the universe. Again [he] made a loud sound and became a dreadful spectacle.
>
> Shaking the full-flowing mane which hung down his neck on both sides, and erecting the humid hairs of his body, he proudly displayed his two most exceedingly white tusks. Then, rolling about his wine-colored eyes and erecting his tail, he descended from the region of the air and plunged head-fore-most into the water. The whole body of water was convulsed by the motion, and began to rise in waves, while the guardian spirit of the sea, being terrified, began to tremble for his do-mains and cry for mercy.[84]

The most famous epic of its kind is the *Mahabharata.* According to the Encyclopaedia Britannica, it was based on actual events that took place from the fifteenth to the eleventh centuries B.C.E., pre-cisely the time period when Atlantis reached the height of its power and succumbed to its doom. Beginning in the *Drona Parva* (Section XI), the destruction of Tripura is set forth. It is described as a wealthy and powerful oceanic kingdom, whose eastern shore faced the coast of Africa.

The *Mahabharata* calls it the "Triple City," after the trident given by the island's creator, Shiva, as an emblem to the residents. The city itself was designed by Maya, "of great intelligence." He raised two more, configuring each one on a massive, opulent scale and "shaped like a wheel" (*chakrastham,* Sanskrit for "circular"). "And they consisted of houses and mansions and lofty walls and porches. And though teeming with lordly palaces close to each other, yet the streets were wide and spacious. And they were adorned with diverse mansions and gateways. Each of these cities, again, had a separate king."[85]

Their identity was described as Daityas, but, in a more basic sense, they were also Asuras, beings that corresponded to Greek Titans—creatures greater than men but lesser than gods. Although originally a virtuous race, they gradually corrupted themselves with earthly delights, outraging the heavenly powers. "Intoxicated with covetousness and folly, and deprived of their moral senses, they began to shamelessly wage exterminating war against the cities and towns established throughout the world. Filled with pride, the wicked Daityas regarded the rest of humanity as inferiors and slaves."

The gods convened to decide a proper punishment, and Brahma, the Creator, ordered his fellow immortals to cast down a celestial projectile containing "the Power of the Universe." They obeyed him at once. "Putting forth his prowess, Mahadeva hurled into the sea the paradisiacal Daitya city. Burning those Asuras, he threw them down into the Western Ocean."[86] A great black cloud arose from the scene of the catastrophe. It blotted out the sun's rays and cast the world into prolonged darkness. Plants withered, animals starved, and the few human survivors wasted away. To prevent all life on earth from dying, Shiva inhaled the planetwide cloud of blackness. Hence, his throat is often depicted as indigo blue for the massive ash cloud he voluntarily inhaled to save the world.

There can be no doubt that the event described in the *Mahabharata* is the destruction of Atlantis. It features all the basic elements included in Plato's *Dialogues*. Tripura's very name derives from its emblem, the trident, the weapon of Poseidon, the sea god who created Atlantis. As described, both cities are filled with mansions,

palaces, and temples; they were arranged in circles with and surrounded by high walls; both were thalassocracies operating from an
island "in the Western Ocean" beyond the shores of Africa. Its inhabitants were called Daityas, "those of Aitya," what in Greek would be
Atlanteans, "those of Atlas."

The Daityas were Asuras, Titans; Atlas and his followers were
likewise titanic. The cities of the Daityas were ruled by their own
king, the same type of imperial confederation outlined in the *Kritias*.
Their society became materialistic and they waged a war of conquest, just as Plato describes. The *Mahabharata* even describes the
convocation of the gods Plato said took place just prior to the
cataclysm. Brahma is the Indian equivalent of Zeus, and both
commanded a heaven-sent power to fall upon Tripura-Atlantis,
sinking it beneath the sea. The agency of destruction is "the Power of
the Universe," in the form of a falling projectile, a wonderful characterization of the approaching comet trailing disaster in its wake.

CATACLYSM ENCIRCLES THE GLOBE

To the south, a Sri Lankan deluge story tells of the twenty-five
palaces and forty-thousand streets "swallowed by the sea."[87]

The *Zend-Avesta* is the sacred book of Persia's Zoroastriaism,
with roots in the thirteenth century B.C.E. In the *Vendidad* section,
which is partially an account of early humanity, the prophet Zoroaster
wrote of Tistrya, a triple-headed star that fell from the sky: "The sea
boiled, all the shores of the ocean boiled, all the middle of it boiled."
Curiously, he makes specific reference to what appears to be the
mid-Atlantic, mentioned in numerous other historical myths as the
location for a comet- or meteor-fall into the sea.[88]

On the Gold Coast of West Africa there are several accounts of
the Deluge among the Yoruba people. They tell how Olokun, the sea
god, became angry with sinful human beings and sought to cause
their extinction by instigating a flood that would drown the world.
Many kingdoms perished, until a giant hero, Obatala, stood in the

midst of the waters and through his *juju*, magical powers, bound Olokun in seven chains. The seas no longer swelled over the land, and humanity was saved.

Atlas can be perceived in this African Obatala, a giant in the middle of the sea, while the "seven chains" that signal the end of the Deluge may coincide with the seven Pleiades.

In the remote region of the lower Congo, oral tradition recalls an ancient time when "the sun met the moon and threw mud at it, which made it less bright. When this meeting happened there was a great flood."[89]

Tale of the Shipwrecked Sailor

Far north of the Congo, the ancient Egyptians told several deluge myths. The best-known account can be reliably traced to the middle of the third millennium B.C.E., although it is certainly older and underwent revisions throughout the centuries.

"The Tale of the Shipwrecked Sailor" tells of a young man on board a vessel in company with fellow copper miners. All are lost after their freighter sinks in a storm, except for the hero, who becomes a castaway on a distant island: "Suddenly, I heard a noise as of thunder, which I assumed was a wave from the sea crashing on the shore. But the trees shook violently and the ground quaked."

These geologic stirrings announced the arrival of the Serpent King, a huge, bearded creature overlaid with gold and lapis lazuli. He carefully picked up his hapless guest "in his great jaws" and carried him to his "resting place." There he told him about "this island in the sea and of which its shores are in the midst of the waves . . . an island of the blest, where nothing is lacking and which is filled with all good things . . . a far country, of which men know not." He is the monarch of an island kingdom with his family of fellow "serpents" . . . "without mentioning a young girl who was brought to me by chance, and on whom the fire of heaven fell and burnt her to ashes."

After a four-month stay, the king loaded his uninvited guest with gifts. "But when you leave this place," he warns, "you shall nevermore see this island. It shall be changed into waves."[90]

The Serpent King is referred to in the story as "Prince of the Land of Punt." His island was seismic ("the ground quaked"), in the middle of the sea ("the shores are in the midst of the waves"), and "a far country of which men know not"—all of which suggest the geologic instability and midocean location of Atlantis.

The impression deepens when the king refers to his domain as "an isle of the blest," a characterization both Greeks and Romans used to refer to Atlantic islands generally and Atlantis specifically. Its rich, natural abundance ("where nothing is lacking and which is filled with all good things") is likewise reminiscent of this passage from the *Kritias:* "The island itself provided much of what was required by them for the uses of life. . . . All these that sacred island lying beneath the sun brought forth fair and wondrous in infinite abundance." Indeed, the Serpent King's words leave no doubt as to the Atlantean identity of his island: "It shall be changed into waves."

Why then was the Serpent King's island called Punt? As Kenneth Caroli makes clear, the Egyptians knew several locations by that description, and it is doubtful the name was ever used to designate a single geographical site.[91] Just as the New Testament writers employed "Babylon" to describe any wealthy city, the Egyptians referred to foreign lands of abundance and with which they were trading on friendly terms as Punt.

The Serpent King is far more than some fabulous creation. The Pyramid Texts read, "Thou, Osiris, art great in thy name of the Great Green [the sea]. Lo, thou art round as the circle that encircles the Hanebu." Howey comments, "Osiris was thus the serpent that, lying in the ocean, encircled the world."[92] This depiction of Osiris as both man-god and culture bearer who voyaged throughout the world, preaching the virtues of civilization and his own mystery cult of rebirth, is itself overtly Atlantean. Osiris was portrayed in Egyptian myth as a "serpent king." His appearance highlights his imperial personage, not as a giant snake, but a powerful ruler. The beard he wore was an emblem of kingship. (Even Queen Hatshepsut had to wear a false beard on occasion during her reign.)

His "scales" of gold and lapis lazuli were, of course, his royal raiment, his usual garb of lapis and gold jewelry. The castaway's transportation to his "resting place" (that is, the palace) in "the great jaws" (guards armed with edged weapons) refers to the king's power of command. The sailor himself appears to have been engaged in the lucrative copper trade that supposedly made the Atlantean capital rich and influential. That his ship loaded with miners should have floundered close enough for him to reach the Serpent King's island strongly implies he was in the immediate vicinity of Atlantis.

The most cogent and otherwise inexplicable feature of the Serpent King's story is the "young girl—on whom the fire of heaven fell and burnt her to ashes." Atlantis means "daughter of Atlas." Is *The Story of the Shipwrecked Sailor* a memory in myth of a catastrophe, "the fire from heaven," that struck the Atlantean "isle of the blest," "and burnt her to ashes"?

With this Egyptian version of the disaster, the Atlantean story has been traced around the world in common mythic themes that connect virtually every society on earth. These examples nonetheless represent but a fraction of the hundreds of known flood accounts. Yet even here, the accumulative impression begins to form of a planetwide cataclysm that touched all humanity so deeply the memory was quick-frozen in the folkish consciousness of humankind. It is impossible that so many shared elements vividly describiing the same event and often held sacred by the people who preserve its memory over generations, are unrelated, merely coincidental. On the contrary, when seen from a global perspective, the Deluge myth in all its variations represents eyewitness testimony of that natural catastrophe—and of the great city it destroyed.

The phenomenon of nostophilia was an instinctive urge in animals compelling their return to some remote homeland or breeding ground, mentioned in chapter 3. Certain eels, rodents, birds, and even butterflies continue to converge on an open area of the Atlantic Ocean, the location of a large, former island, long ago sunk to the sea bottom. Is it possible that we, too, possess a kind of nostophilia for a remote and lost homeland? While the other animals act out their memory in self-destructive behavior, perhaps humans express it in the universal myth of the Great Deluge.

FIVE

How Was Atlantis Destroyed?

From its deep-rooted base the Isle of Flame
stern Poseidon shook and plunged beneath the
waves its impious inhabitants.
Fragment of a poem by Dionysus of Rhodes

Myths are the lucid dreams of mankind. Like personal dreams, they may be filled with concrete, realistic details, but the sense of time is askew. Myths preserve historical truths wrapped in layers of poetic metaphor, although the events they so colorfully, even accurately depict cannot be anchored to any specific period. The function of myth is to describe, not date, the past. Fixing credible time parameters on ancient occurrences is the work of the archaeologist, the historian, the geologist, and the astronomer, not the mythologist. It is up to the "hard scientists" to determine just when and how the world catastrophe mythologized by virtually every human society took place.

The scientific search for the When and How of that catastrophe begins in Egypt. There, in West Thebes, the best preserved New Kingdom ceremonial complex in the Nile Valley may still be visited. Known as Medinet Habu, the Victory Temple (perhaps, "Victory against the Hanebu"), it was built by Ramses III around 1180 B.C.E. to commemorate his triumph over the most dangerous sea invasion his kingdom ever faced. The Hanebu, also known as the Meshwesh, Sea Peoples, were a foreign thalassocracy, a menacing power whose ships ranged throughout the Mediterranean Sea, as far as "the Ninth Bow," possibly the Egyptian equivalent to the Straits of Gibraltar.

A number of related tribes, or perhaps divisions of the Meshwesh, included the Denyen, Kel, Peleset, Sheklesh, and so forth—names that occasionally corresponded with specific locations, such as Palestine or Sicily. The sites appear to have been named after the various Sea Peoples following their occupation of these locations in the aftermath of the war against Egypt. Temple inscriptions describe the far-reaching ambition of these armed seafarers: "They laid their hands on countries to the very circuit of the Earth."[1]

Medinet Habu was erected on a grand scale. An impressive specimen of Pharaonic architecture, it still shows traces of its original paint after more than three thousand years. Its temple inscriptions are not myth, but history, although mythic figures were occasionally used by the scribes who copied down official reports of the Egyptian victory to describe events on a dramatic scale. They wrote that in the year of Ramses' coronation, 1198 B.C.E., terrible omens fell on the land: "Men go about looking like gem-birds [ravens], because there are none whose clothes are white in these times. All are laid low by terror."[2] Sunlight was drastically diminished, the skies were always dark, and the air unusually chill because of "a great darkness" that overshadowed Egypt.

Other documents that have survived into the present, such as the *Ipuwer Papyrus*, speak of the world appearing to turn upside down in a cosmic cataclysm. The Book of Exodus from the shrine of Al-Arish, written by a Jew, Midrashim, repeats the Egyptian accounts.[3] The unusual events were regarded as awful portents for his reign, and, sure enough, five years later, the Egyptians of the Nile Delta were confronted from the northwest (the same direction from which the ash cloud came) by the most massive invasion fleet they had ever seen.

The Hanebu, leading a confederation of other Meshwesh, launched a series of major naval engagements and armed landings. They rapidly swept aside the Egyptian coastal defenses and stormed ashore at various points along the mouth of the Nile. The invasion's inertia carried it over or past all military obstacles set in its way. The Hanebu force, numbering in the tens of thousands, seemed at first an irresistible tide of armed men and warships. They took one city after another, killing, routing, or capturing the defenders. But through the brilliant strategy of Ramses III and the skill of his archers, the invaders were vanquished and pushed back into the sea. Many were taken prisoner and their portraits incised into the walls of the Victory Temple. Their hands were tied behind their backs or over their heads. Bound, one unfortunate wretch to the next, by a long chain strung between neck collars, they were paraded before Pharaoh, his family, the court, soldiers, and crowds of spectators.

Before their execution, the Hanebu officers were interrogated and their testimony recorded. Why, they were asked, did they invade Egypt? The defeated enemy replied that they were desperate after the loss of their homeland. The Medinet Habu inscriptions read, "The head of their cities has gone under the waves. The great heat of Sekhmet mingled with their heat, so that their bones burned up in the midst of their bodies. The shooting-star was terrible in pursuit of them . . . a mighty torch hurling flame from the heavens to search out their souls, to devastate their root. The Kel and the Meshwesh of the sea, they were made as those that exist not. The land of the Meshwesh was destroyed all at once."[4]

This last line parallels Plato's description of the length of the Atlantean cataclysm—"in a single day and night." The substance that turned the Egyptians' white linens to sooty black and caused the cold darkness that frightened the people was fallout from heavy ash clouds, effects from the eruption of Mount Atlas, driven by the prevailing westerly winds across the Mediterranean to the Nile Valley. Sekhmet was the Egyptian lioness-headed goddess of fiery annihilation. And the homeland of the Sea People she destroys is called Netero, the Sacred Island. Its description is similar to that of Plato's sunken capital. At Medinet Habu, the most important elements associated with that lost city—the Atlanteans' war against Egypt and the celestial event that brought about the deluge of their island home—come together, not in speculative myth, but recorded history. Clearly, the only event in ancient history that fits this graphic portrayal is the destruction of Atlantis.

"A CHAIN OF DESTRUCTION"

The testimony written in stone on Ramses' Victory Temple opens a unique door to the past that had been hidden until this moment. It affords the perspective needed to see Atlantis in the context of the real world, and, therefore, brings it into focus more clearly than ever before. The epoch in which the Sea Peoples invaded Egypt and Netero went under the waves was one of widespread destruction not confined to the Atlantic Ocean. The magnitude of annihilation was nothing less than transcontinental. Its scope was horrific and devastating. Before the catastrophe's sudden arrival, Western Civilization had reached a high level of cultural excellence. Egypt stood at the zenith of her splendor. The Mycenaean Greeks, described in Homer's epics, ruled the Eastern Mediterranean while their Trojan rivals dominated the commercially strategic Dardanelles from their opulent capital of Ilios. The Hittite Empire spread throughout most of Asia Minor, and the Assyrians to the south controlled the central Near East. The slow inner decay that infected so many societies since was not in evidence. On the contrary, all these kingdoms were economically prosperous, militarily vigorous, artistically rich, and at the height of their powers.

Yet, within a few decades, all of them (with one exception) were wiped out, their capitals and most of their towns incinerated, their surviving populations hiding in the high mountains. Only Egypt escaped destruction, but she went into a steep decline from which she would never recover. Along with the better-known powers, the Babylonian Kassites, a formidable people that had troubled the Hittites for centuries, disappeared, as did Elam. The Shang Dynasty in distant China, which was deluged with rains of ash, collapsed suddenly. The short years bridging the thirteenth and twelfth centuries B.C.E. witnessed the obliteration and abandonment of literally hundreds of cities and towns across the civilized world. The very foundations of civilization were shattered, and humankind rapidly slipped back into a dark age of savagery, lawlessness, and ignorance for the next five hundred years. Government, science, art, architecture, literacy, medicine, seamanship, economics, agriculture—everything that had risen to lofty stratas of achievement between 3000 to the 1200 B.C.E. vanished in an instant.

In Anatolia (present-day Asia Minor), every important Bronze Age site and many insignificant ones, including all of the important settlements belonging to the hitherto unvanquished Hittite Empire, were utterly destroyed by fire sometime around 1200 B.C.E. In the centuries that followed, a few cities were occupied by handfuls of squatters; the rest were forgotten until their discovery by modern archaeologists. At the ruins of Hattusas, the imperial capital, researchers found copious amounts of ash, charred wood, and slag from mud bricks melted at some inconceivably high temperature—evidence of an intense fire. Identical evidence was uncovered at nearby Alaca Hoeyuek, where a thick layer of ash covered the entire metropolis. The fortress-city of Alishar, its mighty defensive wall still standing unbreached, had been gutted from end to end by a monstrous fire.

About sixty miles to the east, the powerfully built border outpost of Mashat Hoeyuek, which stood for centuries as a successful bulwark against invasion, went up like a matchstick. Faraway to the west, the great city of Milawata watched over the Aegean coast from behind its unassailable ramparts. It, too, burst into all-consuming flames sometime around 1200 B.C.E. At that same moment, hundreds of miles to the southeast, the fortress-towns of Tarsus and Mersin were obliterated by a common conflagration. An unnamed Hittite castle-town guarding the strategic headwaters of the Seyhan River was incinerated at about the same time. Numerous forts, cities, and villages along the upper Euphrates River in eastern Anatolia were burned in what Drews called "site-wide" destructions. Lidar Hoeyuek, Tille Hoeyuek, Norshuntepe—the list of settlements great and small is a catalog of fiery exterminations, complete and unsparing.

The physical evidence of destruction throughout Anatolia proved that the ancient historians had written the truth when they recorded cataclysmic upheavals in Asia Minor soon after the Trojan War. The Roman scholars Pliny the Elder and Strabo, and, earlier, the Greeks Pausanias and Democles, reported that "entire villages disappeared" during an unprecedented series of geologic violence that struck Lydia, Ionia, and the Troad.[5] They described Troy as having been "submerged" during this time, and marshes suddenly expanded to become lakes. These abrupt transformations were probably caused by a gigantic tsunami set in motion by either an extraordinarily powerful seaquake or the fall of a large meteorite in the Ionian Sea off the coast of northwestern Anatolia.

In Virgil's *Aeneid*, Aeneas and his family witnessed a powerful meteor fall on the last day of the Trojan War. In fact, evidence of serious geologic damage has been established at Ilios. (It should be mentioned here that "Troy," although traditionally used in the same context as its chief city, was actually the name of the country surrounding Ilios, the Trojan capital.)

Nearby Mount Sipylus "was overturned." As it collapsed, a city on its slopes crashed into the depths of a chasm, which was filled by a deluge to become Lake Saloae. According to Pausanias, the city's ruins could be seen on the lake bottom until, over time, they were silted over.

Ugarit was among the oldest, largest and most powerful cities in the Near East. At the time of the Trojan War, it too was subjected to such an all-embracing and violent conflagration that everyday life came to an immediate stop. Present-day excavators working on the archaeological site found clay tablets in an oven, as though their creators were surprised in the midst of their daily affairs. A much smaller, nearby coastal town, Ras Ibn Hani was similarly obliterated. Along the length of the Orontes River, city after city was laid waste in charred mounds of smoldering ruin. Typical was the smaller site of Alalakh, discovered by the famous archaeologist Leonard Wooley. Despite the millennia separating him from the destruction, he was awed by what he found: "The burnt ruins of the topmost houses show that the city shared the fate of its more powerful neighbors."[6]

The holocaust reached into the southern Levant, devouring the great city of Lachish in flames and bathing in fire the entire stretch of territory from Syria to the Egyptian border known in later Roman times as the Via Maris. All of the Egyptian pharaoh's imperial holdings in this wide area, large cities and small hamlets alike, trading centers and fortresses, were reduced to heaps of ash. B. Hrouda, an archaeologist who excavated sites in the Levant for twenty years, wrote about the ash deposits, "These burnt strata are evidence of a major catastrophe."[7] Wiesner, who also spent decades excavating Bronze Age sites in the Near East, writes of "a chain of destruction" from Troy to Palestine.[8]

THE INCINERATION OF HOMERIC GREECE

In Greece, "almost all the great mainland centres had been destroyed by fire, several being deserted thereafter," according to mid-twentieth-century archaeologists excavating dozens of settlements in the Peloponnesus dated to the end of the Bronze Age.[9] Of the 320 Greek cities and towns standing in 1200 B.C.E., perhaps forty were still inhabited ten years later. From the far-northern palatial site of Iolkos to the harbor city of Xeropolis on the Euboean coast, human settlements were reduced to metropolitan-sized cauldrons of flame. Mycenae itself burned so thoroughly that not one square inch inside the Citadel was untouched. The very masonry melted in temperatures difficult to comprehend. In the distant Argolid, in the northeast of the Peloponnesus, some one hundred settlements of varying size and importance were either hastily evacuated or totally burned to ashes.

Magnificent Tiryns, its formidable bulwark recently erected against some major threat from the sea, was blasted so severely that the metropolis and everything in its immediate vicinity, including the neighboring city of Midea, were virtually atomized by heat. The ruins were then swamped by a devastating flood, as was Iolcos. The river city of Menelaion, together with a large, fortified palace, was entirely consumed in flames, its charred ground unoccupied for the next four centuries. In Greece proper, as in Peloponnesus, an accounting of incinerated, abandoned settlements is very long. As many as two hundred towns or villages, most of them small, were suddenly evacuated at the same time that the fabulous Palace of Nestor, at Pylos, was consumed by fire. An identical fate struck every major city in the region, as far as the Messenian Gulf.

The cataclysm of 1200 B.C.E. was by no means confined to the mainland. It swept throughout the Aegean. The island of Paros's citadel burned to its foundations, while Crete suffered no less than Mycenaean Greece. The palatial cities of Knossos and Mallia, along with smaller centers such as Kydonia, were gutted by fire. Without exception, every major city on Cyprus was burned beyond recognition or abandoned at the same time.

EGYPT SUFFERS

Egypt may have been more affected by these neighboring events than the physical evidence revealed thus far. The *Ipuwer Papyrus* reads, "Gates, columns, and walls are consumed by fire. The sky is in confusion."[10] And the wall texts of Medinet Habu report, "The

House of the Thirty [a huge, luxurious palace for the chief nobles] is destroyed. The Earth shakes. All the water is useless."[11] Caroli has suggested that "comets contain poisonous metals and gases which could be released during an impact or mid-air explosion, contaminating land and water."[12] The Medinet Habu text continues in the same vein: "The Nile was dried up and the land fell victim to drought. Egypt was without shepherds."[13]

These Egyptian accounts are underscored by the Old Testament's Second Book of Moses. Better known as Exodus, scholars generally agree it describes conditions in Egypt during the mid-thirteenth century B.C.E., precisely the period of the worldwide cataclysm. The Medinet Habu statement "All the water is useless" is supported in chapter 7, verses 20 and 21: "All the waters that were in the river were turned to blood. And the fish that were in the river stank, and the Egyptians could not drink the water of the river. And there was blood throughout all the land of Egypt." Volcanic out-gasing results in prodigious quantities of ash, which is often blood-colored due to high levels of reddish tufa. Sufficient volumes of ash falling into rivers and lakes would turn them scarlet and render them undrinkable.

In addition to this widespread water pollution, "there was a thick darkness in all the land of Egypt for three days. They did not see one another" (Exodus 10: 22, 23). Again, Exodus closely parallels the pharaonic records and similarly describes a dust-veil event caused by large-scale volcanic activity or the collision of an extraterrestrial body with Earth. Since volcanoes never existed in the Nile Valley, the ash clouds either drifted from outside sources or may have arisen from celestial debris falling on Egypt. Plagues of animals are also known to be among the occasional consequences of major geologic upheaval. For example, the sudden appearance of thousands of snakes in China has long been used by seismologists there to anticipate imminent earthquake activity.

A devastating meteor fall is graphically described in Exodus 9: 23, 24, and 25: "And the Lord sent thunder and hail, and lightning ran along the ground. And the Lord showered hail upon the land of Egypt. So there was hail and flaming fire mingled with with the hail, very grievous, such as had never been in all the land of Egypt since it became a nation. And the hail smote throughout all the land of Egypt all that was in the field, both man and cattle. And the hail destroyed all the herbs of the field and broke every tree."

The inscriptions of Ramses' Victory Temple describe even worse conditions in Libya, which, until then, was considered a relatively fertile, prosperous country: "Libya has become a desert. A terrible torch hurled flame from heaven to destroy their souls and lay waste their land. Their bones burn and roast within their limbs."[14] The language is remarkably similar to that used in depicting the destruction of Netero, the Egyptian term for Atlantis.

EUROPE ABLAZE

In effect, Greece, Crete and the smaller islands of the Eastern Mediterranean, Anatolia, and the Near East (and, to an unknown, although probably lesser extent, Egypt and Libya) all simultaneously burst into flame. Because these were the most civilized and heavily populated areas of Europe and northern Africa, their accounts of the catastrophe are fairly well documented. In other, less civilized areas, researchers need to rely on additional clues. Much of Germany burned. The sphagnum bogs of the eastern Alps, which lie 7,800 feet above sea level, contain the remains of forests that, according to pollen analysis, burned before the eleventh century B.C.E.

Pollen analysis also revealed that the entire Black Forest region, predominantly pine until around 1200 B.C.E., was wrapped in flames. Mountain pines cannot be set afire by lightning; they must be deliberately burned. But the Black Forest contained no large human populations at the time, so something else must have been responsible for the devastation. Peat-bog remains dating from the turn of the twelfth century B.C.E. indicate that Western Europe was parched by perhaps the greatest drought it ever experienced.[15]

THE GREAT KILLING

Far more than palaces and empires disappeared. Precisely how many people perished in the catastrophe is impossible to estimate. Some idea of the loss of life may be gathered from the fact that, thirty-two centuries ago, Anatolia, Greece, and even Britain were almost entirely depopulated. The Greek population was reduced to a mere one-hundredth of its size after 1200 B.C.E. Caroli writes that in only a few years, "populations in the areas affected dropped from a fourth to a tenth of their former numbers."[16]

Archaeological evidence of an extraordinary devastation occurring around 1200 B.C.E. is supported by climatic and geologic data. Many of the doomed sites suffered earthquake damage, some severe. But quite a few others show no signs of seismic activity. Moreover, all locations, near population centers or in remote areas, were destroyed by some remarkably intense fire that in many instances was certainly accompanied by earthquake activity. Nevertheless, the primary cause of destruction does not appear to have been seismic; only some of the sites had their stone foundations badly cracked by tremors.

Most scholars are hard put, perhaps reluctant, to explain the fiery annihilation that occurred during the Bronze Age. Their speculations range from prolonged droughts to earthquakes. But none of these causes could have effected the enormity of the cataclysm that decimated civilization.

Some believe that the advent of new weapons technology, especially improvements in sword design and manufacture, was responsible for the Mediterranean region's depopulation. They hypothesize that armed, nameless barbarians rapidly overthrew their more civilized victims.

It is certainly true that some of the locations wracked by flames were victims of raiders involved in the Atlantean War described by Plato. But the cities the invaders hit were coastal and amounted to but a tiny fraction of all the destroyed sites. Ilios was burned by the Achaean Greeks, but not so thoroughly as at many other locations throughout Anatolia, because the Trojan capital was reoccupied for the remainder of the twelfth century B.C.E. shortly after it was sacked. There is no real evidence for the anonymous barbarians who supposedly toppled civilization without resistance. Until the great conflagrations, all the Bronze Age kingdoms were at the peak of their strength. It does not seem logical that the Mycenaeans, fresh from their victory at Troy, or the Hittites, conquerors of most of Anatolia, would have fallen without a fight to undisciplined savages, no matter how well equipped.

Believers in attacking hordes must also accept that these unknown barbarians were so benighted that they burned large cities and tiny villages for sport; the invaders made no attempt to occupy these victimized sites, nor to take any valuables with them. Raiders interested only in plunder would have bypassed insignificant towns and hamlets for the riches of the big cities. But the small settlements in Greece, Anatolia, and so forth, were no less devastated by fire than the palatial sites.

Evidence of fire extends beyond the destroyed settlements into the sea. A Swedish expedition in 1947–48 led by Hans Peterson drilled core samples from the bottom of the Mediterranean and retrieved deposits of foraminifers (small shellfish) overlaid with thick layers of ash dated to the close of the thirteenth century B.C.E.[17] Thus, the ash covering the land sites could not be a result of human action. It would have required many millions of alleged raiders to devastate so vast an area in only a few years time. In view of the worldwide scope of the catastrophe, all military explanations dwindle to nothing.

The cause of so widespread, sudden, and complete a catastrophe must lie elsewhere. Around 1200 B.C.E. temperate or southern Europe grew suddenly colder and wetter, while the Mediterranean became arid due to great amounts of ash being pushed into the atmosphere. Climate records for the Atlantic Ocean reveal a sharp cold snap, beginning in the thirteenth century B.C.E., that spiked in

1159 B.C.E. with the massive eruption of Iceland's Hekla volcano.[18] This event was not an isolated geologic incident, but signaled the end of a series of related cataclysms that had been going on for forty years.

The cold weather was not limited to the Atlantic; temperatures dropped worldwide. Along the entire west coast of North America, from present-day southern California to Alaska, climatologists have documented a sudden cooling trend beginning in 1200 B.C.E. Archaeo-climatologists found that the level of Great Salt Lake dropped suddenly at that time. Simultaneously, what they refer to as the Eayan Phase (a prolonged period of steady, warm temperatures), as evidenced along the eastern shores of Vancouver Island, ended abruptly. Archaeologists noticed that the dramatically changing climate coincided with the rapid abandonment of central California by Windmiller culture people. Its population was apparently dispersed in all directions. Researchers have found evidence of violent mass deaths and extensive burning.[19]

Earth's cold phase peaked around 1100 B.C.E., and lasted for roughly the next four hundred years. This period of reduced sunlight and plummeting temperatures caused by a massive dust-veil event almost perfectly coincides with the appropriately termed Dark Ages that separated the end of the Bronze Age from the beginning of the Classical Period. A chart in *Science* magazine shows the dramatic temperature deviation occurred with unique suddenness in 1200 B.C.E.[20] Interestingly, the Mediterranean region, once as warm as the Caribbean, grew cold after 1200 B.C.E.

The Swedish climatologist, Otto Peterson, demonstrated that Britain's Bronze Age climate was permanently altered after 1200 B.C.E. A huge area of low pressure descended over Britain, resulting in rains so heavy they may only be described as a deluge. In nearby Ireland, tree rings virtually disappeared during this time period.[21] Caroli observes, "It is worth noting that there were two dust-veil events with worldwide effects, the first in 1628 B.C. [the Thera eruption], the other more than four centuries later. Combined, they represent the greatest out-gassing in the Holocene Epoch, and signify one of its principal shifts. Since the entire Holocene is only separated by four main climate divisions, this fact points up the extreme geologic destructiveness of the second millennium B.C. If catastrophic impacts took place in water, steam would replace dust to a considerable extant. The water vapor that failed to become so-called 'diamond dust' in the upper atmosphere would fall back to Earth as torrential downpours on the scale of a true deluge."[22]

WORLDWIDE VOLCANIC ERUPTIONS

The catastrophe and its fiery devastation burst the bounds of Europe to affect the rest of the world. An unprecedented level of volcanism accompanied the conflagrations and ash clouds. Caroli writes, "This period surpassed even the dangerous fifth and eighth millennia in violence. There were more known eruptions here than at any other time in the Holocene. Close passes by a major comet, as well as actual meteoric impacts, would exacerbate stresses on the Earth's crust. Plate boundaries were particularly vulnerable. Similarly, volcanism would be instigated by impacts and/or close cometary passes. In the close approach of a comet, the total mass of its body together with its relative distance from the surface of Earth was crucial."[23]

The mass of the Bronze Age killer comet would have been of sufficient mass to exert horrendous stresses on the seismically active Earth. Historical investigator Joseph Jochmans points out, "Recent computer simulations reveal that if a comet or asteroid hit the Earth on one side, the seismic waves it generated would be transmitted through the planetary interior. By being focused on account of the Earth's curvature, the waves would meet together at the other location directly on the opposite side where the impact took place, and the high stress energy released could disrupt the surface area, causing a tremendous outpouring of volcanic activity."[24]

In southwestern Italy, Mount Vesuvius, notorious for the destruction of Pompeii and Herculaneum in 79 C.E., was convulsed by a trio of violent eruptions beginning in 1200 B.C.E. and lasting for the next hundred years. Another Italian volcano suddenly awoke in Ischia. At the same moment, an unnamed volcano in southern Arabia, inactive before and since, began a prolonged, massive outgassing. Near the Pacific Ocean, in far eastern Russia, the Avachinsky and Sheveluch volcanoes on the Kamchatka Peninsula burst into flame. Meanwhile, Japan's Omuroyama-amagi group of volcanoes on Honshu became active. Among them, the gargantuan Atami-san erupted, and its entire eastern wall collapsed into the sea. (Atami-san is so large the modern city of Atami, with more than fifteen thousand residents, in located inside its dormant crater.)

Across the Pacific Ocean, the Americas were shaken with volcanic activity. Mount Saint Helens launched into three major eruptions: the first beginning in 1200 B.C.E., the next fifty years later and the last around the turn of the twelfth century B.C.E. Washington's Mount Baker awoke in a protoclastic display at about the same time. From 1200 to 1100 B.C.E., California's Mount Shasta and Oregon's Newberry Volcano and Belknap Crater illuminated the northwest. In Central America, El Salvador's San Salvador volcano exploded as well.

Researcher Henriette Mertz postulated a geologic cause and added an additional element to the catastrophe. She proposes that "the Caribbean plate did in fact collide with the North American plate sometime around 1200 B.C. . . . and the Caribbean plate bent down sliding under the leading edge of the north plate, crumpling the edges as it disintegrated into the depths of the Puerto Rico Trench. What tragic consequences would it have created along the Atlantic seaboard, as well as along the Gulf Coast! What a towering tsunami! How inconceivably high would that wave have been and with what force would it have traveled over land and sea!"[25]

As evidence for the seismic wave, she cites Alabama's deep Russell Cave, which was flooded with an incomprehensibly massive inundation thirty-two hundred years ago.[26] Mertz was certainly right in claiming massive geologic upheavals for the Caribbean within the dates she calculated. Mount Pelee, on the island of Martinique, erupted during this time, as did Saba on Saint Eustatius, and there is similar evidence for a volcanic event on Grenada in addition to three other known eruptions of uncertain magnitude in the Antilles.

Ice-core samples taken from Greenland and Antarctica show a mounting ash layer beginning around 1200 B.C.E. and peaking in 1159 B.C.E. with the eruption of Iceland's Hekla volcano.[27] It was here, in the Atlantic, that the scene was set for the greatest concentration of volcanic violence. From Ascension Island in the South Atlantic to Hekla in the North, the ocean was in tumult. Candlemas Island, in the South Atlantic, erupted with such vehemence that it threw ash for at least twenty-five hundred miles. Far to the north, Mount Furnas (Furna de Fernao Jorge), in the Azores, blew up with a level-4 explosion, a magnitude greater than the eruption that destroyed Pompeii and Herculaneum. A calibrated date for the event in the Azores is circa 1178 B.C.E. As long ago as 1935, researcher James Churchward directly connected the eruption of Mount Furnas with the Atlantean catastrophe.[28]

Since the first modern investigations of the sea floor began in the late 1940s, oceanographers have been astonished to find prodigious amounts of ash on the bottom of the Atlantic. The presence of so many thick layers proves that phenomenal volcanism once took place along the fifteen-thousand-mile Mid-Atlantic Ridge.

The Canaries, the islands closest to the suspected location of Atlantis, were especially hard hit. Gran Canaria, Fuerteventura, and Lanzarote all suffered through volcanic outbursts. So massive were these combined out-gasings that all twenty-eight hundred square miles of the seven islands were covered with layers of lava and ash. Wooden beams and tree trunks on Gran Canaria were embedded with lava 3,075 years ago, plus or minus a hundred years, according to Dr. H. O. Schminke of Germany's Mineralogical Institute in Bochum. Greenland ice-core dating for these dramatic events ranged from 1191 to 1194 B.C.E., plus or minus twenty-five years, hitting a postulated date for the destruction of Atlantis virtually on the nose. At the same time, within sight of Lanzarote, the North African coast writhed in geologic spasms.[29] The first-century B.C.E. Greek historian Diodorus Siculus wrote that prolonged earthquakes deformed the shores along Mauretania (modern-day Morocco) in the years after the fall of Troy. His testimony was borne out more than two thousand years later by the investigative team of geologists Borchard and Herrmann, who discovered that the rim of the Atlantic coast along northwest Africa (the Draa Depression) dropped suddenly "as a result of large faulting movements" circa 1250 B.C.E.[30]

ATLANTEAN DESTRUCTION: A WORLDWIDE CATACLYSM

From the vantage point of an imaginary satellite orbiting Earth just after 1200 B.C.E., an awesome spectacle unfolded. A transcontinental conflagration engulfed southern Germany, the Balkans, Crete and the Eastern Mediterranean, Anatolia, the Near East, and possibly parts of Lower Egypt and Libya. East of this flaming holocaust, volcanoes were erupting from Arabia to Russia and Japan. Volcanoes also detonated across the American northwest, south to the Antilles and into El Salvador. A ruinous ash fall transformed the climate and killed many thousands of people in Britain and China. But the most awful sight would have been presented by the mid-Atlantic, where the volcanic ferocity was concentrated. Even before the full fury of the destruction was spent, rising, thickening billows of smoke and ash wrapped the entire planet in a dust veil, reducing both sunlight and world temperatures.

These simultaneous developments represented, in the consensus of scholars, "a catastrophe which was one of the worst in world history" [31]; among "the most frightful in the history of the world." [32] Atlantis had the terrible misfortune to be located in the central vortex of this calamity. But what could have possibly caused such earth-wide destruction? Geologic explanations seem woefully inadequate.

However, running through world myths that describe the Great Flood is the consistent theme of some celestial precursor, most often depicted as a terrifying comet, that crashed in the sea to initiate the Deluge.

Historic accounts contemporary with the calamitous events of the late thirteenth and early twelfth centuries B.C.E. likewise report the appearance of a remarkably frightening comet. The wall texts at Medinet Habu read, "The shooting-star was terrible in pursuit of them [the invading Sea Peoples]. . . . a mighty torch hurling flame from the heavens to search out their souls, to devastate their root."[33] Sekhmet, the lioness-headed goddess of fiery destruction, was said to have set this cataclysm in motion. According to inscriptions dating to the reign of Seti II (among the last pharaohs of the Nineteenth Dynasty, he reigned until 1210 B.C.E.), Sekhmet was regarded as "a circling star that spread out her fire in flames, a fire-flame in her storm," spewing forth heat that "burned the forests and meadows of the Nine Bows."[34]

It is not clear if all of the territories within the Nine Bows (from the Straits of Gibraltar to Syria) were burned or just the land specifically located at the Ninth Bow. If the latter, than this is a definite reference to the immediate vicinity of Atlantis, an interpretation made more persuasive with the mention of "forests and meadows" that, as Plato affirmed, were abundant on the island. A later Egyptian text quoted by Wainwright reads, "The fire was to the end of heaven and to the end of the Earth," which, in view of the worldwide magnitude of the catastrophe, is no overstatement. We have seen, too, that the Egyptians believed the Libyans were slaughtered because "a terrible torch hurled flame from heaven to destroy their souls and lay waste their land."[35]

The Ras Shamra inscription from Ugarit, in Syria, a magnificent city completely burned in the early twelfth century B.C.E., seems to foretell the impending doom: "The star Anat has fallen from heaven. She slew the people of the Syrian land and confused the two twilights and the seats of the constellations."[36] Caroli comments, "[the term] 'Syria' was used mainly for the plain east of the Orontes and west of the bend of the Euphrates. In later days, even the region near Hattusas was also called 'Syria,' so this may well be an oblique reference to the obliteration of the Hittite homeland, which ruled Ugarit."[37]

While Assyrian armies battled the Hittites for control of northern Iraq in 1244 B.C.E., their emperor, Shalmaneser I, was astounded by the sight of an enormous comet illuminating the heavens and had the event recorded on clay tablets.[38] His grandson Ashurdan I had his court reporters write of the awful comet that streaked through the skies of his crumbling Assyrian Empire circa 1179 B.C.E.[39] In Babylon, an alarming comet troubled the reign of Nebuchadnezzar I around 1124 B.C.E.; its appearance was duly recorded by his palace scribes.[40] The same comet even appears in a contemporary report from China, where it was characterized as "a great star whose flames devoured the sun."[41]

By the middle of the thirteenth century B.C., the civilized world stood at the apogee of its cultural splendor. Around the turn of the next century, the far-flung Hittite empire lay in ashes, Egypt entered a decline from which she would never recover, and the Homeric Age of Greece and Troy was burned to a cinder, while the great forests of Western Europe burst into flames. The destruction of Atlantis described by Plato was part of this extensive cataclysm. Scorched remains testify to the nature of that catastrophe, the most devastating experienced by civilized man, in the excavated ruins of the Near East and among the peat-bog finds of Bavaria. Of the Atlanteans' fate, however, nothing survives but myth.

THE EVER-PRESENT POTENTIAL
FOR GLOBAL DISASTER

How credible is the possibility of a comet powerful enough to have brought about the end of civilization more than three thousand years ago? Until very recently, most scientists ridiculed the idea that such a thing actually happened. "Catastrophism," the belief that natural disasters play a role in shaping human affairs, was all the rage among professional and amateur researchers until the middle of the nineteenth century. But the theory of evolution postulated that change in nature was gradual, taking place over millions of years. Geologists made this Darwinian observation a tenet of their own science, resulting in a viewpoint known as "uniformitarianism."

Proponents of the new dogma conceived of Earth as a stable mechanism where physical alterations took place with progressive slowness over epochs of time. To be sure, earthquakes, volcanic eruptions, and even the rare meteorite impact occurred with destructive suddenness. But their effects were deemed no more than incidental to the fundamental geologic and evolutionary processes that crawled with almost immeasurable inertia.

Uniformitarianism dominated the natural sciences for most of the twentieth century. Into the early 1980s its advocates were still preaching peaceful gradualism, although, by then the inconsistency of their doctrine was often obvious. A case in point was the nationally televised series entitled *Cosmos,* scripted and hosted by America's best-publicized astronomer, Dr. Carl Sagan. At the beginning of the fourth episode he poked fun at the world traditions that portrayed comets as dangerous phenomena and compared these astronomical phenomena instead to dirty but wonderful "snowballs" whirling innocently around the sun. Later, in the same episode, Sagan told his audience with a straight face that the Tunguska Event of 1908, a twelve-megaton blast that leveled seven hundred square miles of Siberian forest, was caused by debris from a passing comet. He then went on to lament that Earth might be destroyed if a similar event took place during the Cold War, because the impact could be mistaken for a nuclear attack, sparking a mutually retaliatory and annihilating exchange. Had the Tunguska explosion occurred over London, it would have killed three-hundred thousand people and flattened all buildings within a twelve-mile radius of the city. So much for the quaint innocence of comets!

Such muddy thinking had already grown circumspect by the 1970s, when material evidence demonstrated that some celestial impact wiped out many species. Theories on the sudden worldwide disappearance of the dinosaurs blamed either a single large object, perhaps an asteroid that fell into the Caribbean Sea, or a "swarm" of large meteorites that bombarded the entire globe with a heavenly artillery barrage. Or a combination of both. In any case, the decades following this discovery have brought forth an accumulating abundance of supporting evidence, and even most skeptics have been forced to admit some cosmic collision triggered a mass-extinction of sixty-five million years ago.

The general acceptance of some sky-borne catastrophe as the agency for abrupt and planetwide change cast the dogma of uniformitarianism in a doubtful light. That light shone brighter for a week in July, 1994, when a comet impacted our largest planetary neighbor in plain sight of Earth's telescopes. Shoemaker-Levy plunged into Jupiter, resulting in a series of explosions equivalent to forty million megatons. Had it missed Jupiter and crashed into our world instead, every living thing on the face of the globe would have been exterminated. For astronomers and scientists of all kinds, Shoemaker-Levy was a wake-up call. Even before that graphic display of astronomical collision, some noticed a disturbing correlation between several known sudden mass-extinctions on Earth and the periodic near-misses of asteroids and comets in the past. They wondered if the evolution of life on our planet had been shaped by the recurring visitations of celestial cataclysms.

It has become generally accepted that of all the species of creatures that ever existed on Earth, some two-thirds of them became extinct because of an extraterrestrial cataclysm. A few die-hard uniformitarians try to argue that Jupiter actually protects Earth from such mishaps, because potentially dangerous debris is pulled into its great mass. But they fail to appreciate the downside to this Jovian theory: Its broad gravitational field also acts like a far-flung fisherman's net, drawing comets or asteroids and meteorites toward the solar system's inner planets.

We like to imagine that Earth travels securely through space. And even though catastrophes such as the one that killed off the dinosaurs do happen, such events are separated by many millions of years. So, the chance of a similar occurrence taking place in the history of civilization, to say nothing of our own lifetimes, is so remote as to be virtually impossible. That blissful assumption was rudely dispelled as recently as March 23, 1989, when astronomer Henry Holt, using Mount Palomar's Schmidt telescope, discovered that an asteroid had missed our planet by just 450,000 miles.[42] That might seem a very safe margin, but had it crossed our orbit just six hours later the object would have collided with Earth and shattered civilization. The asteroid had a 500- to 1,000-foot diameter; its impact would have caused a two-thousand-megaton explosion and firestorms within a fifty-mile radius.

Nor was the 1989 near-miss a freak encounter. In February 1936 a different asteroid had a brush with our planet. It belonged to the Apollo Group, a cluster of asteroids orbiting in relatively close proximity to Earth and was a monstrous six and a quarter miles across. The asteroid came so close to our planet that its own orbit was slightly distorted. Had it struck, no living creature on Earth could have survived the impact.[43] The September 1986 issue of *National Geographic* carried a remarkable photograph taken on August 10, 1972. It shows a huge meteor streaking through the daylight skies over Johnson Lake, Wyoming. Astronomers studying the photograph concluded that the object narrowly missed our planet, because its trajectory was marginally deflected by Earth's thick ionosphere. They calculated its weight at approximately 1,000 tons, enough mass to have exploded with the force of a 5-megaton bomb. Had its attitude been at an angle sharper to that of the ionosphere, it would have hit us.[44]

Catastrophic celestial events have indeed taken place in historic times. In 1490 C.E., some ten thousand persons were killed during a meteor shower that swept over central China. On September 22, 1979, a U.S. tracking satellite observed a small "nuclear" blast in the South Atlantic about four hundred miles southeast of Cape Town, in the area of Prince Edward Island. At first the South African government was accused of secretly testing an atomic device. But before year's end scientists realized the event was actually the result of a sizeable meteorite striking the sea.[45] Had it arrived about two hundred miles farther southwest, it would have collided with the Atlantic-Indian Ridge, a spur of the geologically unstable Mid-Atlantic Ridge. In that case, the world might have witnessed the same kind of cataclysmic, seismic chain reaction that destroyed Atlantis.

With rapid technological developments in modern space telescopes, astronomers are beginning to identify asteroids that are close enough to endanger Earth. By the mid-1990s, observers at the U.S. Geological Survey and the University of Arizona found about 150 bodies "of the size that could eliminate human society."[46] At least six have diameters in excess of five miles, large enough to extirpate our world of humans. The astronomers' study is far from complete, but they estimate that as many as four thousand asteroids, each more than half a mile in diameter, cross Earth's orbit annually. An impact with any one of them would close down civilization. At least fifty, smaller, but nonetheless potentially deadly meteors, with diameters ranging from 16 to 160 feet, pass within 240,000 miles, nearer to us than the moon, according to David Rabinowitz of the University of Arizona.[47] A meteorite with a diameter of 150 feet created Barringer Crater twenty-seven centuries ago (see chapter 2). Had it struck Athens instead of the Arizona desert, Classical civilization would have perished in its infancy and the course of human development inconceivably changed.

Astronomers are plotting the movements of literally thousands of comets and asteroids whose paths intersect ours. The vast majority are not on collision courses with Earth, despite a handful of close calls. Nonetheless, it is becoming increasingly clear that asteroids of all sizes are numerous enough to form a cloud in the vicinity of our planet, like so many hornets buzzing around a nest. If another celestial body of sufficient mass and velocity were to pass within some proximity of this cloud, many of the asteroids would be sent careening toward Earth in a "swarm" of meteorites that could devastate human civilization, if not all life. It has happened before. Perhaps more often than we know. A large object worrying astronomers does indeed follow a course along Earth's orbit and could eventually collide with our planet. It is known officially as "asteroid 2340 Hathor," the same name, ironically enough, the Egyptians gave to the extraterrestrial menace that destroyed Atlantis, the Sea Peoples' island home.

Calculating possible collisions will not be possible until every threatening object in near-space has been identified. Even then, outside factors, such as a comet, can throw estimates into disarray. Still, both scientific and government authorities are taking an extraterrestrial threat far more seriously, especially since Jupiter's experience with Shoemaker-Levy. At a 1992 conference of leading astronomers, physicists, and politicians at Los Alamos, New Mexico, Edward Teller, the Father of the H-Bomb, outlined several proposals for tracking and destroying incoming asteroids. At the close of the conference, the NASA panel endorsed a "stand off" plan, in which an atomic device delivered by a guided missile is detonated in front of a threatening object to deflect its course away from Earth. There is even talk of using the Star Wars program as a defense against extraterrestrial debris.[48]

The distinguished astronomers Victor Clube and Bill Napier conclude there was at least "an even chance" of a cosmic collision registering one to ten thousand megatons during the past three thousand years.[49] A blast of the magnitude they mention would have produced the catastrophic effects that did indeed sweep around the world at the end of the Bronze Age.

THE BULL OF HEAVEN

But does astronomy or geology offer any really credible evidence that a comet or asteroid caused those effects? Clues to the answer may be found by studying a meteor shower that takes place each summer and fall, when the night skies are flecked with shooting stars from the constellation Taurus. Because of their apparent origin, they are referred to as the Taurids. Some of the fireballs are bright enough to illuminate the landscape momentarily, but they seem harmless. The Taurid meteor stream is made up of pale debris, individually bright but mostly innocuous grains, "the fossil remnants," as Clube described them, of a great cosmic serpent that once dominated the skies of Earth.[50]

Accompanying the Taurids in their biannual visitations is a comet named after the astronomer who calculated its orbit, Johann Franz Encke. Having determined it has the shortest orbital period (about 3.3 years) of any known comet, he also discovered its uniqueness. All other comets are so affected by close encounters with Jupiter that they are eventually tossed out of the solar system. Encke alone continues in a stable orbit outside Jupiter's gravitational grasp, possibly making it the oldest phenomenon of its kind. It is also the only comet in an Apollo Group orbit, which brings it closer to Earth than any other comet.

Over time, Encke has lost mass and grown so feeble that it is only a faint celestial light, despite its recurring proximity. The years have taken their toll on what, only ten centuries ago, was a far more impressive event. During medieval times the "Taurids were the most powerful shower," according to Russian astronomers Ivan Astapovic and Dmitri Terenteva, spewing forty-two fireballs. "No shower, not even the great ones, could be compared with them as to activity." It is clear that the Encke we barely see today has been going through a gradual disintegration from its or its progenitor's originally formidable intensity. In 1200 B.C.E., the time of the catastrophe that put an end to the Bronze Age, proto-Encke must have appeared a flaming monster, the most horrifying apparition humans ever looked upon in the sky.

Today's enfeebled Encke has a traveling companion known as Oljato, an unusual rock one mile across. Although it appears to be an asteroid, Oljato is actually the severed head of a dead comet, probably Encke's close predecessor. In 1982 and again the following year, the unmanned *Pioneer Venus* spacecraft subjected Oljato to close examination; abrupt changes in the object's magnetic field were detected by on-board magnetometers. These readings implied that the space probe, when following close behind the asteroid, entered a stream of magnetized gas—the chemical fingerprint of a comet. Even earthbound observers using telescopes were able to see a faint trail of gas streaming from Oljato. Clube and Napier insist that the chances of just three asteroids sharing an orbit with Encke are less than one in a million. Yet, they point out, as many as two hundred asteroids, each a little less than a mile in diameter, belong to Encke's Taurid meteor stream.

Surrounding all the Taurid stream is a vast, tube-shaped envelope of smaller meteoric flotsam. Named after its Czech discoverer, the Stohl stream is forked, the result of an asteroid collision that occurred nearly five thousand years ago when the stream was moving in its highly elongated orbit between Mars and Jupiter. This immense, bizarre collection of dust, gas, asteroids, and trillions of meteoric fragments all traveling together and regularly near-missing the Earth is the cosmic skeleton of a body that once pulsated with astral fire some sixty thousand miles long. This is how Oljato's comet appeared at the time Atlantis was destroyed. No other single cause could account for the earthquakes, floods, erupting volcanoes, dramatic climate alterations, fires, droughts, dust veils, and ash falls that began around 1240 b.c.e. and continued with growing intensity for almost a hundred years thereafter.

The celestial trigger that appears to have brought Encke-Oljato on a near-collision course with our planet was discovered as recently as fall 2001. According to Caroli, "Recalibrations ascertained and published by astronomers at California's Jet Propulsion Laboratory (*J.P.L. Newsletter,* vol. 13, no. 11, 30 September 2001, La Jolla) reveal that the Earth passed through the tail of Comet Halley in 1198 B.C., when Pharaoh Ramses III recorded the fiery sinking of Neteru, an apparent reference to Atlantis. The same kind of close encounter took place in the early 20th Century, minus disastrous consequences. But the brush with Comet Halley and with Encke-Oljato 3,100 years earlier added the extra gravitational impetus needed to push the latter comet into a more confrontational attitude with Earth. The arrival of two major comets in 1198 B.C. coincides all too well with the mass-destruction known to have swept around the world at that time" (Caroli, personal correspondence, 9 November 2001).

The ominous comet must have been visible for years, gradually drawing closer to Earth with each pass. Returning to Exodus, "And the Lord went before them [the Hebrews] by day in a pillar of cloud, to lead them on the way; and by night in a pillar of fire, to give them light, so that they may travel by day and night. The pillar of cloud by day and the pillar of fire by night never failed to go before the people" (13:21–22). Again in chapter 14, verse 24: "The Lord appeared to the Egyptian army in a pillar of fire and of cloud, and threw the Egyptian army into confusion."

An impending assault from the heavens was undoubtedly obvious to human observers long before it began. When it did come, the catastrophe probably consisted not of a single asteroid colliding with Earth, but an almost regular barrage of extraterrestrial debris varying in magnitude from thick showers of fireballs, most of which burned up in their descent through the mesosphere (a layer of our atmosphere about 30 miles above Earth), to meteorites perhaps hundreds of feet across and large enough to reach Earth's surface. The majority of this extraterrestrial material probably fell into the sea, because two-thirds of Earth's surface is covered by water. But the prolonged intensity of the attack, which resumed every summer and autumn for almost a century, made many collisions with land inevitable. In either case, the results were disastrous. Even if only a small fraction of meteorites reached Earth's surface, the amount and number of impacts on sea and land would have been cataclysmic, given the hundreds or even thousands of rounds of heavenly artillery the fearsome comet was then capable of delivering.

Although some Atlantologists concluded that the Great Flood was caused by a celestial event, it wasn't until 1997 that the scientific community generally conceded that a killer comet was responsible for the demise of Bronze Age civilization. During a three-day symposium in July, leading astronomers, geologists, and climatologists met at Fitzwilliam College in Cambridge, England, at an international conference of the Society for Interdisciplinary Studies. Speakers included such notables as astrophysicist Mark E. Bailey, director of the Armagh Observatory in Northern Ireland; Marie-Agnes Courty, a geologist from the French Center for Scientific Research; and Bas Van Geel, a paleo-ecologist at the University of Amsterdam. Many of the one hundred participants came from as far afield as Japan, North America, and Australia. Their consensus was that an abundance of physical and cultural evidence confirmed that periodic close encounters with a large comet from the fifth millennium B.C.E. to the early eleventh century B.C.E. were responsible for several eras of widespread destruction on Earth's surface, including the end of the Bronze Age.

Swedish physicist Lars Franzen, of the University of Goeteborg, and archaeologist Thomas B. Larsson, of the University of Umea, pointed out that general cooling, above average precipitation, and catastrophic flooding before 1000 B.C.E. were earmarks of a celestial cataclysm. They concluded, "It is obvious that these events were sudden and occurred worldwide." They mentioned a particularly sharp change in climate was noticeable in Europe, the Americas, the Near East, as far north as Alaska, and as far south as the Antarctic, circa 1200 B.C.E. Lake levels increased drastically; Turkey's Lake Van rose as much as 240 feet. Larsson said the abrupt rise in lake levels has been verified in Sweden (Federsee), Ireland (Loughnashade), the United States (Great Salt Lake), Canada (Wald Sea Basin), Bolivia (Titicaca), and Argentina (Lago Cardiel). Franzen told how Swedish, English, and Irish oak bogs preserve a record of above average, sudden rainfall around 1000 B.C.E. At Steng Moss, in Northumberland, there was a sixfold increase in peat moss accumulation.

While such findings are generally unknown to the public, they have long been recognized by climatologists as conditions of the Plenard Period, from 1250 to 1000 B.C.E. World temperatures suddenly fell nearly two degrees Celsius and rainfall was prodigious. British anthropologist Richard Desborough said of the Plenard Period, "the changes that came about were little short of fantastic. The craftsmen and artists seem to have vanished almost without a trace: there is little new stone construction of any sort, far less any massive edifices; the metal workers' techniques revert to primitive, and the potter, except in the early stages, loses his purpose and inspiration; and the art of writing is forgotten. But the outstanding feature is that by the end of the twelfth century B.C., the population appears to have dwindled to about one-tenth of what it had been little over a century before. This is no normal decline, and the circumstances and events obviously have a considerable bearing on the nature of the subsequent dark ages, and must be in part at least a cause of its existence."[51]

Franzen and Larsson locate the focus of the Bronze Age catastrophe in the vicinity of Atlantis itself. "We even suggest that relatively large asteroids or comets (c. 0.5 km diameter) hit somewhere in the eastern Atlantic, possibly at the shelf of the Atlantic west coast of Africa/Europe . . . mainly affecting the Mediterranean parts of Africa and Europe, but also globally."[52]

A BLOW-BY-BLOW DESCRIPTION OF THE ATLANTEAN WORLD CATASTROPHE

As Earth turned on its axis, the proto-Encke comet, Oljato, bombarded everything from above the Equator to below the Arctic

Circle, depending on the comet's inclining angle to Earth. Passing over the Caribbean, it fired down an object one mile across. Moving a hundred times the velocity of a 9mm bullet, the asteroid plunged through the water and exploded with a force equal to one million megatons, excavating a 900-foot-deep crater on the seafloor. The resulting 1,000-foot-tall wall of water swept inland as far as Alabama, killing every living thing in its path. The explosion set off volcanoes from the Antilles to El Salvador.

Over North America, the comet let loose a barrage that created a nuclear bomb–like event in the Ohio Valley and triggered a hellish series of volcanic outbursts in Washington, Oregon, and Wyoming. Cosmic bombs falling across the Pacific Ocean raised roaring walls of water that obliterated whole island populations. In the Hawaiian Islands of Lanai, Maui, Molokai, and Oahu, deposits of unconsolidated coral were placed nearly a thousand feet above sea level by a monstrous wall of water. Tsunamis, waves set in motion by submarine earthquakes, never begin to approach the thousand-foot-high swell that was necessary to wash over the Hawaiian Islands. Only a wave caused by the plunge of a large meteorite or asteroid could have attained such enormous proportions.

Approaching Asia, Oljato caused volcanic and seismic devastation throughout Japan and eastern Russia. The face of China was obscured by catastrophic storms of corrosive ash, as atomspheric nitrogen and oxygen combined with nitric acid released by the relentless impacts of celestial debris thousands of miles away. India and the Middle East were tormented with geologic violence from the merciless onslaught high overhead.

But Europe and the Near East, the cradles of Western civilization, were especially hard hit by Oljato. As it passed over Anatolia, the moment of "the Fire from Heaven" had arrived. A veritable deluge of flame descended in waves of thunder from out of the sky. Hattusas, capital of the mighty Hittite Empire, erupted in a fiery holocaust. Hundreds of cities and towns with hundreds of thousands of their residents all across Asia Minor were abruptly incinerated. Burned in great flashes of flame were Palestinian commercial centers and Syrian fortresses. Unrelenting earthquakes smashed Pharaoh's monumental temples to smoking ruins, while the divine wrath threatened Lower Egypt with death by fire. Libya, her once-fertile neighbor, was seared to a barren desert.

Across the Aegean Sea, the people of Crete fled into the high mountains to escape the flaming, quaking doom of their cities and towns below. In mainland Greece, the light of civilization went out, replaced by a monstrous glow as hundreds of her settlements, citadels, palaces, and temples were girdled in flames. Conflagrations in coastal cities and harbors were quenched by overpowering floods that were scarcely less devastating. The same sea that nourished the Greeks for a thousand years had become their murderer.

Several large rivers which converge in the Hungarian Plain suddenly spilled over their banks to innundate this vast area of low-lying land. The entire region was covered with a ferocious flood that wiped out several prosperous Bronze Age cultures. It had come, in the words of Swedish archaeologist Adolf Aberg to "an unexpected end, after which the country is without any discoverable sign of occupation and seems deserted."[53]

Europe's largest fire consumed the Black Forest down to the Swiss Alps. An ash-fall covered Britain, killing the majority of all living things there.

The worst was yet to come. Leaving the continent in flames, Oljato dispatched a salvo of cosmic bombs hurtling toward the ocean at twenty-thousand miles per hour. As each broke the sound barrier, they filled the air with reverberating thunder. At least one meteorite hit the geologically sensitive Mid-Atlantic Ridge. It awoke like the enraged Midgaard Serpent of Norse myth. Sea quakes caused five-hundred-foot tsunamis crashing at 150 miles per hour across the face of the deep. Volcanoes roared in furious choruses of streaming magma and piling cloudbanks of ash from Ascension and

Candlemas Islands in the South Atlantic to Iceland's Hekla in the North. The Canary Islands of Gran Canaria, Fuerteventura, and Lanzarote exploded with flames as the nearby coast of North Africa writhed in seismic anguish.

Stabbing like sharp pain through a raw nerve, geologic violence shot along the length of the Mid-Atlantic Ridge and across the fault boundary on which Atlantis was situated. A trembler moving close to the speed of sound struck the submarine foundations of Atlas, detonating the sacred mountain. Unable to vent the sudden force of so much erupting magma, one wall of the volcano blasted out laterally. An inconceivable wall of the sea rushed into the gaping wound, where water and fire combined to destroy the entire island. The opulent, powerful, corrupt capital, with most of its screaming inhabitants, sank to the bottom of the ocean it had dominated for centuries—the same ocean to which it had given its own name.

THE GREAT SERPENT MOUND

As Oljato rained down worldwide destruction, earthly survivors preserved the experience in myth. A cometary near-miss would have terrified human observers. It would have been dramatic enough to make an indelible impression in the traditions of any population that witnessed and survived such a cataclysm. Due to its great size, close proximity, and intensity, Encke-Oljato would have been visible twenty-four hours a day, a horrifying sight, bright enough after sunset to disperse the dark with an unrelieved, eerie twilight.

But what other evidence exists to show that some cosmic event was really the cause for the catastrophe? Most of the meteors were lost at sea; those that did hit land have since eroded. Of the few remaining traces, three bear awesome testimony to the worst natural disaster in the history of civilization. Twenty tons of meteorite are on display at the New York City Museum. Its companion piece may be found in Copenhagen, Denmark. Both originally belonged to a two-hundred-ton nickel-iron object that fell onto Cape York, off the northwest coast of Greenland, sometime before 1000 B.C.E. The gigantic wave it undoubtedly produced was on a par of havoc with the celestial cataclysm that aimed Cape York's meteorite and its annihilating companions at our planet.

Another impact site, and a bizarre example, is one of the foremost archaeological parks in North America. Located near Locust Grove in the Ohio Valley, the extraordinary Great Serpent Mound is a 1,254-foot-long earthen effigy of a monstrous snake writhing in seven humps across a high, wooded ridge. It disgorges an egg from its gaping jaws. Five feet high, with an average width of twenty feet, its tail ends in a large spiral. Although clearly discernable at ground level and even better from a forty-foot-tall observation tower provided by the local museum, the effigy may be fully appreciated from the air, two or three hundred feet above the ground. From any point of view, however, its perfect proportions confirm the technical and artistic sophistication of its creators.

Whoever they were, they thoroughly cleaned up after themselves. No trace of tools, implements, or weapons of any kind have been excavated in the mound's vicinity. The construction involved careful planning. Flat river stones were selected for size and uniformity, and lumps of clay were placed along the ground to form a serpentine pattern. Then basketfuls of soil were piled over the pattern and sculpted into shape. Not only does the effigy imply the cooperation of an organized labor force with artistic and engineering genius, but a standard system of measurement and orientation. In the early 1990s, archaeo-astronomers determined that the serpent's humps are aligned with various significant celestial phenomena, including solstice sunrises. The site was never inhabited, so it must have served instead as a ceremonial center.

The Great Serpent Mound is unique for more than the outstanding perfection of its construction. It sits atop a singular formation. Within a 4-mile-diameter circle, the bedrock has enormous cracks. Some of the resulting blocks were forced steeply downward, others sharply upward. Early investigators concluded this feature was created by the upward pressure of a volcanic force from below that never quite reached the surface, hence, it is described as "crypto-volcanic." It has since been concluded that only impact of an object approximately two hundred feet in diameter, traveling at some forty-five thousand miles per hour, could have produced the cracks and blocks similar to the features found at Arizona's Meteor Crater. In view of the Great Serpent Mound's location atop the ridge of a major astrobleme, it is apparent that this effigy memorializes the grand cosmic event responsible for its crater. The celestial orientation of the seven humps underscores a celestial connection.

The Mandan Indians, the earliest people known to have resided in the vicinity of the mound, said it was built by a race that preceded them. They were powerful, even fearsome, descendants from survivors of a "tidal flood" in the Gulf of Mexico.[54] The Mandan were not only forbidden to visit the Great Serpent Mound; they were not even allowed to look in its direction. Eventually, the Mandan found conditions under the domineering mound-builders unbearable and migrated west to the Missouri River. What is particularly remarkable about their memories of the Serpent Mound is that the Mandan, of all the Plains tribes, preserved the most elaborate ceremony commemorating the Great Flood. Known as the Okipa, it was witnessed by George Catlin, portrait artist and explorer of the early American West. Documenting the Okipa in words and paint, he described how an entire Mandan village reenacted the drama of the Deluge. The Indians daubed themselves with dyes made from plant fibers to impersonate the red-headed, white-faced survivors who arrived in a large, wooden ark. A re-creation of this vessel itself was placed at the center of the village.[55]

The egg and serpent symbols do not appear in the tribal cultures of any other Plains Indian nation, although several tribes in the southwest, such as the Hopi, practiced ophiolatreia, snake idolatry.[56] The Hopi version of the Great Serpent Mound contains many Atlantean elements. They claim their ancestors were raised by a related tribe, the Snake Clan, who escaped the destruction of their island homeland far out into the Eastern Ocean. Remembered as "the Third Emergence," the Snake Clan's migration was made possible through the leadership of Pahana, the "White Brother." He piled people and animals into fleets of large reed boats, which floated them to a new life in America. Soon after landing on the East Coast, they set up a shrine to the serpent-god in gratitude for their survival from the catastrophe. The serpent was, after all, the spirit of regeneration, and they had escaped the violent destruction of their homeland.

Migrating westward, they passed into the Ohio Valley, where they raised the Great Serpent Mound, naming it Tokchii, the Guardian of the East, commemorating the direction from which they fled the Deluge. Descendants of the Snake Clan still wear seashells to memorialize their oceanic origins.[57] It is remarkable that the Hopi should claim descent from the Snake Clan, survivors from a lost island in the Atlantic Ocean and designers of the mound representing a serpent disgorging an egg. The Greeks, separated from the Hopi by half a world and thousands of years, recorded that their ancestors were the Ophites, a Serpent People, from the Western Sea, whose emblem was a snake with an egg at its mouth.[58]

THE SCOTTISH SERPENT MOUND

Ohio's Great Serpent Mound has a material counterpart in, of all places, Scotland. Found on the shore of Loch Nell, near the coastal town of Oban, it shows a snake disgorging an egg from its jaws, even though it is badly eroded. The Scottish serpent is about one hundred feet long and has three humps. But its tail, like that of the Ohio structure, ends in a spiral. The egglike formation of the Loch Nell effigy is a stone cairn, an apparent difference from the earthen oval of the Ohio mound. However, "a small circular elevation of large stones much burned once existed in its [the Ohio effigy's] centre, but they have been thrown down and scattered by some ignorant visitor under the pervading impression probably that gold was hidden beneath them."[59] The stones of the Scottish cairn were also used as an altar and burned material (earth, charred nutshells, and bones) have been uncovered.

The Mandan's Okipa ceremony and Hopi traditions of the Snake Clan shed light on the Ohio geoglyph. But of its Loch Nell brother local folklore is silent. The precise location of the Scottish serpent is Glen Feochan, in western Scotland, in the hamlet of Dalnaneun, or Place of Birds, and seagulls do indeed still flock there in large numbers. A few miles inland from the Hebridean coast, close to the shores of tranquil Loch Nell, the bioglyph squirms across a low hill in view of the triple-cone of Mount Ben Cruachan.

The effigy has long inspired regional awe. George Blackie, a nineteenth-century poet of some renown, wrote, "Why lies the mighty serpent here, let him who knoweth tell; with its head to the land and its huge tail near the shore of fair Loch Nell."[60]

Perhaps a hundred yards from the mound is a small, subterranean temple of circular stones. Dalnaneun had been continuously occupied from early Neolithic times into the Late Bronze Age, and was famous throughout prehistoric Argyllshire for its cultic significance, according to findings preserved at Oban's Archaeological Museum. It is estimated that the Ohio figure was constructed around 1200 B.C.E. Physical resemblance between the American and Scottish serpents and their similar ages tend to confirm an Atlantean identity for both structures. Just as the Locust Grove geoglyph appears to represent the meteoric cataclysm that caused the "crypto-volcanic" landscape on which it lies, the Scottish serpent mound suggests its immediate environment. The surrounding region was once alive with geologic violence, visible in the massive lava flows still very much apparent for miles around Oban, particularly the extensive shoreline of petrified magma. It seems that these two remarkably similar effigies, separated by the Atlantic Ocean but united in time, symbolically portray a natural catastrophe so enormous it simultaneously impacted both continents.

Comets are traditionally represented as dragons or serpents, from the Bible to Aztec myth. Their sinuous motion across the sky bears an obvious likeness to the snake. The Ohio serpent's size, together with the "egg" being spat from its mouth, strongly suggests that its creators intended to portray a comet ejecting the meteorite that excavated the crater in which the effigy is located. The builders of the Great Serpent Mound must have witnessed the meteor fall. The earthwork has been dated to 1000 B.C.E., plus or minus 200 years, and was, therefore, caused by the "fire from heaven" that decimated Earth.

A sky-serpent spitting a meteoritic oval can be found beyond the Ohio Valley and Scotland. Classical Greeks told of their Atlantean predecessors, calling them Pelasgians, the same Sea Peoples documented by Pharaoh Ramses III's scribes at his Victory Temple in West Thebes. The Pelasgians were said to have emerged from the Cosmic Egg disgorged "from the fangs of Ophion."[61]

The oldest creation myth in Greece held that Ophion (Serpent) was swimming alone in the primeval sea before the beginning of time when Boreas, god of the north wind, accidentally dropped a seed into the waters. Ophion swallowed it and soon after the Cosmic Egg sprang from his mouth. It seems clear that this story contains the same ideas implicit in the Great Serpent Mound, perched on the western rim of an astrobleme. The "seed" accidentally dropped by Boreas, personification of tumult in the sky, was the meteorite that fell into the ocean, triggering the geologic upheavals from which the Atlantean Sea Peoples emerged as survivors and culture bearers.

SIBERIAN FIREBALL

Encke-Oljato's capability to bring about an earthwide cataclysm thirty-two hundred years ago was verified early in the past century. Since its ancient onslaught, the old comet has lost almost, but not

all, of its destructive powers. Six years before the man-made catastrophe of World War I, an object detonated five miles above Yuzhnoya
Boloto, a southern swamp in the central Siberian plateau. Its explosive force equaled a twelve-megaton blast and charred twelve hundred square miles of forest, incinerating fifteen hundred deer thirty
miles from its flash point and setting people on fire sixty miles
away. Some four to five hundred feet in diameter, the Siberian
object released as much energy as the 1980 Mount Saint Helens
eruption. The causes of what has since come to be known as the
Tunguska Event were many and various, from a huge chunk of
cosmic ice (shades of Martin Hoerbiger, as opined by Carl Sagan, of
all people!) to the crash of an alien spaceship. Trees affected by the
blast were closely examined eighty years after the mysterious explosion established that an asteroid had been the culprit.[62]

The Beta Taurid meteorites, both asteroids and numerous smaller
pieces of debris brush our planet each summer between June 24 and
July 6. The amount of material falling into Earth's atmosphere peaks
on June 30, the same date that the Tunguska Event occurred in
1908. It is clear, then, that this is still a dangerous comet, even in its
advanced age. What it was capable of producing in its prime, thirty-
two centuries ago, beggars the imagination.

SIX

When Was Atlantis Destroyed?

For you, you are divine, and you have the gifts of memory
and story. But only the faintest echo of the
great tale has come down to me.
Virgil, The Aeneid, *Book VII*

Atlantis is most often located on a continent that suddenly sank to the bottom of the Atlantic Ocean 11,600 years ago. Centuries of cultural development must have preceded such an event, since the Atlanteans were alleged to have attained high levels of civilization before their demise. Consequently, their society could have arisen in the eleventh millennium B.C.E. or even earlier.

Unfortunately for the advocates of a continental Atlantis, their position has been progressively eroded by rapidly evolving underwater technology that has provided oceanographers with an expanding view of the world beneath the waves. There is no evidence for anything even remotely resembling a true continent in the mid-Atlantic. A very large island, approaching the size of modern Portugal, may have existed there as recently as only two or three million years ago. But few Atlantologists suggest that anything approaching a civilized society was present then. While more are beginning to admit Atlantis could have been on an island, others still believe in a lost continent that has not yet found.

It is difficult to imagine how a whole continent could continue to elude the extensive explorations and satellite mapping of the ocean bottom undertaken by highly trained investigators of a dozen nations since the late 1940s. A compilation of these findings was published in 1995 by Scripps Institution of Oceanography.[1] These maps show nothing to suggest a sunken continent in the Atlantic. They reveal that there was no continent to lose—the tectonic mechanisms of our planet do not allow for a large landmass to have existed and then sunk when and where its proponents claim it did.

While many Atlantologists are willing to downgrade Atlantis's setting from a continent to an island, they still hold on to a mid-tenth millennium B.C.E. date for its destruction. This, by implication, places the date for its civilization's establishment even earlier, almost certainly more than twelve thousand years ago. The humans who lived in Upper Paleolithic, or the Old Stone Age, belonged to the Magdalenian culture and were nomadic hunters. They sheltered in caves in winter and in tents during summer.

Occasionally, these nomadic groups came together in temporary riverside villages of as many as six hundred inhabitants.[2] The Magdalenians made stone tools and fit them into bone or antler handles. They wore animal skins and shell necklaces. Their outstanding achievement was the creation of polychrome cave paintings that portrayed hunting scenes. Although animals were depicted with masterful realism, representations of humans never advanced beyond stick figures. The best examples of this Stone Age art are found in the wall paintings of Lascaux, France, and Altamira, Spain. Paleolithic artists also fashioned small cult objects, stylized statuettes of faceless women with an emphasis on sexuality and fertility. These Venus figurines appear to have signified an attempt by hunters to gain some measure of control over the forces of nature.[3]

Thus, the level of culture reached in the late Upper Paleolithic was generally similar to that attained by the Plains Indians of North America prior to the sixteenth-century arrival of Europeans. The Magdalenians built no cities, crossed no large bodies of water, created no monumental statues, possessed no written language, did not work in metals, knew nothing of agriculture or irrigation. Although they made use of fire from natural sources and may even have understood something about the properties of flint, they had no fire-starting tools; the fire-drill stick would not be invented for another two thousand years.

Technologically, they were very primitive compared to the civilized Atlanteans of the *Dialogues*. While culturally interesting, the Magdelanians cannot be said to have created anything approaching civilization, yet they did represent the high point of human achievement at that time. Even so, these are not Plato's seafaring, empire-building Atlanteans. Items such as eyed needles and the bow and arrow were new innovations. The Atlanteans' chariots, even horse-drawn carts, were many thousands of years away. There were no ships, no harbors or canals. The Atlantis described by Plato is an identifiably Bronze Age city, not an Old Stone Age site.

ATLANTIS FANTASTIC

Upper Paleolithic humans doubtless crossed the still-standing land bridges from present-day Portugal to the almost-island of Atlas. But the conditions they encountered there did not match those described in the *Kritias*, which told of a temperate, almost balmy climate that allowed for year-round farming. The Fourth (Wuerm) Glacial Period, a time of low sunlight and intense, dry cold, held sway eleven thousand years ago. Little but scrub brush could take root in the frozen ground.

If one believes that the civilization of Atlantis existed during the Old Stone Age, one must also accept that it made absolutely no impact on either European or African cultures for the centuries in which it was said to have dominated parts of both continents. An Upper Paleolithic Atlantis would have stood so far above all other human societies that it had to have been totally removed from the context of the times in which it supposedly flourished. Envisioning such an advanced society in the Late Stone Age is akin to imagining Noah riding out the Flood in the Queen Elizabeth II. There is no evidence from Magdalenian times that implies a contemporary Atlantis. So far as the archaeological and anthropological records are concerned, the island and its civilization were invisible. It does not seem logical that an abundance of artifacts from small, scattered populations of Paleolithic hunters have a better chance of surviving into our time than a single stick from a civilization that allegedly flourished for centuries or millennia over much of Earth.

Placing Atlantis in the Paleolithic wreaks complete havoc with Plato's narrative. The Saite archives, which he said contained the original account, were surely not eight thousand years old. As Caroli points out,

> Researchers who insist on the literal dates for Atlantis must show evidence that there was not only writing twelve thousand years ago, but that it was known in Egypt and could still be read coherently in Classical times. There is no evidence for recognizable writing of any kind in the Nile Valley prior to the late fourth or early third millennium b.c. To accept Plato's literal dates we must believe that writing existed there for five to seven thousand years without leaving a single trace, and that the Egyptians of circa 570 to 385 B.C. still possessed these ancient archives, which they could read perfectly, then translate them with no mistakes into Greek.
>
> Granted, the educated priests of Sais, where Solon and/or Plato heard the story of Atlantis, were the Egyptians most likely to have been able to translate ancient documents into foreign languages. But the notion that eight-thousand-year-old records survived intact and were still readily translatable stretches credulity far beyond the breaking point.[4]

The very mention of readable, written records in Plato's discussion of Atlantis limits the timing of his subject to the late fourth millennium B.C.E. at the earliest. The oldest Egyptian king-lists extend to Hor-Aha and Scorpion, rulers who immediately preceded Menes or Narmer, the first pharaoh to rule over a united kingdom in 3100 B.C.E. Records possibly, if not probably, went back several centuries earlier, perhaps to the institution of the first nomes, or governorships in the Nile Valley, beginning around 3500 B.C.E. There are surviving written references to the *Smsu-Hor*, "Followers of Horus," and the *Mesentiu*, "Harpooners," culture bearers who founded Egyptian civilization.

If conditions in western Europe were bleak during the Late Old Stone Age when some researchers argue Atlantis flourished, the situation in the eastern Mediterranean was worse. "Between circa 9600 B.C. and perhaps 5600 or 5200 B.C.," according to Caroli, "Egyptian 'history' is almost blank. The Aegean was similarly empty. There is virtually no evidence Greece was even inhabited in the mid-tenth millennium B.C., let alone capable of fighting a major war."[5] In other words, the period assigned by Plato for the Atlantean war against Athens and Egypt occurred thousands of years before the Greek city was built and the Nile Valley civilized.

A MISTAKE IN TRANSLATION

A continental, Stone Age Atlantis is self-invalidating. The city Plato so meticulously describes in the *Kritias* could have never existed in Upper Paleolithic times. Both the climate conditions and the Magdelenians' relatively low cultural level render Plato's Atlantis an anomaly.

The buildings found in Plato's Atlantis are, however, typical of Bronze Age palatial construction found in Mycenaean Greece, Tyre, or Troy. Atlantis differed from these locations in that it appears to have been superimposed on (or grown up from) an earlier Neolithic, or New Stone Age concentric settlement typical of Atlantic sites such as the Canary Islands (Gran Canaria), coastal Morocco (Zora), Britain (Stonehenge), and Ireland (New Grange). These circular stone ruins date from the late fourth millennium B.C.E. Atlantis became a thoroughly Bronze Age civilization, according to Plato's description. And it is only within the context of the period from 3000 to 1200 B.C. in which it may be found.

Researchers have long been troubled by the glaring disparity in Plato's account—realistic details and unrealistic dates. In the early 1950s, Immanuel Velikovsky decided, "There is one too many zeroes here. We do not know of any vestiges of human culture, aside from that of the Neolithic age, nor of any navigating nation, nine thousand years before Solon."[6] At about the same time, L. Taylor Hansen, in her monumental book, *The Ancient Atlantic*, confessed her confusion: "We have complications in what we have learned. There are either two dates for the deluge or there were two catastrophes."[7]

The source for a twelve-thousand-year-old Atlantis is none other than Plato himself. He assures us on several occasions in the *Dialogues* that his narrated events took place nine millennia earlier. According to the chronology he establishes in the *Timaeus* and *Kritias*, Athens was founded at the same time war broke out with Atlantis, nine thousand years before Solon's time, which was about 550 B.C.E. An Athens of that great age is out of the question. No one, not even the Atlanteans, were capable of mounting sea-borne invasions at that time. Clearly, there is something wrong with the figures Plato uses.

The Minoan revisionists thought so too, and argued that he made a mistake in translation. Plato or possibly Solon accidentally added a zero when translating from Egyptian into Greek, as Velikovski suggested. By simply dividing the *Dialogues'* nine thousand years by ten, the Athenian war with Atlantis takes place in 1470 B.C.E., a desirable result for anyone who wanted to believe that the Minoan and Atlantean empires were identical.[8] Until the early 1990s this date was generally accepted for Thera's eruption and collapse into

calendar, as the pharaohs had millennia before.[9] Closer to the period in question, Eudoxus of Cnidos, one of the earliest pioneers in astronomy, who studied in Egypt, described how his teachers, all priests of various temples, employed a lunar calendar.[10] Plutarch, the Greek historian of the second century C.E., wrote in *Lives*, "The Egyptian year at first, they say, was of one month. They have the credit of being a more ancient nation of any, and reckon in their genealogies a prodigious number of years, containing months, that is, as years."[11] Herodotus, Manetho, and Diodorus Siculus wrote that the Egyptians meant "month/lunation" when they spoke of "years."[12]

Bailey writes, "An ancient Semitic use of the word 'year' was 'month' when the moon had been man's prehistoric time-keeper, and his year meant not a solar cycle but a lunar cycle."[13] A cogent example is found in the allegorical tale of the Egyptian Osiris, whose reign of twenty-eight "years" actually signified the twenty-eight days in the lunar month. Bailey cites the case of Methuselah, who according to the Old Testament, died at 969 years of age; in lunar years, he would have lived into his eighties. Doubtless, the priests in charge at the temple where the carved or painted columns that recounted the story of Atlantis were kept likewise used a lunar calendar. The lunar calendar was also known in Greece, so the priest who made the translation for Solon may have assumed his guest understood that he was speaking in terms of lunar, not solar years.

According to the astronomers Clube and Napier, "There is evidence that the Egyptians at this time (500 B.C.) were considered by the Greeks to be counting in months rather than years, though it is possible also that the Greeks did not fully understand the Egyptian reckoning of time based on extant priest-lists going back to the first dynasty (around 3000 B.C.). Probably, therefore, the Egyptian time-scale should be reduced by a factor of twelve or ten, although the exact figure remains unknown. . . . Thus the drowning of Atlantis seems to relate to events observed in the sky at or before 1200 B.C., the apparent inversion in the extended zodiacal sea, events during which mankind also suffered at the hands of invading hordes from the zodiacal band. The Atlantis story deals thus with a seemingly visible assault from the cosmos, whose structure was broadly known . . ."[14]

The destruction of Atlantis has also been dated to 1200 B.C.E. by the renowned astronomer Professor Harold A. T. Reiche.[15] Other noted researchers who separately arrived at the same date include Jurgen Spanuth, James Bailey, Eberhard Zangerer, Henriette Mertz, and Comyns Beaumont.

THE ATLANTIS CATASTROPHE, 1240 TO 1159 B.C.E.

During the dark ages that befell Greece around 1200 B.C.E., no single calendar was in universal service, and it was not until after 500 B.C.E. (following Solon's death) that the solar calendar was adopted as standard. Manetho, a third century b.c. Egyptian historian from whom modern Egyptologists compile their chronological histories, explained that his ancestors thought in terms of lunar years. He lived during Ptolomaic times, when Greek culture dominated Egypt and most of the old institutions were replaced with Hellenic ones, including the solar calendar. "The year I take, however, to be a lunar one," Manetho said, "consisting, that is, of thirty days. What we now call a 'month,' the Egyptians used formerly to style a year. The total [of some previous groups of kings he was describing] amounts to eleven thousand years. These, however, being lunar periods, or months."[16]

The same applies to Plato's dates. If his "nine thousand years ago" date is converted into the lunar years used by the priests who preserved the Atlantis account, the actual date for the Atlantean war and destruction begins in the year 1250 B.C.E. This is not a contrived revision to make the evidence fit some preconceived theory. "Ironically," Caroli points out, "even 'traditional' chronology supports a circa 1200 B.C. date, despite Plato himself. He set the end of the Atlanto-Athenian War just prior to the ascent to power of Theseus. Legend said he died within no more than a decade of the Trojan War after occupying the throne for a long time. His reign would have begun around 1220 to 1250 B.C."[17]

Additional evidence supports this time line. The precessional age of the Pleiades began around 2200 B.C.E. and came to a conclusion in 1100 B.C.E. It seems likely that this precession coincided with the menacing approach of Encke-Oljato in the late third millennium B.C.E. and culminated during the catastrophe that climaxed in the twelfth century B.C.E. In human myth and ceremonies around the world, the Pleiades were related to catastrophic floods or natural disasters of transforming magnitudes. The constellation undoubtedly received its name sometime after those occurrences, connecting its stars in myth to Atlantis as "Atlantides," or "Atlantises."

Of course, the most important correlation to the 1250 B.C.E. date in Plato's account is the planetwide holocaust that did indeed begin just then. As Velikovski concluded, "At the time when Atlantis perished in the ocean, the people of Greece were destroyed: the catastrophe was ubiquitous."[18] The very existence of that catastrophe is alone sufficient to place the Atlantean flood within the exact context of Plato's documented history. But its mid-thirteenth century B.C.E. date is more than confirmed by human events around the world. A single year sometime near 1200 B.C.E. was the most important date in the history of civilization, a sharp delineation of universal, often fundamental change not experienced since.

In Egypt, Ramses III recorded the destruction of Atlantis in 1198 B.C.E. on the walls of the Victory Temple he erected to celebrate his defeat of the Sea Peoples. But he was also the last of the great pharaohs, and, with his assassination, Egypt went into a decline from which it would never recover. Around 1200 B.C.E. the entire Near Eastern Bronze Age came to a stop at the same time the gigantic copper mines of Michigan's Upper Peninsula were abandoned with such alacrity it appeared as though the miners, who left their tools and cribs in place, would return to their work the next day.

At the same time the Hittite Empire, which dominated Asia

Minor, vanished, as did all the great cities of the Levant. Assyria went into decline. Troy fell. Mycenaean Greek civilization was overthrown. An enormous migration of Celts was driven through France and Belgian from their wooded homeland in southern Germany, its forests transformed into an ocean of fire. In Britain, development on Stonehenge suddenly ceased. The Balearics, along with Sardinia, Corsica, Majorca, and many other Mediterranean islands were invaded by the Sword People, Ramses III's Atlantean "Sea People." As they battled across North Africa, they were known as the Garamantes.

Serpent mounds symbolizing the cataclysm were simultaneously raised in the Ohio Valley and near the shores of Loch Nell. Poverty Point arose in the northeast corner of Louisiana. The oldest city in North America, it is a reproduction of Atlantis itself, built of concentric rings of alternating land and water, intersected by canals. Mesoamerican civilization suddenly went into high gear with the rise of the Olmecs. The New Fire Ceremony, maintained by the Olmecs' Aztec descendants, began in 1197 B.C.E. (Counting back from the last known Fire Ceremony in 1507, using the Aztecs' seven- and six-year cycles of the 52-year periods they employed at 364 and 312 years, respectively, we arrive at a date just a single year different from Ramses III's date for the destruction of Atlantis.) In South America, the seminal Andean Sechin-Chavin Culture, which featured monumental building styles similar to those found in Morocco (Lixus) and Egypt, came into existence. The Shang, China's oldest dynasty and one of immense power and wealth, suddenly collapsed under the deluge of ash-storms that ravaged the land at the zenith of a 644-year reign. All of these huge, transforming changes occurred within a few years of 1200 B.C.E.

The catastrophe wrought by Encke-Oljato spread over an eighty-year period. It began with the fall of Troy in 1240 B.C.E., peaked during the destruction of Atlantis in 1198 B.C.E., and culminated in 1159 B.C.E. with the massive eruption of a volcano in the North

Atlantic, Hekla. The opening shot of the cataclysm appears briefly in the Aeneid (Book 2: 680–698), when Aeneas gathers his family to escape the burning Trojan capital. As they were about to leave, the long, fine hair of his son began to stand out from the boy's head, around which "a light tongue of flame seemed to shed a gleam and, harmless to its touch, lick the soft locks." Hardly had this strange illumination settled on little Iulus, "when, with a sudden thunder, a star shot from out of heaven trailing a fiery tail amid a flood of light. We saw it flame over the palace and crash into the forest of Mount Ida. There was everywhere the reek of scorched sulphur."[19]

The incident, regarded as a portent confirming Troy's doom, was otherwise a very minor incident in Virgil's epic. It nonetheless appears to have actually happened. Meteorites sometimes break the sound barrier, creating sonic booms, and are known on occasion to generate static electricity (which could have caused Iulus' hair to stand and glow) during low-altitude passes, particularly those mete-ors that survive their plunge through the atmosphere to impact the earth. It seems remarkable that a first-century Roman would have known about such phenomena, unless he had at his disposal a report describing real events. More cogent to this investigation, the mere mention of a meteoric occurrence at the same moment Encke-Oljato was raining down its fiery destruction on Anatolia indicates that the incident very probably took place.

Atlantis was destroyed within a very few years before or after 1200 B.C.E. The wall texts at Ramses III's Victory Temple are the only known source to specify a date. Unfortunately, modern Egyptologists cannot agree on a precise dynastic chronology, and they still debate the year of Ramses' coronation (the same year the destruction oc-curred), placing it from 1198 to 1171 B.C.E. Given supporting evi-dence from the many other sources cited, it appears that the earlier date is the more likely. The abundance of material (astronomical data in conjunction with persistent cultural traditions) also allows the month and even the last day of Atlantis to be determined.

BULL'S BLOOD FOR HUMAN BLOOD

As stated earlier, two Taurid meteor showers accompany the comet Encke and appear near our planet at two different times of the year. The summer shower reaches the height of its intensity on June 30, the same day an asteroid exploded over Siberia in 1908. The second shower takes place in fall, from November 3 through the 15. At the time Atlantis was destroyed, the length of this Alpha shower was longer, lasting from late October into early November. The Taurid meteors appear to come from a small area in the constellation of Taurus the Bull, hence the name.

In the *Kritias*, Plato describes an important, unusual animal sacrifice undertaken by the imperial high priests of Atlantis.[20] Assembling every fifth and sixth year, regents from the ten related realms, who were also the high prists of Atlantean religion, met in the Temple of Poseidon, located at the very center of Atlantis. They surrounded a pillar gleaming with orichalcum, the brilliant, high-grade copper that was the basis of Atlantean prosperity. On this pillar the Laws of Poseidon were inscribed by the island's first kings. In the presence of this sacred object, the regents debated national and legal matters. Before instituting new policies or passing judgments, they prayed to Poseidon for assistance in securing a proper sacrifice, then repaired to an adjacent corral where they engaged in a ritual hunt among the fine bulls bred for this purpose. (The bull was Poseidon's sacred animal.)

Using only clubs and nooses in order to commemorate their ancestors who hunted with primitive means, they caught one of the great beasts, dragged it back inside the temple, and cut its throat atop the orichalcum pillar, allowing the blood to flow over the inscribed laws. The carcass was then consecrated in fire, while a bowl of wine was mixed with a clot of bull's blood. The pillar and general premises cleansed, each of the ten priestly kings drew a golden cupful of wine from the bowl and poured a libation into the fire, swearing an oath to give judgment in accordance with the venerable, eternal principles enumerated on the pillar.

In the zodiac, said to have been founded by Atlas, the bull is Taurus, so perhaps there was some connection between this ritual sacrifice and the Taurid meteor stream that menaced the Earth for centuries before the great cataclysm. Encke, with its biannual showers of at least occasional destructiveness, would have been observed in the sky by a fearful humanity as a major, growing object long before the comet became deadly in the thirteenth century B.C.E. The Atlanteans may have sought to avert an impending natural catastrophe through the supernatural influence of sympathetic magic. By slaughtering, then giving over to consecrating flames the living symbol of the constellation threatening them with fire, they hoped to avoid its dangerous consequences, which must have appeared more apparent each time the comet swept closer to Earth and its Taurid showers brought an increasing number of meteors.

The so-called scored lines of the Great Pyramid at Giza aligned with the star Alkyone in the Taurus constellation at noon of the spring equinox in 2141 B.C.E. It is perhaps not coincidental that the last Age of Taurus lasted from 4500 to 2300 B.C.E. The former year is a possible candidate for the establishment of Atlantis. Astronomers believe the Taurid meteors, originally belonging to a single stream, diverged into two different showers circa 2700 B.C.E. after a collision with a large body while Encke was in Jupiter's space. The split may not have been noticeable from Earth until some time after that encounter.

Twenty five years before Clube and Napier published these findings about the Taurid meteor showers, mythologists Gertrude and James Jobes concluded, relying on the internal evidence of a Cherokee flood legend, that "the fall of one star may be connected with a Deluge story; possibly the fall of a Taurid meteor is echoed here."[21]

THE DAY OF THE DEAD

While the Beta, or summer, Taurid meteor stream was equally capable of bringing about the destruction of Atlantis, there are significant reasons to assign that event to the fall shower. The Day of the Dead, celebrated around the world, takes place during the autumnal meteor shower. The Celtic Samhain was a fire festival during which the spirits of the deceased returned to Earth from October 30 to November 4. Halloween, on October 31, is directly descended from Samhain. According to Caroli, "It was a time of year when the world of the dead was nearest that of the living, with cross-overs between the two planes. Several theorists believe Halloween and other, similar festivals memorialize ancient catastrophes."[22] Samhain was celebrated throughout the British Isles, where November was known as "the blood month." It was on such prehistoric traditions that the Roman Catholic All Souls' Day was instituted. It is celebrated on November 2 (November 3, if the second falls on a Sunday). Priests wear black vestments, and they say three requiem masses, because the office of the day is that of the dead.

In India, the Hindu Durga was a celebration for the dead held during the first days of November, referred to in an ancient Brahmin calendar at Trivalore as Kartica, the month of the Pleiades. An annual festival conducted during the first three days in November by Australian aborigines, who paint their bodies to resemble skeletons, is meant to honor the Pleiades. Throughout much of Polynesia, islanders traditionally pray for the spirits of the dead in early November, a practice already found in place by the first Christian missionaries.

The Days of Death celebrated in early November were among the most important Aztec festivals, and appear to have dated back into Maya or even Olmec times, in the thirteenth century B.C.E. As mentioned above, the Aztecs began their ceremonies with the heliacal rising of the Pleiades. Atemoztli, or Falling Waters, took place every November 16, when the end of the Fifth Sun or "Age," which had been brought about by a world flood, was commemorated. The Atlantean origin of this festival is affirmed by Tlaloc, the god who presided over it, portrayed in temple art as a bearded man bearing the cross of the sky on his shoulders, a Mesoamerican Atlas. Indeed, a variant of Tlaloc's name was Atlatoc. And more than a philiological correspondence existed between the Aztec Atemoztli and Atemet, the Egyptian goddess Hathor, in her guise as Queen of the Sea; sacred art depicted her wearing a fish-shaped crown, signifying the oceanic character of the goddess (in her guise as Sekhmet) who destroyed Netero, the Egyptian version of Atlantis.

The Maya throughout Yucatan and Peten hung small packets of cake on the branches of the sacred ceiba, especially where the tree was found standing among clearings in the forest or at crossroads. These offerings were made of the finest corn available and intended for the spirits of the dead, as indicated in their name, *hanal pixan*, "the food of the souls." The hanal pixan decorated this most sacred tree, a living memorial of the Great Flood, for the first three days of November. The Incas performed the Ayamarca, or carrying the corpse ceremony, every November 2. In so doing, they sought to establish a direct link between their deceased relatives and the Ayar, an ancestral people who perished in a great flood. Only a few were believed to have survived by escaping to South America, where they sired the Inca race.

The appearance of the Pleiades also signaled the beginning of ancient Hawaii's most important celebration, the annual Makahiki festival. It honored the arrival of a white-skinned, fair-haired "god" Lono who recently escaped a catastrophic deluge at Kealakekua in the Kona district on the Big Island of Hawaii. Lono was associated with all manner of cataclysmic celestial events, together with devastating earthquakes and floods.

At the western end of the Pacific, celebrants still participate in the Loi Krathong. On the night of the full moon (as the name of the festival indicates), in early November, they launch model boats carrying lit candles into the Gulf of Thailand. Designed to honor a sea goddess, the lotus-shaped little vessels made of banana leaves bear flowers, incense, and a coin to the spirits of their ancestors who perished in the Great Flood.

Ancient cultural links between Thailand and Japan are slim. Yet the Japanese have traditionally celebrated Bon, the Feast of the Dead, in a manner virtually identical to the Loi Krathong since prehistoric times. They set adrift fleets of burning lanterns to guide ancestral spirits across the sea. The ceremonies last for several consecutive nights, and include the Bon Odori, hypnotic outdoor dancing that often occurs in cemeteries. Bon was partially appropriated by Buddhism in its early struggle with native Shinto traditions, and so the annual date of its celebration was probably shifted to the middle of the seventh lunar month; today it takes place around August 14.

But another Japanese ceremony of the dead does indeed take place from the last week of October to the first days of November—the Tsunokiri, or ritual antler cutting, at the Kasuga Taisha shrine, in Nara. Sacred bucks are lassoed by a priest who carefully saws off their antlers, which, through their recurring velvet, signify life. Deer also symbolize the sun, so cutting their antlers implies the sun's loss of power, that is, darkness.

The relationship between early November and a day of the dead is not only a worldwide phenomenon but a very ancient one as well. The Assyrians conducted elaborate rituals on behalf of the dead during Arahsamna, their month that included the end of October and the beginning of November. It was then, they believed, that the sun god and the god of the Pleiades entered the land of the dead to rule the underworld. The ancient Persian new year began after November 1, known to them as Mordad, the month sacred to the Angel of Death. Mordad derived from the earlier Marduk of the

Babylonians. They revered him as the Lord of the Deep, who caused the Great Flood, and November belonged to him.

The Old Testament, in chapters 7 and 8 of Genesis, reports that the world-ravaging Deluge began on the seventeenth day of the Second Month, concluding on the twenty-seventh day of the Second Month the following year. In the ancient Hebrew calendar, the Second Month was known as Cheshvan, equivalent to the end of October and the start of November. Both the seventeenth and twenty-seventh days occur in early November. Nonbiblical Jewish tradition relates that Noah regarded the appearance of the Pleiades at dawn of the seventeenth of Cheshvan as an omen signifying the onset of the flood.

The Egyptian version of the Deluge happened during Aethyr, a name associated with the Greek Alkyone, because the month was regarded in the Nile Valley as "the shining season of the Pleiades." Aethyr, like the Assyrian Arashamna, corresponded to late October–early November. The name has several important connotations in Egyptian myth, proving its importance over a long period of time. In the story of Osiris, the man-god who, through the mysteries of Isis, his wife, achieved new life, was locked in a coffin that was thrown into the sea on the seventeenth day of Aethyr, which corresponds to November 2. It was henceforward known as a day of death and rebirth. Aethyr is a variant of Hathor, the goddess who, like Atlas, guarded the pillars that supported the sky. She also had her own flood myth.

The sun god, angry with humanity, commanded Hathor to punish the world. Her onslaught was catastrophic, and the other gods, fearing all humanity would perish, unloosed a deluge of beer. Drinking it up, she became too intoxicated to proceed. Her great festival was among the most popular in the Nile Valley, held for several days around November 1. As though foreshadowing Halloween, her small son, Ihi, was portrayed playing his sistrum, a rattlelike musical instrument, driving the evil spirits of the dead away from his mother's celebration.

She herself was sometimes depicted in sacred art as a cow walking away from a funeral mountain. The earliest name by which she was known appears to have been At-Hor, Mountain of Horus, an apparent philological relation with things Atlantean. Her funeral mountain is suggestive of death-dealing Mount Atlas and November associations with days of the dead. The lioness-headed goddess, Sekhmet, was used by the Egyptians to describe the fiery comet that brought about the destruction of Atlantis. She was actually Hathor in her vengeful mode—the two deities were aspects of the same goddess. The Pleiades are associated with her, too.[23]

Astronomy combines with historical myth to provide the precise date for the catastrophe. Encke's autumnal meteor shower very closely, if not exactly, corresponds to Day of the Dead festivals held around the world for thousands of years. Most of the festivals were and are celebrated on the first days of November, just when the Taurid stream reaches its intensity. Plato reported that the island of Atlas sank into the sea during "a single day and night." In other words, it might have occurred over the better part of a day and an equal portion of the night, bridging two days.

Writing in the nineteenth century, R. G. Haliburton wondered, "[The Day of the Dead] is now, as was formerly, observed at or near the beginning of November by the Peruvians, the Hindoos, the Pacific islanders, the people of the Tonga Islands, the Australians, the ancient Persians, the ancient Egyptians, and the northern nations of Europe, and continued for three days among the Japanese and the ancient Romans. This startling fact at once drew my attention to the question, How was this uniformity in the time of observance preserved, not only in far distant quarters of the globe, but also through that vast lapse of time since the Peruvian and the Indo-European first inherited this primeval festival from a common source?"[24] Haliburton's question is answered by evidence from the festivals themselves. Together they describe a natural cataclysm that killed many of their people, some of whom survived to replant civilization in other lands. The only event that measures up to this universal Festival of the Dead is the destruction of Atlantis.

Arriving at a precise time for the Atlantean catastrophe is by no means arbitrary. The date is corroborated by numerous, important, and complementary testimony. Applying the lunar calendar to Plato's account results in a period that perfectly coincides with a date Ramses III inscribed on the walls his Victory Temple to mark the sinking of the Sea Peoples' homeland. That date likewise parallels a global cataclysm at the time confirmed by geology, the contemporary size and proximity of Comet Encke, the sudden and simultaneous collapse of civilizations in one part of the planet and the rise of new ones in another, and a Day of the Dead celebrated around the world on a date corresponding to the height of the Taurid meteor shower. This evidence cross-references itself to produce a date at once credible and inescapable.

It appears, then, that the destruction of Atlantis took place around the first three days of November, 1198 B.C.E.

SEVEN

Life in Atlantis

Close to Ocean's margin and the setting sun—on the edge of
the world, where giant Atlas holds,
turning on his shoulders—the pole of
the universe inset with blazing stars—
The Aeneid, *Book IV*

As discussed in chapter 6, while Plato's physical description of Atlantis is real enough, his numerical values are exaggerated. More than just the timing of the events was distorted by failure on the part of his translator to correctly recalculate Egyptian numbers into Greek—the dimensions of the city and its public features given in the *Kritias* are all out of proportion.

Just how unrealistic its figures are has been graphically brought to light in *Atlantis Illustrated*, by H. R. Stahel.[1] His architectural drawings were sketched in faithful accordance to the specifics provided by the *Dialogues,* and consequently result in what is certainly the most believable picture of the capital's physical features. For the first time, investigators were presented with a very good notion of Atlantis' physical appearance. But Stahel's strict adherence to the text demonstrates Plato's utterly unacceptable dimensions. The elephants harnessed for construction are reduced to the size of crickets by comparison with the city's outsized architecture. Their human overseers are mere specks beside mountainous palaces and temples. The subterranean docks look like Zeppelin hangars, while Stahel's rendering of the encircling racetrack resembles a major airfield. Clearly, these oversized features would have been far beyond the capabilities or even the needs of any ancient civilization, no matter how powerful or opulent.

The Egyptians employed many units of measurement for architecture, geography, irrigation, navigation, sculpture, and so forth. The system they used to define the dimensions of Atlantis for Solon when he learned its story in the Temple of Neith, at Sais, was not identified. It appears that the system they applied to Atlantis was based on a unit of measurement known as the *aroura,* or "side." It was equivalent to 150 feet, or one-fourth of the stadium used by Plato in the *Kritias.* When the aroura is substituted for Plato's stadia, Atlantis instantly downsizes from overblown fantasy to proportions entirely commensurate with the late Bronze Age cities of Mycenae and Troy. For example, when Plato describes an Atlantean irrigation ditch as equivalent to an incredible 18.9 miles long, a scaled-down length, using the aroura, is some 4 miles. While still impressive, this, at least, was entirely possible. Incidentally, its 4-mile length is similar to surviving trenches left by the Atlantean copper miners at Isle Royale, in the Great Lakes, more than three thousand years ago.

No one, then or now, would have use for the one-hundred-foot-deep canal that Plato mentions; this, perhaps more than any other single detail, proves that the figures are patently incorrect. But when the same canal, described as an unnecessarily long 5.1 miles, is refigured using arouras, it becomes almost a mile and a half in length and twenty feet deep, well within the limits of ancient engineering. The biggest Bronze Age ships, even fully loaded with cargoes of copper ingots, probably drew less than ten feet. Such a deep canal can be explained by the varying water levels produced by incoming and outgoing tides common to any island in the Atlantic Ocean. With a twenty-three-foot depth, the Atlantean canal, would have accommodated the lowest tide, and allowed access to even heavy ship traffic at all times.

Use of the aroura also reveals something extraordinary that further justifies its use to properly recalculate Plato's figures: If the dimensions he gives for the citadel of Atlantis are transposed into arouras, it becomes equal to the area of the Great Pyramid's base, 13.4 square acres. This important relationship underscores the aroura as the most probable unit whereby to reconstruct Plato's lost island and its capital city.

To be sure, the Atlanteans' construction of canals, cyclopean walls, massive towers, resplendent temples, and the rest was a mighty accomplishment on a par with and exceeding, in at least certain particulars, the achievements of the Trojan or Hittite imperialists. Re-creations found in the pages of *Atlantis Illustrated* are undoubtedly close in form, if not actual size. But the picture can be brought down into proper scale by reducing Plato's grossly overblown numerical values, thus attaining some level of credibility.

Kenneth Caroli compares Atlantis with the dimensions of large-scale public works built by contemporary, complementary cultures, such as the Mycenaean Greeks, Phoenicians, Trojans, and New Kingdom Egyptians. Using arouras, he calculates that the citadel of Atlantis was somewhat greater than 13 square acres. The circumference of its orichalcum-plated walls was 10,000 feet, covering an area of 160,000 square feet. It was constructed upon the crown of the old hill; the elevation of the base of its walls was about 90 feet above the inner canal's waterline (a total of about 110 feet above the canal bed).

The citadel contained two ship berths or dry docks excavated out of the banks of the central island and roofed over with native rock. These docks were 263.8 by 208.3 feet. Since the ships of the period were roughly 60 feet long with 10- or 15-foot beams (oars more than double the width), two ships per dock seems likely. Their masts would be 20 to 35 feet high. But if the masts were removable or segmented, high ceilings would not have been necessary. Some ships were much larger. *Menechou* and *bair* were ship classifications that referred to seagoing vessels up to a hundred feet in length, such as the capacious freighters of Ramses III's expedition to Punt, the last voyage of its kind after more than a thousand years of trade with that elusive country. Warships belonging to the Atlantean Sea Peoples he fought, depicted on the walls of his Victory Temple at West Thebes, were substantially larger, although their precise dimensions are uncertain.

A fifth century B.C.E. Greek leviathan, the three-masted *Alexandris*, was 420 feet long, with an 11-foot draft. Although the largest known ship in the Ancient World, it was not without rivals. Another Greek warship, the *Demetrius*, was almost 300 feet from bow to stern. Contemporary Phoenician transports carried several hundred passengers per vessel in colonizing expeditions that began in Carthage, then sailed out of the Mediterranean Sea through the Pillars of Melcart (the Straits of Gibraltar) and down the Atlantic coasts of North Africa to found cities as far away as Guinea. Roman freighters later hauled many tons of grain from Egypt throughout *Mare nostrum;* most of the Empire's population depended on this steady supply for their sustenance.

The natives of Poseidon's island did everything with a flair for the stupendous, and the very word *Atlantean* has come to signify anything done on a monumental scale. Without doubt their ships were in keeping with this penchant for large-scale magnificence, necessitating the large, deep canals. Interestingly, those canals were capacious enough to allow efficient passage for a vessel the dimensions of the *Alexandris*—some indication, perhaps, of the size to which Atlantean ships were built.

THE INNER ISLAND OF ATLANTIS

The walls in the central part of the citadel were probably no more than 30 feet high and 10 to 20 feet thick. Watchtowers were arranged at regularly spaced 100-foot intervals. Each gate would have larger towers than those along the intervening walls and a bridge to the next zone of land. These bridges were 10 feet wide and 60 feet long. They were sufficiently high and had piers widely spaced enough for a ship to pass underneath. Each bridge also included an aqueduct to supply the citadel and disperse waters of the island's hot and cold springs to places where needed. These freshwater springs were common throughout the city and its surrounding countryside.

Within the reddish orichalcum–plated walls of the citadel, were located the palace, the Temple of Poseidon, barracks for the imperial bodyguard, and the Grove of Poseidon, in which his sacred bulls roamed. The temple was 150 feet long (one aroura) by 75 feet across. It was of "proportionate height." The roof formed a dome similar to the contemporary (1300 B.C.E.) *tholos* or "beehive" Tomb of Agamemnon at Mycenae. Also known as the Treasury of Atreus, the ceiling is a pointed dome of overhanging or corbelled blocks with a base and height of fifty feet. The configuration and dimensions of the Greek *tholos* appear to closely approximate the Atlantean Temple of Poseidon. Its exterior was silver covered, with gilded pinnacles, a roof frieze, and gold crenellations. The facade exhibited a simple monumentality, a spare cleanliness of sweeping line that implied imperial power. Windows, high up in the walls, were long slits, admitting light enough to create the hallowed interior milieu of a sacred space.

Several colonnaded courtyards stood within the enclosure. Nearby, yet separate, was a shrine dedicated to Kleito, the mortal, primeval islander who lay with Poseidon to sire semidivine Atlantean royalty. Pillars within the temple were plated in orichalcum, as was much of the interior. Two rows of five columns each stood on each side of the processional aisle, representing the imperial houses.

Arranged near the walls, small shrines displaying golden statues of the ten monarchs stood in company with equally splendid representations of their queens. These were the founding emperors listed by Plato. The pillars and statues may have symbolized each day in the week of a sacramental calendar. If so, they suggest the ten-day decan used by the Egyptians. The temple's gold and silver exterior also implies a lunar-solar calendar likewise known in the Nile Valley. In Greek myth, Atlas was depicted as having invented the first lunar-solar calendar. The presence of so much orichalcum probably honored either Venus or Sothis/Sirius.

The ceiling and sections of the temple walls were decorated with carved ivory panels. Its extensive use, as described by Plato, suggests the abundance of elephants he said inhabited the island. Although primarily stone, many pillars were made of wood (the Atlantean mountains were reputedly rich in timber); both were plated with gleaming precious metals. The high altar stood directly before the colossus of Poseidon. It was massive, ornately contrived, and contained built-in closet space for the blue ceremonial robes worn by the conferring kings as well as the golden law tablets. The texts were inscribed with heavy styluses in Atlantean, which resembled a curious combination of astrological signs, rune-like characters, more like Sumerian-style cuneiform or Aegean linear letters than Egyptian hieroglyphics or curvelinear Arabic scripts.

Close to the Pillar of the Law was a fire pit for burned offerings and an accompanying skylight through which smoke was allowed to rise toward heaven. Poseidon's house was a public building, unlike Kleito's shrine, which may have been an underground cavern-temple, as were many places where goddesses were worshiped in other parts of the world. If not actually situated inside a cave, the effect was probably simulated. Kleito may have been an Earth Mother deity.

The emperor's palace was large and tastefully embellished over the course of generations. Constructed of the red, white, and black volcanic rock so abundant throughout the island, its interior was a maze of corridors with adjacent courtyards of various sizes. The building was multistoried, rising on several terraced levels above the hill on which it was situated. Within the palace were numerous storerooms and private quarters, their inner chambers graced with wall paintings, such as those large, colorful scenes created by the Etruscans, Egyptians, and Minoans. Variations of flame, wave, maze, and pyramid basket weave patterns were common motifs. Corbelled or "false" arches were typical of Atlantean architecture. A slant or obliquity to walls, doors, and windows was another architectural theme.

Atlantis benefited from temperate weather, so its building styles followed known Mediterranean models. But Plato hints that, while in a warm, verdant locality, the capital still experienced winters cold enough to require covered, heated baths, the water provided by the island's abundant natural hot springs. Water temples, where ritual bathing and ablutions took place, were built near and sometimes directly over such springs. Most of the remainder of the citadel consisted of groves dedicated to Poseidon. Sacred trees—ash, oak, poplar, cedar, and sycamore—were tended, along with palms and citrus, whose oranges were the famous "golden apples" entrusted to the Hesperides (one of the daughters of Atlas) in Greek myth.

TOWARD A CREDIBLE ATLANTIS

Beyond the citadel, the innermost canal moat was 75 feet wide and 20 feet deep. The first ring-island was 750 feet across. It had both an outer and inner wall decorated with polished sheets of tin, blinding in the bright sun. This ring featured the headquarters and privileged barracks for the imperial bodyguards and their officers. A royal road linked the citadel to a bridge. From there it passed through a tin-decorated gate to another bridge over the next watercourse. Beneath the island's surface was a tunnel roofed over by natural rock, allowing ships to pass through to the innermost canal moat. The second ring-island was about 300-feet wide, with a circumference of 9,375 feet, and surrounded by a wall of dazzling bronze.

The ship canal that ran beneath the second land ring was roofed over with an artificial, rather than a natural or terra-formed ceiling. Vessels were towed through these tunnels, a process that required ledges for the stewards who performed that function. For the bigger ships, elephant-power assisted efficient passage. The larger, outer land ring featured public gardens, gymnasia, stadiums, and numerous statues of the gods. There were also numerous shops offering refreshments to the huge crowds of spectators who attended the races here. Seating was awarded according to privilege and status: pavilions and seats for the nobility, aristocrats, and military officers; grassy earthen embankments for the less privileged. This ring island was 450 feet wide, with a circumference of 4,687 feet, and served as one of the largest racetracks of the ancient world.

The sea canal was 8,100 feet long; the gargantuan main gate to the citadel was nearly two miles from the ocean. This sea canal was lined with warehouses and market stalls. The entire outer land ring was crowded with visitors both day and night. It was here that the common people resided. They consisted of various miners, metalsmiths, craftsmen, merchants, laborers, fishermen, dock workers, low-level bureaucrats, tavernkeepers, sailors, and low-ranking soldiers assigned to police the beggars, pickpockets, brawlers, suspicious foreigners, drunks, and prostitutes endemic to seaports.

The city was nearly four miles across. Its outer wall, constructed in tricolored bands of native tephra, pumice, and lava, ran for sixty thousand feet, more than ten miles. Its parapet was wide enough to drive a chariot around the top. It was guarded by soldiers quartered within the thickness of the wall itself, together with their war horses. Stalls and accommodations for chariots were also built in. While this outer wall was certainly impressive, it was by no means beyond the abilities of ancient engineers to raise. The outer fortifications were only little more than half the extent of the twenty-seven-foot-thick walls that were known to encircle North Africa's Carthage for twenty miles.² Altogether, the area of the Atlantean capital within the outer wall was approximately 5,080 square acres.

Outside the imperial city, a great plain stretched for 4,830 square miles. It was crisscrossed in a checker pattern of numerous irrigation canals watered by mountain rivers. A total population figure upward of five to six hundred thousand Atlanteans, particularly at the zenith of their prosperity, is not unrealistic. Of these, the armed forces comprised some 30,000 infantry, sailors, and marines according to Plato's estimate.

The extensive irrigation networks may have consisted of up to one thousand miles of canals; the verdancy of the plain was as much the result of man as nature. The number of canals implies that part of the plain was originally dry, while Plato's mention of swamps and marshes indicates some large areas needed to be drained. But the volcanic soil was fertile and productive, enough to have supported a large population.

Atlas comprised approximately 6,000 square miles, a figure in accord with a sunken feature in the near-Atlantic Ocean known as the Horseshoe Seamounts, directly fronting the Straits of Gibraltar, Plato's Pillars of Heracles. Though hardly a continent, it was large and fertile enough to nourish a prosperous nation over the course of many generations, and to support the magnificent capital of a world power.³

Even so, oceanographers are reluctant to accept that the sea is capable of swallowing a 6,000 square-mile landmass "in a single day and night." To be sure, precedents for such a deluge are few and actually outside the normal geologic parameters of the volatile Mid-Atlantic Ridge. But the cataclysm of 1198 B.C.E. was an extraordinarily powerful influence, the magnitude of which was potent enough to push those parameters beyond their usual limitations. As mentioned in the previous chapter, just at this time, physicists Franzen and Larsson found that asteroid-sized debris from a comet struck the eastern ocean, the very location of Atlantis itself. Under such a celestial onslaught, the already unstable Mid-Atlantic Ridge was tormented into extremes of geologic violence otherwise excessive even for this explosive region of the ocean floor. Thus battered by a nuclear-like barrage of cometary material, the entire length of the Horseshoe Seamount on which the civilization of Atlantis perched so precariously collapsed into the depths.

Atlantis served as a site for the chief city of an empire measuring its extent, not in land, but across the surface of the ocean. Consequently, its power was not matched until the advent of the British Empire. Early masters of the seas, the Atlanteans knew they could travel faster and access distant riches easier than any landlocked imperial enterprise. The island and the city were one in Atlantis. It was only the starting point, the political linchpin of a civilization that dominated much of three continents and all the peoples in between for at least a thousand years. While Atlantis was never a continent, it was more—it wielded transcontinental power from the Americas to Asia Minor.

PUTTING A FACE ON THE ATLANTEANS

But what of the Atlanteans themselves? What did they look like? What were their origins? What language did they speak? Did any survive the destruction of their civilization? If so, do their descendants still exist? These questions are more difficult to answer than those about geology or archaeology. Humans are more perishable than a sunken volcano or a cyclopean wall. Yet, even here, evidence is not entirely lacking.

A point of reference may be the Guanches, natives of the Canary Islands discovered by the Spaniards in the early fifteenth century. The Guanches were white, light eyed, and fair haired. Many were blond. They were tall and robust, with ruddy complexions. But their population appears to have become inbred. Skeletal remains showcased at the Santa Cruz Museum in Tenerife display numerous physical deformities often associated with inbreeding. They appear to have been a people in genetic decline, because of their geographical isolation, even before they were exterminated by the Spanish. They built stone step-pyramids and concentric temples, mummified their dead, preserved traditions of a great, sunken island from which their ancestors came, and worshiped Atlas.[4]

The Guanches were certainly an Atlantean people, perhaps the last surviving population. Their racial description coincides with Atlantean accounts in other parts of the world, such as stories of the Feathered Serpent, known to the Maya and the Aztecs as the tall, fair-skinned, yellow-bearded man from across the Atlantic Ocean who founded Mesoamerican civilization. In South America, he was known as Sea Foam, a poetic metaphor for the bow wave of his ship, and remembered as red-haired. In North America, virtually every Indian tribe similarly recalled the White Brother, who arrived after the Great Flood; he was known to the Winnebago as Red Horn for the color of his hair.[5] Most of the traditional myths of culture bearers or Atlantean survivors describe them as red-haired.

Several depictions of Atlanteans survived the millennia. The most important may be found in the portraits of individual Meshwesh captured by Pharaoh Ramses III after their defeat at the Nile Delta. These portraits are realistic profiles cut into the walls of Medinet Habu at West Thebes. Wearing horsehair helmets and prisoners' collars, the beardless Atlanteans have sharp, aquiline features, determined mouths, somewhat oval heads, and a slight upward slant to the eyes. They appear to have been taller than the Egyptians and looked more like Western Europeans, their hair wavy in comparison to the Egyptians' straight locks, their physique trim but sturdy.

These same characteristics may be seen on an Etruscan mortuary terra-cotta piece representing a husband and wife. Although this work was probably made about five centuries after the destruction of Atlantis, it testifies to the survival of the Atlantean race in western Italy. It was here, according to Plato, that the Atlanteans extended their power, and Etruscan civilization certainly possessed many earmarks of Atlantis. With their legendary origins as a result of the Trojan War (Plato's Atlanto-Athenian War), command of a thalassocracy said to stretch beyond the Pillars of Heracles as far as the Azores, and physical resemblance to the Sea People illustrated at Medinet Habu, the Etruscans preserved an Atlantean identity until their assimilation by the Romans sometime before the second century c.e.

Another terra-cotta masterpiece portrays an Atlantean woman of obvious importance. Known as the Lady of Elche, the statue was found in 1897 at an archaeological site near the Rio Vinalopo in the Alicante province of southeastern Spain, in a town known as Ilici to the Romans. But the Lady predates their Iberian conquest by many centuries. She has the same, singular facial features as the Etruscan couple and the captured Meshwesh. It is remarkable that all four surviving representations of the Atlantean type should be found in those locations most directly influenced by warriors and civilizers from Atlantis; namely, the Atlantic islands inhabited by the Guanches; Ramses III's Egypt, scene of the Atlanto-Athenian War; Etruria, occupied by the Atlanteans, according to the *Kritias*; and the southeastern coast of Spain, where an Atlantean domain was ruled, according to Plato, by King Eumelos.

ATLANTEAN PHYSIOGNOMY

The Atlanteans' racial characteristics as portrayed in surviving artwork and oral tradition correspond to those of a people living for many centuries on a temperate island. Windy conditions would result in the evolution of a near-epicanthic fold seen in some representations of their eyes (which, again according to various traditions, were blue or gray). Their reportedly ruddy complexions would have been caused by exposure to moisture and abundant sunlight. The Atlanteans were exceptionally tall for their time. Indeed, when they appeared among the relatively diminutive natives of South America, they were regarded as giants. The Spaniards often remarked on the stature of the Guanche descendants of Atlantis. One Guanche woman warrior, while engaging the invaders in combat, picked up a Spanish officer in her arms and ran off the battlefield with him! It was not for nothing that the Atlanteans were remembered by the Greeks as "Titans."

Their robust physique appears to have been inherited from Cro-Magnon ancestors. The Atlanteans were a very ancient people indeed, belonging to a pre-Aryan, even pre-Caucasoid race. In hominid history, humans migrated from their African genesis responding to environmental changes as they went, evolving over time into the Cro-Magnons of the Atlantic isles, then moving on into northern Europe and beyond to the steppes of central Russia, homelands of the Nordic, Caucasian, and Indo-European peoples of today. The Atlanteans separated at the beginning of this mass movement that left Africa behind in the evolutionary past for Europe.

Far more significantly than their general physical appearance, the Atlanteans were a people of incomparable genius, expressed in their technological achievements. The scope of their copper mining enterprise in Michigan's Upper Peninsula was not equaled until the mid-eighteenth century. They explored and mapped the world at least five thousand years before the men of the European Renaissance. Most impressive of all, they built a monument that still stands in Egypt on the Giza Plateau.

The Atlanteans were an outgoing, vigorous people who delighted in sports and spectacles. After all, an entire Atlantean land ring was used as a racetrack. They were capable and audacious seafarers. But rather than isolating them, the sea urged them toward the expansion of their culture through economic and military domination. They were aggressive imperialists, joyful warriors who delighted in conquest. Everything about them was outsized, from their physical stature and monumental architecture to their colossal mining operations and transcontinental empire. But they were also susceptible to flamboyant luxury and the excesses of materialism, perhaps resulting from the fabulous wealth that befell them through their discovery and monopoly of the international copper trade.

As their population grew to form a single society and then a civilized state, the Atlanteans developed that somewhat introverted national personality peculiar to islanders, and regarded the outside world with suspicion and defensiveness. This insular attitude contributed to a feeling a superiority fueled by their vaunted skills as navigators and copper barons. With great wealth came great paranoia, as Atlantean arrogance and fear lengthened the lists of enemies—real, potential, and imaginary. This contributed to the massive, walled fotifications of Atlantis and the incessant activities and expansionist policies of her armed forces. For most of their history, Atlantean genius was directed toward spiritual values, as enumerated in the various mystery cults based on the observation of natural law. Only after their burgeoning population began to upset a proper balance with the island's environment did the Atlanteans begin their decline into vulgar self-indulgence.

ATLANTEAN EVOLUTION AND LANGUAGE

Atlantean origins may be traced back to humanity's early evolutionary history on the nearby continent. *Atlanthropis* is a genus name assigned by the French anthropologist, Camille Arambourg, to *Homo erectus* finds in Terrifine, Algeria. Also referred to as *Homo erectus muritanicus*, *Atlanthropis* represents a slight development (considered "superfluous" by some scholars) of type along the Atlantic shores of North Africa, but may nevertheless represent sufficient change to indicate that populations of coastal *Homo erectus* hunters followed migrating animal herds across land bridges onto Atlantic islands. There the abundance of game and a temperate climate fostered further evolutionary steps toward becoming Cro-Magnons (recall the abundance of elephant remains found at more than forty different sites along submerged land bridges leading from North Africa into the Atlantic Ocean). This hypothesis is bolstered by many Cro-

Magnon finds throughout the Canary Islands. In fact, a Harvard expert on the Canary Islanders, Dr. Edward Hooten, demonstrated that they possessed numerous Cro-Magnon features.[6.]

The Guanche language was at least partially Indo-European, although unlike any other known Aryan tongue. It had surprising affinities to Greek, Gothic, and Old High German (including *zonfra,* zone; *fayacan, veiha* or priest"; and *magada, Magd* or maid, respectively).[7] But Canary Island speech contained so many non-Aryan elements, some apparently related to Euskara, the Basque language, and even ancient Egyptian languages that a thorough translation was never possible. In other words, Guanche was made up of influences from many different sources and, therefore, typical of a people who had dealings with widely disparate foreigners. The Atlantean language must have undergone a similar development, at least in its imperial days. The Canary Islanders may, in fact, have spoken the same tongue heard in lost Atlantis. Tragically, only several dozen of their words have come down to us.

Whether or not some original Atlantean stock still survives anywhere in the world cannot be credibly ascertained. Surely, the Guanches were Atlantean. But since their extinction, it is difficult to tie any modern population group to Atlantis with equal certainty. One such group may be the Basques of the Pyrenees Mountains. Their language is not Indo-European and is unrelated to any other modern tongue. Interestingly, Euskara shares some affinity with Finno-Urgic Patumnili (spoken in ancient Troy), Etruscan, Guanche, and Nahuatl, which was spoken by the Aztecs. These long-dead languages are themselves only imperfectly understood. But the fact that Euskara contains cognates with the languages of four peoples descended from Atlantis is most significant.

Perhaps the word most cogent to our investigation is *Atalya,* the name of an ancient ceremonial mound in Biarritz, in Basque country. Atalya is also the name of a holy mountain in the Valley of Mexico venerated by the Aztecs. Atalaia is a site in southern Portugal featuring Bronze Age tumuli, or domed tombs, dating to the late period of Atlantean florescence, the thirteenth century B.C.E. Gran Canaria's Atalya is a mountain with its valley sloping steeply toward the sea in a scene straight out of Plato's *Kritias*. It is clear that Atalya carries the same meaning in Euskara, Nahuatl, Portuguese, and Guanche; namely, the description of a sacred eminence, either a mound or mountain. It appears to derive from "Atlantis," daughter of the sacred summit. The Atalya of the Basques, Aztecs, Iberians, and Guanches was probably meant to commemorate, in word and configuration, the original Mount Atlas. What conceivable connection could have otherwise existed between such dissimilar and widely separated peoples?

The Basques share additional links with the now-extinct Canary Islanders. The Guanches practiced a goat cult that was virtually unique. Yet, the ancient Basques, too, employed its arcane rituals during Roman times.[8] They likewise displayed occasional Cro-Magnon cranial features, similar to skull remains among the Canary Islanders. Isolated as it is from other tongues, Euskara has nonetheless influenced languages hugely separated by time and distance. For example, our word "bronze" is not Indo-European, but derives from the Basque *broncea*. This could be a very important discovery (pointed out by Ignatius Donnelly more than one hundred years ago[9]), because, if Euskara is indeed descended from the Atlantean language, then our word is the same as that spoken in Atlantis. The Atlanteans were, after all, its foremost manufacturers and exporters, responsible for and dominating the Bronze Age, which abruptly ended with their demise.

The modern use of words from a long-dead civilization by a completely different culture is not without precedent. For example, the Etruscans were a pre-Roman people who died out by the first century C.E. Yet the English language uses several of their words as part of its vocabulary. "Ceremony" derives from the Etruscan city of Cere, noted for its many festivals. "Histrionics" is another Etruscan word with the same meaning in English. These and other examples are all the more remarkable, because the Etruscan language is almost completely indecipherable to modern scholars. Doubtless, a number of words uttered by our ancestors in Atlantis are still spoken in the languages of all those lands they touched.

On the other side of the world, the use of Quechua, the language of the Incas, predated them by unknown centuries. It is still spoken by some five million inhabitants of the Peruvian highlands. The Quechua word for "drizzle" is *garua*. In Euskara, *garua* means "dew." Even more cogent, northwest of the ancient Inca capital at Cuzco stands a sacred mountain in the Andes. Both the summit and a village on its southern slope are known as Atalaia. The Incas, like the Guanches, told of fair-haired culture bearers, Sea Foam being but one, who arrived after some natural catastrophe in the Atlantic Ocean.

The Basques have their own sunken-city myth. They still recall the name Amaiur, whom later Christian theologians equated with the biblical Tubalcain, Noah's grandson. This Basque flood hero led his fellow Aintzine-koak ("Those who came before") into the Bay of Biscay. They were survivors from the destruction of an oceanic kingdom, the Green Isle, that was engulfed by the sea. Amaiur and his followers finally resettled in the Pyrenees, where they became the Basques' progenitors. In view of Euskara's affinity with pre-Columbian language in Middle America, an alternate name for the Green Isle is provocative: It is also remembered as the Mound of Maia.[10] Moreover, in Greek mythology, Maia was the oldest and loveliest of the Pleiades.

Comparative linguistics, archaeology, and myth paint a real-life portrait of the Atlanteans, despite the thirty-two centuries separating their time from ours. They were a tall, robust, oval-headed, fair-complected, light-eyed people, given to occasional red-headedness. They were the mixed descendants of Cro-Magnon hunters who crossed land bridges that linked North Africa to the Atlantic islands twenty thousand years ago. Their language, like their blood, eventually became tainted with the foreign influences that comprised their empire. Those who did not perish in the great cataclysm were eventually assimilated by the native peoples of former colonies. Only two population groups may have survived into modern times—the doomed Canary Islanders and the indomitable Basques, through whose veins the blood of Atlantis may yet flow.

EIGHT

The Discovery
of Atlantis

*To achieve anything really worthwhile in research
it is sometimes necessary to go against
the opinions of one's fellows.*
Sir Fred Hoyle

If the city of Chicago were struck by four two-hundred-megaton bombs and another three detonated in Lake Michigan, deluging the entire metropolitan area, what physical evidence for civilization in northern Illinois might still exist after more than three thousand years? This is the magnitude of the problem facing anyone in search of Atlantis.

Critics scoff that such a place never existed, yet their conclusion is prejudiced by the simple fact that no scientific expedition to look for the sunken capital has ever been undertaken. The reasons for not having done so were sound. Much embarrassing nonsense on the subject has been espoused by so many overenthusiastic sciolists (both pro and con), singleminded debunkers, dreamy-eyed occultists, and crackpots of every stripe that any professional who suggested Plato's island should be looked for would have never again been taken seriously by his colleagues. And where would they begin to search? One author claims Atlantis lies under the South Pole, another says it was really Minoan Crete. Others insist it is covered by only 19 feet of water in the Bahamas or 2,200 feet near Cuba. They describe it as a huge continent that boasted a super-civilization before it sank in a geologic moment 11,600 years ago. It is no wonder that serious, trained investigators whose lives are dedicated to the no-nonsense disciplines of archaeology, geology, or oceanography refuse to even consider such an absurd fairy tale.

With this book's investigation, however, Atlantis is removed from the realm of fantasy in which it was too long held captive and placed squarely within the context of history and the earth sciences. Now that there is a fairly good notion of how, when and where it was destroyed, all that remains is to look for it. Happily, such a task is at last within reach. Modern scientists have sent space probes to the ends of the solar system. Surely the same technology is capable of probing the *inner* space of our own planet. The search is on for civilizations on other worlds, while the motherland of earthly civilization awaits its discovery on *this* world. In fact, the lost city of Ubar, consigned for more than a thousand years to the realm of Arabic legend, was found by studying images from a Landsat orbiting survey in the late 1990s.

We are an extremely privileged generation. The Atlantis Question has been debated since Plato penned his *Dialogues* twenty-four hundred years ago. But only now are the means available to settle the argument one way or the other. The fabled oceanliner *Titanic*, lying in utter darkness under miles of ocean for seven decades, was located and thoroughly photographed, inside and out, in 1986. Up to the moment of its discovery, hope of finding the *Titanic* seemed unfounded. Just two years later, another legendary ship, the *Bismarck*, was discovered under equally daunting conditions. If these relatively tiny deep-water targets can be detected in the obscuring vastness of the ocean bottom, locating a city should prove less formidable, but far more significant. Indeed, the recovery of Atlantean remains is not so improbable when we remember that the Roman cities of Pompeii and Herculaneum were buried under similarly hardened lava and fable for seventeen centuries.

Homer's Troy was almost universally regarded as myth until the German-American amateur archaeologist dug it out of the Turkish soil. In the opening years of the twenty-first century, the search for Atlantis compares with the quest for Troy, at the end of the nine-teenth century. At that time, the overwhelming majority of profes-sionals dismissed Homer's epic as fiction. Only very few scholars, most of them amateurs, were convinced that the *Iliad* was histori-cally correct, if not in all its details, then certainly in tone and spirit. It was up to one of these self-styled archaeologists to prove that the Trojan capital was a real place. The world awaits today's Schliemann who will discover Atlantis and prove the skeptics wrong once more.

Comparing Troy to Atlantis is appropriate in more ways than archaeological. Both cultures flourished during the same time at either end, geographically, of the Bronze Age World. After Ilios, the center of Mycenaean civilization came to light, followed by the Minoan and Hittite capitals. In subsequent years, other "Heroic Age" ruins were unearthed in Italy and the Near East. Atlantis is just the last of these lost cities to be found.

THE ODDS AGAINST DISCOVERY

This is not to imply that discovering Atlantis will be easy. Romantic visions of more or less ideally preserved temples, palaces, and col-umns garlanded with seaweed, patiently awaiting their discoverer in the emerald, twilight depths of the sea are not realistic. The island suffered a geologic catastrophe equivalent to a nuclear attack. What might have survived such an event and the passage of millennia is unknown. The Atlas volcano may have blown out laterally, in the manner of Mount Saint Helens, allowing the sea to inundate its exposed interior. The resulting implosion, combined with the sudden weight of a massive-invasion of seawater, literally dragged the entire island to the ocean floor. If the lateral blast occurred far below sea level and blew out the bottom of the island, the part that stood above the surface would have been suddenly undermined and collapsed into the ocean.

Cedric Leonard, one of the best Atlantologists, suggested that the island perished, not through some volcanic event, but in an earthquake, which brings his investigation closer to Plato's account.[1] There is no mention of a volcano in the *Timaeus* or *Kritias;* seismic upheaval is given as the cause of the destruction. Leonard conjectures that Atlas was a continental fragment composed of sial (a relatively, light, flaccid mixture of silicon and aluminum) that overlay heavier, basaltic rocks of sima (silicon and magnesium). An exceptionally powerful submarine earthquake could have shaken the sima base, abruptly displacing the sial level on which Atlantis was located into the sea.

Something of the kind did indeed happen on June 7, 1692, when Jamaica's Port Royal slid under the Caribbean with two thousand victims. Household objects from that disaster are still being retrieved by divers, so the chances of recovering material traces from Atlantis may be good, if she went down in a similar manner. A volcanic eruption is far more destructive; if that were the geologic mechanism, the retrieval of Atlantean artifacts would be less likely, particularly if they are buried under hundreds of feet of silt, or, worse, encased in solidified lava. But, regardless of unforeseeable obstacles, an attempt is certainly worth the effort. The place was, after all, a major city, and there should be at least some opportunities for locating its physical remains.

There are good, geological reasons for starting an underwater expedition at the Ampere or Josephine Seamounts, roughly 250 miles due west of Gibraltar. But there is also tempting archaeological evidence in their general vicinity. The Guanche inhabitants of the

Canary Islands, with their traditions of an ancestral homeland lost beneath the waves, have already been cited as among the last direct descendants of Atlantis. Near the eastern shore of their largest island, Tenerife, scuba divers found cut stone blocks deliberately set into a nine-hundred-square-foot plaza with broad steps descending toward what appears to have been a port or docking facility. P. Cappellano, leader of the 1981 dive, reported that the pavement was incised with glyphs identical to examples left behind by the Guanches on their cave walls. Similar stonework at the same depth, fifty feet, has been photographed off the coast of Morocco.[2] While neither find has received official attention, both are nevertheless real and strongly suggest a proper target area for investigators in search of the sunken civilization. Underscoring these underwater sites are the dozens of locations around Ampere and Josephine that yield the remains of elephants, confirming Plato's description of the creature's existence on Atlantis.

The discovery of Atlantis will affect the imagination of mankind no less powerfully than the arrival on Earth of intelligent beings from another planet. Recognition of its existence will shake our collective unconscious to the deepest core of its being. Suddenly, ancient myths from around the world will come alive in all the colors of memory, as the recollection of an actual place, a real occurrence. It will cause a major shift in human consciousness. We will understand then, to the bottom of our souls, that we, as a species, once rose to the heights of civilized greatness, sinned against the very forces that brought us into being and, in so doing, called down a global destruction that scoured our civilization from the face of Earth.

Atlantis is waiting in the black depths of the ocean, just as she has for the last thirty-two centuries. What a story she will tell to the one who finds her!

NINE

The Atlantis Story
Told in One Sitting

The island is well-wooded and a goddess lives there, the child of the malevolent Atlas, who knows the sea in all its depths and with his own shoulders supports the great columns that hold Earth and sky apart.
Odyssey, *Book I*

Some one hundred million years ago, a continental fragment in the Atlantic Ocean, trailing land bridges to the eastern landmasses, was born from the gradual separation of the Eur-African and American continents. Over the next eighty million years, this fragment slowly subsided below sea-level and broke apart, exposing a large island smaller in area than modern Portugal. It was connected by slender land bridges to North Africa below present-day Tangiers and to southern Europe, at Portugal's Cape Saint Vincent. Early man, following migrating animal herds, crossed these bridges to the Atlantic island, perhaps half a million years ago.

Over the course of the following millennia, the Portugal-sized landmass had, by geologic increments, slipped beneath the ocean, leaving behind a number of much smaller oceanic territories, one of which, sitting at the end of the land bridge that led from North

Africa, attracted the most numerous human settlements. Its temperate environment and fertile, volcanic soil nourished a growing population and stimulated social development. When, over the ensuing centuries, population density and community cooperation reached a certain, indefinable level of interaction, a civilized society of arts and letters, science and government, began to emerge. Even as Earth's first civilization was coming into being, the last of the dwindling land links to the African and European mainlands vanished beneath the waves, isolating the human populations on true islands.

Long before then, the islanders had become skilled shipbuilders and daring seafarers. From the beginning, theirs was a maritime society. Astronomy developed from the need for accurate navigation. Other sciences, perhaps some since lost and never rediscovered, were developed for similar reasons, because, by 4000 B.C.E., this prehistoric people had mapped the world. They called themselves Atlanteans after their island and their national god, Atlas. The founder of astronomy and astrology, Atlas was envisioned as a bearded Titan supporting the sphere of the zodiac on his shoulders. He was also personified by an awesome, dormant volcano that dominated the island. As they spread across the earth, the Atlanteans colonized favored territories, creating the first empire. The colonial riches funneled back to Atlas provided its inhabitants with tremendous material wealth. They transformed their city into a lavish imperial capital. Its unusual, concentric design of alternating land and water rings was determined by a typical early Neolithic settlement that lay beneath.

In 3000 B.C.E., the Atlanteans discovered the richest copper deposits on earth, in Michigan's Upper Peninsula. They initiated a colossal mining operation, extracting prodigious quantities of ore and freighting it to Atlas, which became the metallurgical depot for the Western world. Arriving at the Nile Delta, the Atlantean copper merchants were remembered as the Mesentiu, or Harpooners. In Greece they were the Pelasgian "Sea Peoples." Among the Menomonie Indians of the Upper Peninsula, they were the "Marine Men."

Everywhere they went, new civilizations sprang from their superior culture. They provided the high-grade copper that made the Near Eastern and European Bronze Age possible. At the height of their power, their empire stretched from the Great Lakes, the Yucatan, and Colombia in the Americas to North Africa, Iberia, and the British Isles in the near Atlantic, through the Mediterranean to Italy and, by royal family alliance, as far as the very shores of Asia Minor. In the early thirteenth century B.C.E., their imperial politics began to alarm other powers in the Aegean and the Near East. A series of military clashes with the Egyptians, Mycenaean Greeks, and Hittites escalated into full confrontation when Atlantis dispatched an army to aid the besieged Trojans. With their defeat, the Atlantean navy turned south to invade the Nile Delta. Initially successful, its marines were eventually repulsed by defending Egyptian forces.

Even as the kings of Atlantis were preparing a renewed assault against Egypt, a large comet made closer approaches to Earth with each yearly pass. Beginning around 1240 B.C.E. it began raining down meteoritic debris with increasing ferocity, causing fires, earthquakes, and volcanism, with catastrophic consequences. The comet and its deadly meteor streams came into closest proximity with Earth and reached the zenith of its destructiveness around the turn of the twelfth century B.C.E. Just then, it was nudged closer to our planet by yet another comet, known today as Halley's. In the daylight hours of November 1–4, 1198 B.C.E., one or more large meteorites or asteroids plunged through the ocean to penetrate the seafloor. The collision set off a cataclysmic chain reaction of geologic violence along the length of the Mid-Atlantic Ridge. Wracked by seismic and volcanic upheavals, the island of Atlantis collapsed beneath the waves "in a single day and night" of fire and storm.

Most of the inhabitants perished. But a few survivors, most of them from the priestly elite, the military, and the aristocrats who had access to sufficient numbers of ships, sought out the former colonies of the defunct Atlantean Empire as places of refuge. Some sailed to the Americas, where they and their descendants commemorated the tragedy of their sunken homeland at Ohio's Great Serpent Mound and Colombia's crater lake of Guatavita.

The survivors were not always welcomed as culture bearers. Storming back into the eastern Mediterranean, they launched their planned invasion of Egypt. Having lost everything outside the Straits of Gibraltar, the Atlanteans and their Libyan allies sought to take over the Nile Valley. But in the person of Ramses III they were confronted by the foremost leader of the age. During a succession of engagements in the country's complex river system, his archers inflicted heavy losses on the invaders. They withdrew their mauled naval forces and circled around to Palestine in an effort to resume the attack against Egypt from the east.

But here their landings were effectively opposed by the pharaoh's armies, and the Sea Peoples' confederation was destroyed. Suffering virtual annihilation from their combined defeats at Troy, Egypt, and the Levant, the Atlanteans ceased to exist as a people. Their last twenty thousand men, surrendered veterans of these disastrous campaigns, were taken into captivity by the victorious Egyptians, whose scribes documented the interrogation of the invaders. They told of their failed military intentions and of the loss of their oceanic homeland through fire from the sky and an overwhelming deluge.

These accounts were inscribed on the walls of Ramses III's Victory Temple at West Thebes and into tablets preserved at the Temple of the Goddess Neith, in Sais, on the Nile Delta. It was here that the story of Atlantis was translated for Solon, the great Athenian lawmaker, sometime around 550 B.C.E. Returning to Greece, he recorded the story in all its detail for an epic he intended to write. He died before undertaking this project, but Solon's transcription was passed on to Plato. He set down the account during the early fourth century B.C.E. in his

Dialogues, which have since been referred to as the chief source for the story.

Unknown but apparently substantial numbers of additional documents pertaining to Atlantis were preserved in Greek, Assyrian, Carthaginian, Roman, and Egyptian temples; the single largest repository was at the Great Athenaeum of Alexandria. When it and all other "pagan" libraries were burned before the close of the fifth century, most of the source materials describing Atlantis were lost. Christian theologians condemned the story as a form of heresy because they believed it was contrary to biblical history. For the next eight hundred years, Atlantis was virtually forgotten.

But with the rise of the Renaissance and voyages of discovery across the Atlantic Ocean, Plato's story was revived. As the renowned American archaeologist Ellen Whishaw pointed out, some of the men who joined Columbus as his crew did so in the hope of finding living descendants of lost Atlantis.[1] They were not disappointed when they heard the numerous Native American flood legends. It was not until the end of the nineteenth century, however, that these traditions were combined with others from around the world, together with contemporary geology, in the first serious investigation dedicated to understanding the subject as an historical phenomenon. The American author Ignatius Donnelly was the founder of Atlantology, the scientific study of all things pertaining to Atlantis.

In 1969 the first ruins of a possible Atlantean civilization were found off the north coast of Bimini, an island in the Bahamas. Only by the late twentieth century had underwater technology reached levels of sophistication needed to make a serious search for the sunken city possible. Future history will record if those methods were properly used for the discovery of Atlantis in the following century.

EPILOGUE

The Atlanteans Ourselves

Lo! Death has reared himself a throne in a strange city lying
alone far down within the dim West, where the good and the
bad and the worst and the best
have gone to their eternal rest.
Edgar Allan Poe, The City in the Sea

A common theme runs throughout world myths describing the Great Flood. From the account by one of Ancient Greece's greatest thinkers to the oral tradition of Polynesian singers in the South Pacific, a universal memory recalls that the pre-Deluge people were somehow responsible for and certainly deserving of the catastrophe that overwhelmed them. Through their lust for wealth or power, they abused Earth, upsetting the balance of nature, which caused a planet-wide cataclysm.

In view of the celestial nature of the destruction, it is difficult to imagine how human beings could have been in any way responsible for it. Still, the people of a super-civilization who could build a technological and engineering feat such as the Great Pyramid doubtless created other marvels on a similar or of an even more stupendous scale that we cannot conceive. The Great Pyramid of Giza is the only such example that remains. Perhaps the Atlanteans did indeed operate a technology of which nothing is known. Carried away with greed, their power became unmanageable. They somehow tampered with the fundamental principles of the universe. We arrogantly deceive ourselves if we deem our society utterly superior to all human accomplishments that have come before. Our time has no exclusivity to individuals of genius and endeavor.

The Menomonie Indians of the Upper Great Lakes Region believe the Marine Men violated Mother Earth by digging into her flesh and stealing her copper bones. It was because of this awful violation that she punished them with a terrible flood. The Menomonie tradition was echoed in the "life readings" of Edgar Cayce, who said that the Atlanteans disturbed Earth's geologic mechanism through massive excavations.

In 1995 and 1996, despite protests from around the world, the French government set off more than 160 nuclear explosions in the South Pacific. These so-called tests were wholly superfluous, if only because the Soviet Union, the lone superpower capable of attacking the West, had already rotted away years before. Moreover, atomic bombs have been produced for more than fifty years, so one wonders what further "testing" might have been required.

The bomb tests at Mururoa and Fangataufa Atolls resulted in an underground waste area that leaked hundreds of kilograms of plutonium and other highly radioactive products of nuclear fission. The interior of Mururoa is now a vast, unregulated, high-level radioactive dump. The famous French oceanographer, Jacques Cousteau, said, "The volcanic stratum of an atoll, totally saturated with water, is the worst choice!"[1] Sea life was decimated by the blasts, damaging the food chain, perhaps permanently, exacerbating fish poisoning by dislodging toxic organisms that live in coral reefs. After a malfunction in which a nuclear device got stuck halfway down its test shaft, an explosion blew away in excess of 130 million cubic yards of coral. Since the French had no apparent need to set off so many atomic tests, they must have done so for national prestige. Their abuse of the planet uncomfortably resembles hubris of the Atlanteans and their large-scale excavations that allegedly contributed to the earthwide cataclysm.

The French are, of course, by no means alone in violating the natural foundations that brought humanity into existence. They are afflicted with a disease that is rampant throughout the industrial world. Elsewhere in the Pacific, United States Air Force pilots have for years carried out regular bombing training runs against a formerly sacred island known to the natives as "the Place of the Gods." It is not the task of this book to make a catalog of man's inhumanity to nature. The subject is well known. For all that, precious little is being done to make good for our sins against the planet. In many countries, particularly those that are the worst offenders, absolutely nothing is being done.

In March 1996 a small item appearing in a few newspapers reported on the results of a two-week conference of international climatologists, geologists, biologists, and other earth scientists. Meeting in Geneva under the auspices of the World Wildlife Fund (WWF), they concluded that our planet is witnessing the greatest mass extinction of animal life in sixty-five million years. Not since the demise of the dinosaurs has Earth lost so many forests, all in the space of a single century. At least fifty thousand species of plants and animals die off each year, mostly because of diminishing forests. The worst offenders are North America and Russia, followed closely by Malaysia and Brazil. WWF spokesman Jean-Paul Jeanrenaud lamented, "It is the survival of the planet that is at stake here."[2] But his statement sparked comment among neither editors nor readers, all more interested in economics, politics, sports, and entertainment. No government (certainly none of those nations cited by the scientists) made the merest effort to amend their policies. "Wisdom cries out in the streets and no man regards it."

In August, only a few months after Jeanrenaud's warning, American naturalists reported that huge swarms of butterflies had migrated to the Pacific Northwest, hundreds of miles to the north of their natural habitat. They have been forced from their southern breeding grounds by higher temperatures brought on by industrial pollution, which had killed millions of the creatures.

In Atlantis, the birds vanished before the catastrophe. Modern parallels are chilling.

A year before the WWF's dire, neglected pronouncement, a similar conference of scientific professionals announced that the concept of industrial-induced global warming was no longer theory but demonstrable fact.[3] They warned that if world temperatures continue to rise at the rate discovered over the past hundred years, consequences will appear in many obvious forms during the twenty-first century. Among those consequences will be partial melting of Arctic ice. Even a small additional rise in temperature could unlock enough water from the polar ice caps to bury all but the highest mountain ranges under a neo-Panthalassa, a planet-wide ocean. The greatest irony in human history could be a world flood caused by our high-technology greed; a replay of the Great Deluge that overwhelmed the Atlanteans' super-civilization.

But let us not confuse effects with causes. The ecological assault on Earth is but the result, the effect. It stems from the entirely unnatural, antinatural way of behaving and thinking into which most of humanity has fallen. It is our emotional and attitudinal estrangement from the concept of Land and People that is the ultimate cause of our deplorable actions as a species. We allow the natural environment to be exploited and abused because we allow *ourselves* to be exploited and abused.

Individual men and women of good will have sacrificed themselves to bring about necessary change, namely, to rebuild human society based firmly on recognition of the principles of natural law. But nothing seems to be able to cure humans of their self-destructive neurosis, from striving in vain for self-fulfillment through materialism. Nature can endure even the worst violation for a long time. She gives the transgressors of her commands generous opportunities to correct their behavior. But those opportunities are not infinite, and when she at last decides on punishment, it is irrevocable and overwhelming. There is no better example in all human history than the story of Atlantis. Once its terrifying significance as a supreme object lesson is generally appreciated, humans may begin to back away from too many decades of taking Nature for granted.

Some believe that the souls of old Atlantis are presently reincarnating in great numbers, hence, today's rising interest in all things Atlantean. More importantly, metaphysicians speculate, these souls are returning to prevent a repeat of the cataclysm that utterly destroyed their glorious civilization and nearly the whole world. Others are supposed to be reincarnating now to reenact the cataclysm, only this time on a truly planet-wide scale. Whether or not one chooses to consider such opinions, it seems nonetheless true that the world is rapidly approaching a point in time remarkably similar to the days immediately prior to the destruction of Atlantis. Our civilization is likewise of global proportions, its inhabitants drunk in a scrambling orgy of vulgar materialism, its societies coming apart at the internal seams with fear, crime, and decay; individuals sense a powerlessness.

"Where will it all end?" people wonder. For the answer, let them look to Atlantis.

Notes

Introduction

1. L. Sprague de Camp, *Lost Continents* (New York: Dover, 1970).

2. Richard Cremo, *The Hidden History of the Human Race* (London: Govardhand Hill, 1994).

3. Quoted in Francis Hitching, *Before Civilization* (New York: Holt, Rinehart & Winston, 1991), 132.

4. James G. Bramwell, *Lost Atlantis* (New York: Harper, 1938), 7.

Chapter II: Where Is Atlantis?

1. E. Orowan, "The Origin of the Oceanic Ridges" *Scientific American,* vol. 224, no. 7, (1969): 34–51.

2. Robert Bolt, *Geological Hazards* (New York: Springer Verlag, 1975), 153.

3. F. M. Bullard, *Volcanos in History, in Theory and in Eruption* (Austin: University of Texas Press, 1966), 55–73.

4. Sigurdur Thorarinsson, *Surtsey: The New Island in the North Atlantic* (New York: Viking Press, 1967), 16, 17.

5. William Wertenbacker, *The Floor of the Sea* (Boston: Little, Brown, 1974), 113–76.

6. "Concrete Evidence for Atlantis?" (*Earth & Planetary Science Letters,* vol. 26, 8), March, 1975.

7. Wilhelm Schreiber, *Vanished Cities* (New York: Viking Press, 1970), 125.

8. Richard Perry, *The Unknown Ocean* (New York: Taplinger, 1972), 103–54.

9. Maurice Ewing, "New Discoveries in the Mid-Atlantic Ridge" *National Geographic* vol. 38 no., issue no. 8, (1949), 24.

10. Dorothy B. Vitaliano, "Atlantis from the Geologic Point of View," in *Atlantis: Fact or Fiction*, edited by Edwin S. Ramage (Bloomington: Indiana University Press, 1978), 141–2.

11. Rene Malaise, "Ocean Bottom Investigations and their Bearings on Geology" *Geolologiska Foreningens I, Forhandlingar*, vol. 17, no. 4, (1957), 6–10.

12. Ibid., 22.

13. Dr. Kenneth Landes was quoted in Wolfgang Hegeney, *Atlantis, Impressions from the Depths of the Ocean* (New York: Van Nos Reinhold, 1984), 27.

14. Kenneth J. Hsu, "When the Mediterranean Dried Up" *Scientific American* 227, (1972), 26–36.

15. H. Williamsand A. R. McBirney, Volcanology (San Francisco: Freeman-Cooper, 1979), 33–51.

16. Ewing, "New Discoveries," 40.

17. Preston Sturat, *Animal Behaviorism* (Cambridge, Mass.: Harvard University Press, 1979), 253–55.

18. Trudie Richardson, *South American Insects* (Carbondale, Ill.: Southern Illinois University Press, 1962), 148.

19. Michael Burke, *Mysteries of the Sargasso Sea* (Chicago: Regnery, 1975), 55–80.

20. A. N. Strahler, *The Principles of Physical Geology* (New York: Harper & Row, 1977), 44–76.

21. Marry Settegast, *Plato Prehistorian* (New York: Lindisfarne Press, 1990), 154.

22. J. V. Luce, *The End of Atlantis* (London: Thames & Hudson, 1969), 11–103.

23. Vitaliano, "Atlantis from the Geologic Point of View," 144–46.

24. Kenneth Caroli, personal communication, summer, 1995.

25. James Mavor, *Voyage to Atlantis* (Rochester, Vt.: Park Street Press, 1990), 24–38.

26. Caroli, personal communication.

27. Andrew Collins, "Has Atlantis Been Found?" *Ancient American* vol. 6, 38 (2001), 14.

28. Frank C. Whitmore, et al., "Elephant Teeth from the Atlantic Continental Shelf," *Science*, vol. 156 (1967), 1477–81.

29. Charles Pellegrino, *Unearthing Atlantis* (New York: Random House, 1991), 19–44.

30. Jurgen Spanuth, *Atlantis of the North* (New York: Van Nostrand Reinhold Co., 1979), 155.

31. Bolt, *Geological Hazards*, 126.

32. R. W. Hutchinson, *Prehistoric Crete* (London: Penguin Books, 1968), 23.

33. Desmond Lee, "Appendix on Atlantis," in Plato, *Timaeus and Critias* (London: Penguin Classics, 1977), 147–9, 159, 164.

34. Caroli, personal communication.

35. Caroli, personal communication.

36. Caroli, personal communication.

37. Robert Drews, *The End of the Bronze Age* (Princeton, N.J.: Princeton University Press, 1993), 8–18.

38. A. Kanta, *The Late Minoan III Period in Crete: A Survey of Sites, Pottery, and Their Distribution* (Göteborg, Sweden: Anstrom, 1980), 326 (translated by Rolf Sigurdson, Maxwell Publishing Co., New York, 1983).

39. Philip Betancourt, *The History of Minoan Pottery* (Princeton, N.J.: Princeton University Press, 1985), 159.

40. James Walter Graham, *The Palaces of Crete* (Princeton, N.J.: Princeton University Press, 1962), 152.

41. Caroli, personal communication.

42. David Zink, *The Stones of Atlantis* (Princeton, N.J.: Prentice-Hall, 1990), 28–48.

43. William Donato, "Bimini and the Atlantis Controversy: What the Evidence Says," *The Ancient American* vol. I, no. 3 (1993), 4–13.

44. Douglas G. Richards, "Archaeological Anomalies in the Bahamas" *Journal of Scientific Exploration* vol. 2, no. 2 (1988), 181–201.

45. Caroli, personal communication.

46. Zink, *The Stones of Atlantis*, 143.

47. Fritz Herzmeyer, Greco-Roman Science and Scientists (Berkeley, Calif.: University of California Press, 1967), 114.

48. In "De Generatione Corruptione," quoted in Richard McKeon, *The Basic Works of Aristotle* (New York: Random House, 1941), 212.

49. Gerhard Herm, *The Phoenicians* (New York: William Morrow & Co., 1962), 54.

50. Herzmeyer, *Greco-Roman Science*, 65.

51. Herzmeyer, *Greco-Roman Science*, 77.

52. Herzmeyer, *Greco-Roman Science*, 78.

53. Herzmeyer, *Greco-Roman Science*, 77.

54. Abraham Salafi, *Islamic Light in the Dark Ages* (New York: Revere Press, 1986), 39.

55. Thorarinsson, *Surtsey*, 154.

56. J. W. Judd, "The Eruption of Krakatoa and Subsequent Phenomena," in *Report of the Krakatoa Committee of the Royal Society*, edited by G. J. Symons (London: Treubner, 1888).

57. Svante Arrhenius, *The Earth and the Universe* (London: Wellington, 1927), 197.

58. Caroli, personal communication.

59. Bruce C. Heezen, et al., "Flat-Topped Atlantis, Cruiser and Great Meteor Seamounts" *Bulletin of the Geological Society of America,* vol. 7, no. 3 (1967), 21.

60. Emily D'Aulaire and Per Ola D'Aulaire, "Return to Krakatoa" *Reader's Digest,* vol. 51, no. 3 (1979), 119–123.

61. Plato, *Timaeus and Critias,* trans. Desmond Lee (London: Penguin Classics, 1977) 146–53.

Chapter III: The Queen of Legends

1. Augustus Le Plongeon, *Queen Moo and the Egyptian Sphinx*, 2nd ed. (New York: self-published, 1900), xiv, xv.

2. Friar Diego de Landa, *Yucatan Before and After the Conquest,* Mark Sharpe, trans. (New York: Dover, 1976), 10–210.

3. Robert Graves, *The Greek Myths* vol. 2 (New York: Brazilier, 1961), 28.

4. Francis Wilcoxen, *Plato's Laws* (Boston: Arthur House Publishers, 1889), 223.

5. Wilcoxen, *Plato's Laws,* 225.

6. Robert Drews, *The End of the Bronze Age* (Rutgers, N.J.: Princeton University Press, 1993), 10.

7. Plato, *Timaeus and Critias,* 122.

8. Wilcoxen, *Plato's Laws,* 228.

9. Wilcoxen, *Plato's Laws,* 227.

10. Wilcoxen, *Plato's Laws,* 229.

11. Frank Joseph, *Atlantis in Wisconsin* (Lakeville, Minn.: Galde Press, 1995), chapters 2, 3, and 4.

12. Wilcoxen, *Plato's Laws,* 228.

13. Edward Andrews, *Sacred Crocodile* (New York: Huntington Publishers, 1990), 126.

14. Hans Brander, trans. *The Geographica of Diodorus Siculis* (Cambridge, Mass.: Harvard University Press, 1889), 237.

15. T. W. Rolleston, *Celtic* (New York: Avenel Books, 1986), 136.

16. My thanks to Robyn Sherard, Administrative Assistant, Meteor Crater Enterprises, Inc., Flagstaff, AZ, for meteor crater data.

17. John A. Wood, "Long Playing Records" *Natural History Magazine* vol. 22 (1981), 60.

18. Roberta Willington, *A History of the Navaho* (Norman, Okla.: University of Oklahoma Press, 1953), 22.

19. G. T. Emmons, *Canadian History and Prehistory* (Vancouver, B.C.: Raverston Publishers, 1942), 97–101.

Chapter IV: The Fire from Heaven

1. Albert Kozinsky, "Statistical Analysis of Universal Flood Legends" *Science Review* vol. 12, no. 3 (1973), 112.

2. Richard Andree, quoted in Lloyd Harbister. *Odds against Everything* (Los Angeles: Rutgers House, 1959), 22.

3. C. A. Burland, *The Gods of Mexico* (London: Eyre & Spottiswoode, 1970), 138.

4. R. van Over, *Sun Songs, Creation Myths from around the World* (New York: New American Library, 1980) 33–41.

5. Pierre Grimal, *Larousse World Mythology* (New York: Putnam & Sons, 1958), 127–32.

6. Lewis Spence, *The Myths of the North American Indians* (New York: Dover Publications, 1989 reprint of 1926 first edition), 99–105.

7. Rudolf Meisters, *South American Mythology* (London: Thames & Hudson, 1966), 88.

8. Zelia Nuttall, *The Fundamental Principles of Old and New World Civilizations* (Cambridge, Mass.: Peabody Museum, Harvard University, vol. II), 139.

9. Ivan Lissner, *The Silent Past* (New York: G.P. Putnam, 1962), 177.

10. Lissner, ibid., 100.

11. Ignatius Donnelly, *Ragnarok: The Age of Fire & Gravel* (1883; reprint, New York: Steiner Books, 1976), 168.

12. Immanuel Velikovsky, *Worlds in Collision* (New York: Dell Publishers, 1951).

13. Otto Muck, *The Secret of Atlantis* (New York: New York Times Press, 1978).

14. Sharon Begley, "The Science of Doom" *Newsweek*, 23 November 1992, 60.

15. Edgerton Sykes, *Man across the Atlantic* (London: Robertson Press, 1958).

16. Plato, *Timaeus and Critias*, 113.

17. Ovid, *Metamorphoses,* trans. H. Gunther (New York: Harster Press, 1927), 41.

18. Plato, *Timaeus and Critias*, 142.

19. Graves, *The Greek Myths* vol. 2, 28.

20. Velikovsky, *Worlds in Collision*, 117.

21. Johann von Goethe, *All mein Gedenken* (Berlin: Brandenburg Verlag, 1929), 48.

22. Plato, *Timaeus and Critias*, 143.

23. *Quintus of Smyrna's Little Iliad,* trans. Westbrook Murphy (New York: Macmillan, 1960), 248.

24. Westbrook Murphy, trans. *The Complete Hesiod* (New York: Macmillan, 1958), 357.

25. R. Cedric Leonard, *The Quest for Atlantis* (New York: Manor Books, 1979), 111–2.

26. René Guénon, *Fundamental Symbols: The Universal Language of Sacred Science* (Cambridge, England: Quinta Essentia, 1995), 80, 81.

27. Ovid, *Metamorphoses,* 44.

28. Frank Taylor, *The World of the Greeks and Romans* (New York: Doubleday, 1959), 62.

29. Taylor, *The World of the Greeks and Romans*, 191.

30. Murphy, *The Complete Hesiod*, 354.

31. Victor Clube and Bill Napier, *The Cosmic Serpent* (London: Faber, 1982), 71.

32. Dr. Richard Englehardt, quoted in Clube and Napier, *The Cosmic Serpent,* 152.

33. Donnelly, *Ragnarok,* 202.

34. Ovid, *Metamorphoses,* 111.

35. Theodore H. Gasten, *Myth, Legend and Custom in the Old Testament* (New York: Harper & Row, 1969), 112–31.

36. Alfred M. Renfrew, *The Flood* (St. Louis, Mo.: Concordia Publishing, 1951), 132–48.

37. Robert Graves and Raphael Patai, *Hebrew Myths, the Book of Genesis* (New York: Greenwich House, 1964), Chapter 20.

38. Werner Keller, *The Bible as History* (London: Hodder & Stoughton, 1965), 132.

39. Fulton J. Sheen, "Life Is Worth Living," NBC Television broadcast, 17 July 1957.

40. Caroli, personal correspondence.

41. The version of the Bible quoted here was translated by Robert Conkey and published in London by Congreaves Publishers, 1895.

42. H. R. Ellis Davidson, *Mythology of the Norse* (New York: HarperCollins 1969), chap. 12 and 14.

43. Donnelly, *Ragnarok,* 146.

44. Steven Reichal, *Gods of Northern Europe* (New York: Grosset & Dunlap, 1963), 202–5.

45. Leonne de Cambrey, *Lapland Legends* (London: Hastings Publishers, 1926), 187.

46. Lewis Spence, *The Myths of the North American Indians* (1926; reprint, New York: Dover Publications, 1989), 315–21.

47. John Boatman, *My Elders Taught Me: Aspects of Great Lakes American Indian Philosophy* (Rochester, Md.: University Press of American Indian, 1992), 128–9.

48. August Le Plongeon, *Queen Moo and the Egyptian Sphinx,* 2nd ed. (New York: self-published, 1900), lix, 1.

49. Benny J. Peiser, Trevor Palmer, and Mark E. Bailey, eds. *Natural Catastrophes During Bronze Age Civilisations: Archaeological, Geological, Astronomical and Cultral Perspectives* (Oxford, England: Archaeopress, 1998), 151.

50. Peiser, Palmer, and Bailey, *Natural Catastrophes,* 148, 151.

51. Ibid., 151.

52. Paul Rutgers, *Apache Law and Myth* (Reno, Nev.: University of Nevada Press, 1975), 119–28.

53. Gertrude Jobes and James Jobes, *Outer Space: Myths, Name Meanings, Calendars* (London: Scarecrow Press, 1964), 185.

54. Donnelly, *Ragnarok,* 255.

55. Frank Waters, *Book of the Hopi* (annotated reprint, Santa Fe, N.M.: Rathers Press, 1970), 177.

56. Arthur Schopenhauer, *Parerga und Paralipomena*, volume 2, #303, author's translation from German.

57. R. van Over, *Sun Songs: Creation Myths from Around the World,* 326.

58. Nigel Davies, *The Ancient Kingdoms of Mexico* (London: Penguin Books, 1982) 386.

59. Pierre Grimal, *Larousse World Mythology,* 521.

60. Genesis 8:20; 9:17.

61. Sylvanus Morley, *The Ancient Maya* (San Francisco, Calif.: Stanford University Press, 1946), 176.

62. Zelia Nuttall, *The Fundamental Principles of Old and New World Civilizations,* 269.

63. Dennis Tedlock, trans. *Popul Vuh* (New York: Simon and Schuster, 1985), 164.

64. Charles Gallenkamp, *Maya* (London: Frederick Muller, 1960), 36.

65. Hans Helfritz, *Mexican Cities of the Gods* (New York: Praeger, 1968), 162.

66. Rudolf Meisters, *South American Mythology* (London: Thames & Hudson, 1966), 134–39.

67. Albert MacKenzie, *The Encyclopedia of South American Myths and Legends* (London: Albert Hall Publishers, Ltd., 1926), 228.

68. Ibid.

69. Ibid., 227.

70. Ibid., 110.

71. Jonas Wolk, *Oral Histories of Polynesia* (New York: New York University Press, 1955), 107.

72. Ibid.

73. Ibid., 78.

74. Abraham Fornander, *Migration Tales of the Hawaiian Islands* (London: Castlewood Publishers, Ltd., 1922), 89.

75. Richard Hochland, *Australia and Its Aborigines* (San Antonio, Tex.: Marvel Craft Publishers, Inc., 1965), 44.

76. Lisa De La Ponte, *Asian Origins in Myth and Folk Tale* (Chicago: Regnery Press, Inc., 1977), 56.

77. Ibid., 69.

78. Professor Nobuhiro Yoshida, *Japanese Myths and Fairy Tales* (Amherst, Wisc.: Ancient American Press, 2000), 23.

79. Ibid., 22.

80. Lien Chou Sei, *Ancient Tales of My Chinese Motherland* (New York: Doubleday & Company, 1969), 331.

81. W. S. Blackett, *A Lost History of America* (London: Trubner & Company, 1883), 145.

82. Jessica Ions, *Egyptian Mythology* (New York: Doubleday and Company, 1962), 33.

83. Pierre Grimal, *Larousse World Mythology* (New York: Putnam & Sons, 1958), 94.

84. Derrick Peterson, *Ancient India: Its Records and Folk Memories* (New York: G. P. Putnam & Sons, 1974), 174.

85. Ibid., 261.

86. Ibid., 257.

87. Ibid., 413.

88. Xena Rashnapuhr, *The Persian Dialogue with Heaven* (London: Harcross Publishers, Ltd., 1939), 361.

89. Robert M. Glastone, *Sub-Saharan Myth and Folk Tale* (San Francisco: Afrocentric Press, 1999), 274.

90. Anthony Mercatante, *Who's Who In Egyptian Mythology* (New York: Clarkson N. Potter, 1978), 155–58.

91. Personal correspondence with Kenneth Caroli, 9 March 2001.

92. Anthony Mercatante, *Who's Who In Egyptian Mythology* (New York: Clarkson N. Potter, 1978), 155–58.

Chapter V: How Was Atlantis Destroyed?

1. William F. Murname, *United with Eternity, a Concise Guide to the Monuments of Medinet Habu* (Chicago: The Oriental Institute of Chicago Press), 1980, 44.

2. F. W. Edgerton & J. Wilson, *Historical Records of Ramses-IIIrd* (Chicago: University of Chicago Press, 1964), 22–26.

3. Jurgen Spanuth, *Atlantis of the North* (New York: Van Nostrand Reinhold Co., 1979), 131–45.

4. J. H. Breasted, *Ancient Records: Egypt* vol. 1 (Chicago: University of Chicago Press, 1927).

5. Robert Graves, *The Greek Myths* vol. 2 (New York: George Brazilier, Inc., 1959), 29.

6. Sir Leonard Wooley, *A Forgotten Kingdom* (Harmondsworth, U.K.: Penguin, 1926), 156–64.

7. Robert Drews, *The End of the Bronze Age* (Princeton, N.J.: Princeton University Press, 1993), 55.

8. Josef Wiesner, *Fahren und Reiten* (Archaeologia Homerica I F), (Goettingen: Vandenhoeck und Ruprecht, 1968), 136.

9. Drews, 58.

10. Spanuth, ibid., 135.

11. Edgerton, 173.

12. Kenneth Caroli, correspondence with the author, summer, 1995.

13. Edgerton, ibid., p. 155.

14. Edgerton, 159.

15. R. Hewitt, *From Earthquake, Fire and Flood* (London: Scientific Book Club, 1958), 117.

16. Caroli, ibid.

17. M. I. Budyko, "On the Causes of Climate Variations," Sverig Meteorological-Hydrological Institute, Stockholm (Sweden) and Cambridge (MD), Series B, vol. 3, no. 28: 6 to 13, March, 1949.

18. Lowell Ponte, *The Cooling* (Princeton, N.J.: Prentice-Hall, 1976), 202.

19. Robert Claiborne, *Climate, Man and History* (New York: Angus and Robertson, 1970), 174–91.

20. *Science,* April, 1959, vol. 42, no. 9, 39.

21. Ponte, 263.

22. Caroli, ibid.

23. Caroli, ibid.

24. Joseph Robert Jochmans, Litt.D., "Cosmic Blitzers and Planet Busters" in *Journeys into Meta-Creation,* P.O. Box-10703, Rock Hill, SC 29731-0703, 1996, 188.

25. Henriette Mertz, *Atlantis, Dwelling Place of the Gods* (Chicago: Swallow Press, 1976), 169–77.

26. Mertz, 184.

27. G.A. Zielinski, et al, "Record of Volcanism since 7000 B.C. from the GISP2 Greenland Ice Core and Implications for the Volcano-Climate System," *Science* vol. 264, no. 5, 13 May 1994, 948.

28. James Churchward, *The Cosmic Forces of Mu* (Albuquerque: BE Books, 1988), 254.

29. Drews, 66.

30. Caroli, ibid.

31. Hewitt, 342.

32. Budyko, 13.

33. Edgerton, 126.

34. Edgerton, ibid.

35. Edgerton, ibid.

36. Michael Astour, "New Evidence on the Last Days of Ugarit," *AJA* 69, July, 1965, 253–58.

37. Caroli, ibid.

38. Gian Ruffolo, *Assyria, Land of Gods and Men* (New York: Harper & Row, 1955), 105.

39. Ruffolo, ibid., 43.

40. Ruffolo, ibid., 119.

41. Ruffolo, ibid., 120.

42. Jochmans, ibid., 51.

43. Otto Muck, *The Secret of Atlantis* (New York: The New York Times Press, 1978), 201.

44. *National Geographic* Magazine, Washington, D.C.: National Geographic Society, vol. 79, no. 7, 10 August 1972, 50.

45. Sharon Begley, "The Science of Doom," *Newsweek*, vol. 46, no. 3, 23 November 1992, 56.

46. Begley, ibid., 59.

47. Begley, ibid., 60.

48. Begley, ibid., 58.

49. Begley, ibid.

50. Victor Clube, & Bill Napier, *The Cosmic Serpent* (London: Faber, 1982), 144.

51. Desborough quoted in *Natural Catastrophes During Bronze Age Civilizations: Archaeological, Geological, Astronomical and Cultural Perspectives,* edited by Benny J. Peiser, Trevor Palmer and Mark E. Bailey (Oxford, England: Archaeo Press, 1998), 337.

52. Ibid., 426.

53. Ibid., 314.

54. George Catlin, *The Okipa Ceremony* (Norman, Okla.: University of Oklahoma, 1958), 39.

55. Ibid., 30.

56. Alexander Karnofski, *Serpent Worship* (Toronto: Tutor Press, 1980), 93.

57. Frank Waters, *The Book of the Hopi* (New York: Viking Press, 1963), 97.

58. Waters, ibid.

59. Ronald M. Douglas, *Scottish Lore & Folklore* (New York: Beckman House, 1982), 94.

60. Douglas, ibid., 95.

61. Fritz Schachermeyr, *Griechische Fruehgeschichte* (Vienna: Oesterreiche Akademie der Wissenschaft, 1984), 102.

62. Jack Stone, *Tunguska, The Siberian A-Bomb of 1908?* (New York: Star Books, 1977), 153.

Chapter VI: When Was Atlantis Destroyed?

1. *Scripps' Letter* vol. 27, no. 9, 1995, Scripps Institute of Oceanography, University of California, San Diego.

2. Elizabeth Wyse and Barry Winkleman, editorial directors, *Past Worlds, the Times' Atlas of Archaeology* (New York: Avenel, 1995), 72–75.

3. Norman P. Ross, editor, *The Epic of Man* (New York: Time, Inc.), 30–41.

4. Kenneth Caroli, correspondence with the author, April, 2000.

5. Caroli, ibid., July 2001.

6. Immanuel Velikovsky, *Worlds in Collision* (New York: Dell Publishers, 1951), 42.

7. L. Taylor Hansen, *The Ancient Atlantic* (Amherst, Wisc.: Amherst Press, 1969), 382.

8. Velikovsky, ibid., 44.

9. *Stern Magazine,* Mannheim, Germany: vol. 22, nr. 3,12 June 1952, 6.

10. Veronica Ions, *Egyptian Mythology* (London: Hamlyn, 1963), 31.

11. Plutarch, *Lives,* trans. John Dryden (New York: Modern Library, 1932), 154, 155.

12. Richard Feyodorovitch, *Greek and Roman Sourcebook* (Chicago: Raster Press, 1954), 328.

13. James Bailey, *The God-Kings and the Titans* (New York: St. Martin's Press, 1973), 122–26.

14. Victor Clube & Bill Napier, *The Cosmic Serpent* (London: Faber, 1982), 153.

15. Professor H. A. T. Reiche, "The Language of Archaic Astronomy: A Clue to the Atlantis Myth?," *Technology Review* vol. 2, no. 5, December 1977, 85.

16. Feyodorovitch, ibid., 296.

17. Caroli, personal correspondence, October 12, 2001.

18. Velikovsky, ibid., 142.

19. Virgil's *Aeneid,* trans. Hubert Fox (London: Antiquarian Publishers, 1910), 44, 45.

20. Plato, *Timaeus and Critias,* trans. Desmond Lee (London: Penguin Classics, 1977), 134.

21. Gertrude & James Jobes, *Outer Space: Myths, Name Meanings, Calendars* (London: Scarecrow Press, 1964), 185.

22. Caroli, ibid.

23. R. G. Haliburton, "Festival of the Ancestors: Ethnological Researches Bearing on the Year of the Pleiades," cited by Augustus Le Plongeon in *Queen Moo and the Egyptian Sphinx* (New York: self-published, 1900), 111.

24. Ibid.

Chapter VII: Life in Atlantis

1. H. R. Stahel, *Atlantis Illustrated* (New York: Grosset & Dunlap, 1982).

2. Kenneth Caroli, personal communication.

3. Gilbert Charles-Picard, *Daily Life in Ancient Carthage* (New York: Macmillan, 1961), 19.

4. Eileen Yeoward, *The Canary Islands* (Devon, England: Arthur H. Stockwell, Ltd., 1975), 44.

5. Frank Waters, *The Book of the Hopi* (New York: Viking Press, 1963), 156.

6. E. P. Hooten, *The Ancient Inhabitants of the Canary Islands* (Cambridge, Mass.: Harvard University Press, 1915).

7. Dietrich Woelfel, *Die Kanarischen Inseln: Die Westafrikanischen Hochkulturen und das Mittelmeer* (Bamberg: G. Bauriedl, 1950), 117.

8. M. O. Howey, *The Cults of the Dog* (London: Ashington, 1972), 44–45.

9. Ignatius Donnelly, *Atlantis,* 258.

10. A. Tovar, The Basq*ue Language* (New York: Macmillan, 1957), 271.

Chapter VIII: The Discovery of Atlantis

1. R. Cedric Leonard, *The Quest for Atlantis* (New York: Manor Books, 1979), 174–76.

2. Charles Berlitz, *Atlantis: The Eighth Continent* (New York: Ballantine Books, 1984), 93.

Chapter IX: The Atlantis Story Told in One Sitting

1. Elena Maria Whishaw, *Atlantis in Spain* (1929; reprint Kempton, Ill.: Adventures Unlimited Press, 1994), 62.

Epilogue: The Atlanteans Ourselves

1. Stanley Hopkins, "WWF Conference in Geneva," *Saint Paul (Minnesota) Pioneer Press,*12 March 1996.

2. Robert Dales, "Global Warming News," *Chicago Tribune,* 2 February 1995.

3. Patrick O'Connell, "World Geophysical Symposium Meets in Switzerland," *The Chicago Tribune,* 20 April 1994.

Index